200
10000
ДЕСЯТЬ ТЫСЯЧ
10000 РУБЛЕЙ
100

Exhibit 1.1

Inflation (monthly rate)

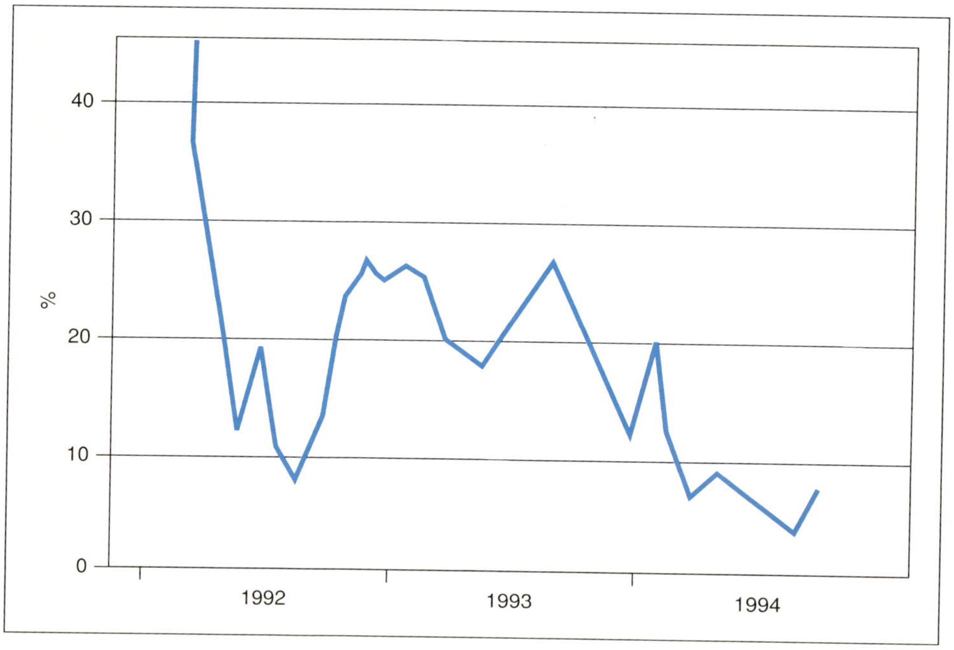

Source: Central Bank.

Exhibit 1.2

Real incomes and consumer price index in 1992–94

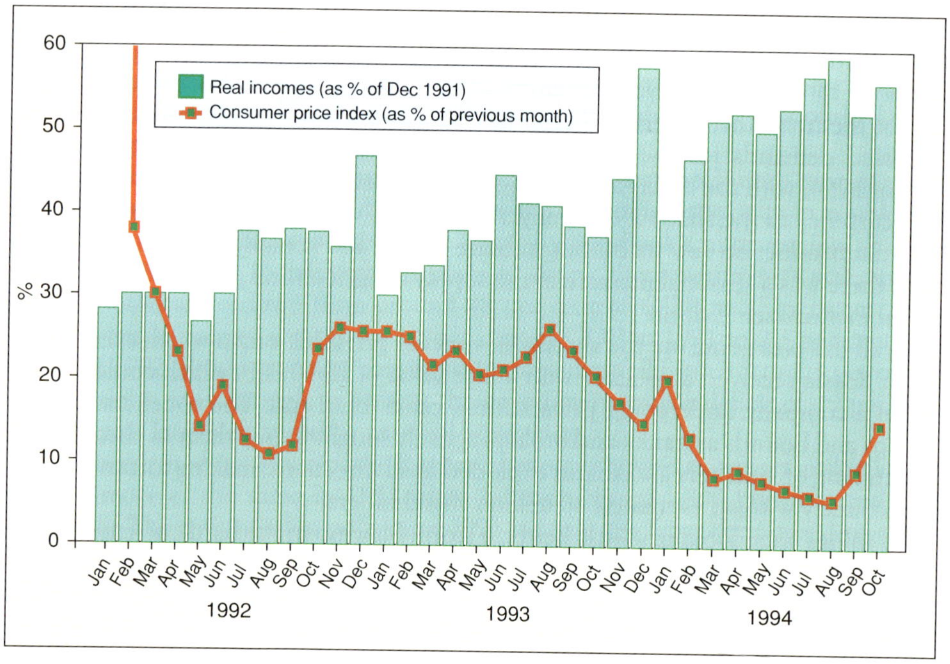

Source: EPIcentre.

While the current economic instability is causing concern, it is generally recognised as an inevitable part of the difficult transition to a market economy

promoted to first vice premier and given overall charge of the basic economic ministries. Chubais convinced a couple of the authors of the old '500-Day Plan' to join him and was able to trumpet 'a new team of reformers'. The new economics minister is the plan's joint author, Yevgeny Yasin, and another recruit was Tatyana Paramonova, acting chairman of the Central Bank, well known as an advocate of anti-inflation measures.

In spite of the inflationary growth during the last months of 1994, the rate finished in the region of 180 per cent for the year, further evidence that something at least was working in the rather chaotic 'self-generated' transition to something increasingly resembling a market economy. Indeed, the battered and shrinking economy is probably at a decisive turning point. The government plans a tough economic programme that aims to bring down inflation to single digits (less than 2 per cent a month) by the end of 1995. It has rejected any idea of resorting to Central Bank credits to finance its forecast 7.8 per cent budget deficit and stopped printing more money for that purpose in the last quarter of 1994. The 1994 budget deficit is estimated at around 10 per cent (see Exhibit 1.4). The government will bridge the gap by issuing state bonds and borrowing some US$13 billion from the international financial institutions. The World Bank has earmarked about US$3 billion in loans and a US$4 billion standby loan from the International Monetary Fund (IMF) has been agreed, subject to Russia meeting budget targets. Moscow also wants a US$6 billion stabilisation fund from the IMF, to defend the rouble.

The economy is officially seen as shrinking in 1995 by over 6 per cent, which is an improvement on the 22 per cent reduction recorded in 1994. However, such figures as October 1994's 4 per cent GDP increase over the previous month, accompanied by a monthly rise of 9.5 per cent in industrial output, have raised expectations for the future. The government also forecasts that Russia's trade surplus will rise from US$18.3 billion in 1994 to US$19.1 billion in 1995, although some of the gain could reflect a further fall in imports. The government has stood firm in defence of its frugal 1995 draft budget, in spite of attacks from the opposition parties, the industrial nomenclature and the military, because it knows that any substantial deviation from its declared budget aims would endanger the inflow of international funds it needs to help stabilise the economy. According to official sources, the government hopes for as much as US$14 billion from the international institutions in the course of 1995.

Both Yeltsin and Chernomyrdin remained firm about the budget through the rows with the state Duma, telling it to pass a tight package or take responsibility for the consequences. Yeltsin claimed that the budget would raise the economy out of crisis and thrust it into a period of rapid growth. Chernomyrdin said 1995 could be a year of financial stabilisation followed by recovery in 1996 and major growth in 1997. The prime minister told the Duma that some changes to the budget were possible, but that the government's deficit financing plans were not negotiable. The sources of funding for the forecast 7.8 per cent deficit were still not clear at the end of 1994. An IMF delegation arrived in Moscow in December to consider releasing the awaited standby loan and the stabilisation fund.

The biggest consumer of state funds is the defence sector which currently claims over 6 per cent of GDP. While this is considerably less than the 15 per cent it got three or four years ago, it is still more than is spent on defence in many democratic nations. Unfortunately, the war in Chechnia has given the military an additional axe to grind. At the same time, public health care has been allocated only 0.5 per cent of Russia's increasingly modest GDP and cuts in health spending have been greater than the fall in defence spending. The Rb12 trillion earmarked for law enforcement and the security agencies compares with the combined Rb11.4 trillion for spending on social, cultural and education projects, including kindergarten subsidies, science, health and leisure.

The ups and downs of the Russian economy since the fall of the Soviet Union have seen several hesitations along the road, but it is clear that the determination to pursue reform is still there, in fact public statements towards the end of 1994 stressed the need to create a new economic climate. There will, government spokesmen said, be an end to subsidies and soft credits to losing enterprises. Policy will concentrate on encouraging existing and new businesses which attract a mixture of state and private capital. The second or 'cash only' phase of privatisation will be accompanied by measures to stimulate private investment, both by companies and individual savers. There is a pledge to encourage foreign investors and the forecast that foreign investment could run at over US$5 billion annually from 1995. But it is equally clear that the government feels Russian industry, in its current state, is in no condition to face foreign competition. There will be what one official termed 'reasonable protectionism'.

It is estimated that about 60 per cent of the Russian economy is in some sort of trouble. The old style economy is weakening rapidly with heavy industry owing the equivalent of US$48 billion and agitating for the soft credits it had for so long, and the farming sector faced by one of the worst harvests in years. The arms industry has no orders and is undergoing a subsidised conversion. Elsewhere, plants are cutting working time and pay. The rest of the economy, both public and private, is enjoying some growth and comparative prosperity. Today 90 per cent of the small companies and 80 per cent of the service sector are in private hands. In all, some 70 per cent of the economy has been privatised and two-thirds of the jobs in basic industry are in the private sector, where employment is increasing. The fact that so much has emerged from nothing and grown in such chaotic conditions must bode well for the future.

Even a provisional verdict on the evolution of the Russian economy to date is a difficult undertaking. The results are definitely mixed. For all the fits and starts of policy, the hesitations, the U-turns, and sometimes irritating procrastination, there are clear gains. Inflation is (comparatively) lower and has gone down from year to year. The reforms are going in the right direction, although seemingly without guide or compass. The first round of privatisation was successfully completed and the second is under way. Among foreign observers there is growing confidence that Russia can stay the course. Last, but not least, the foundations have been put down for democratic institutions. Now economic stabilisation must remain the government's chief priority, particularly in the nation's finances, which remain extremely vulnerable. The grip of the old communist bosses on industry must be loosened if it is to develop in a true market economy. A social safety net is a

Exhibit 1.3

Industry in Russia, 1989–94

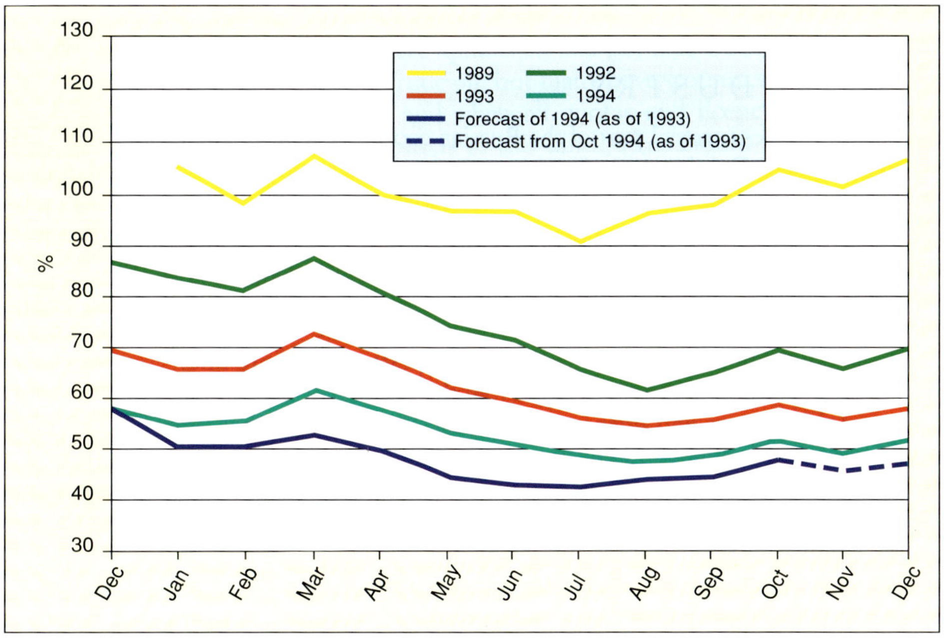

Source: EPIcentre.

Exhibit 1.4

Federal budget of Russia, 1992–94

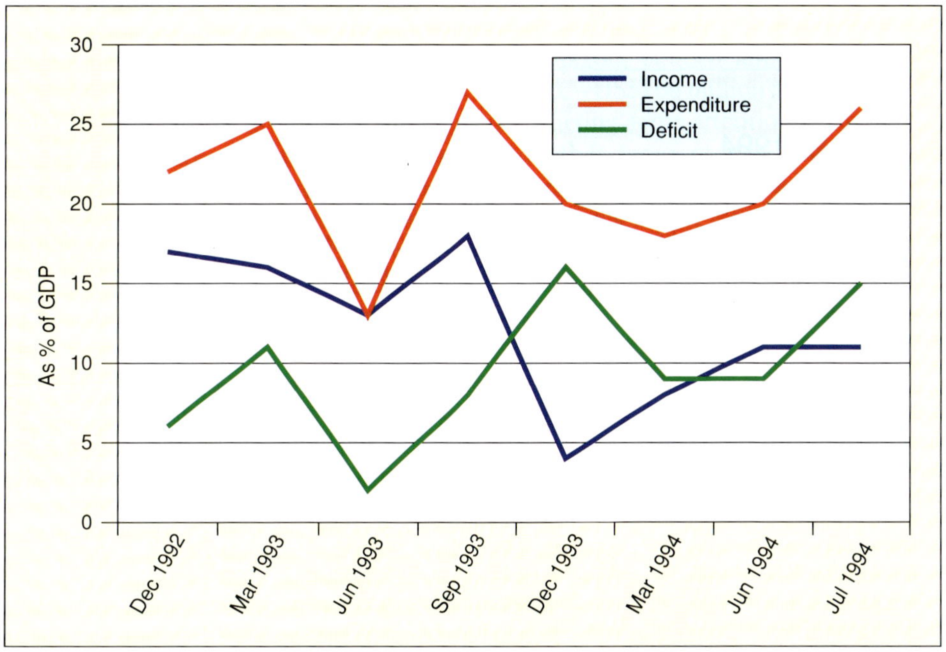

Source: EPIcentre.

standards within which rational competition could flourish. There are varying measures of chaos in such areas as computers, television, telecommunications technology, legal codes, taxes, import tariffs, monetary policy and banking. The nation seems to have gone from a state of excessive centralised planning to no planning at all. The transformation of the Russian economy has been achieved in confusion and its second phase, now underway, could well result in bank mergers and bankruptcies.

With the number of banks growing rapidly, few still have computerised links to the Central Bank. Banks are offering incompatible debit card systems that threaten retail outlets with total confusion. Laws, decrees, judicial decisions are unclear and often in conflict. The respected financial magazine *Delovie Lyudi* considers 'this lack of standardisation to be one of the central issues confronting and impeding honest business at the moment in Russia and the Newly Independent States'. Banking today is the most active commercial sector in the Russian economy, it points out. 'Vast sums of money are being made largely because of an unequal distribution of information and information technology.'

Russia's markets evolved very quickly and Russian capitalism is still in a no-holds-barred phase where the right connections or a bright idea can make instant millionaires. Government connections have always been important in money-making. Today access to information technology, computer services and real-time data are becoming indispensable, but many Russian banks are far behind their western equivalents. Nevertheless, the variety and intensity of financial activity is surprising. A Russian bank will take anything as loan collateral, as long as it is saleable: building leases, boats, planes, product inventories, paintings. They will open a debit card account, sell industrial plant, play the rouble market, and transfer hard currency to foreign banks (it is estimated that two-thirds of a bank's foreign currency assets will be abroad).

Communications remains a serious problem. Telephone lines are unreliable even when they work and high volume satellite connections are far too expensive in Moscow and St Petersburg. Some banks have installed their own fibre-electric cables through metro tunnels. The best computers in Russia are not in the space agency but in the larger banks.

Fortunes have been made in currency speculation. The rouble–dollar and rouble–Deutschmark rates do not run in tandem and an alert dealer can make 5 per cent a day on capital by transferring money out of Russia then back again. The Moscow Interbank Currency Exchange (Micex) is the country's most important currency market, responsible for setting the dollar–rouble rate and some currency trading. In mid-1994 the Micex went on-line, using an advanced multi-user package from Hewlett-Packard and now boasts it is equal to the world's most advanced exchanges.

The remodelling of the Central Bank had yet to reach its important clearing centres at the end of 1994. The payments system is essential for the supervision of money circulation and enabling companies to be paid, as well as facilitating the liquidity of the banks. In a sophisticated system, clearing and payments take place daily. But the Central Bank's potentially profitable clearing centres are still virtually useless for the commercial banks, because the institution does not have the funds to modernise properly. The payment systems left by the Soviet regime are technologically backward and few commercial banks have computerised links to the Central Bank.

The Central Bank effects transactions through several levels of its hierarchy and executes them via telex, followed by a hand-written letter, and a deal can take up to two weeks to close. In consequence, some commercial banks are uniting to establish their own clearing houses for member banks. So far, the Central Bank has set up four different testing bases, with four incompatible computer solutions from four potential suppliers.

The bank has also moved very slowly in developing the country's currency markets. It is only now thinking in terms of interest rate policies and creating short-term money markets and interbank deposit markets. The official excuse has generally been that Russia 'the world's biggest country and that linking its 11 time zones would be an impossible task for the near future'. As information technology improves in banks and trading institutions, the windfalls produced by the Central Bank's inefficiency will cease to exist and traders are already turning to other options. There are trading opportunities for banks in the new currencies of the countries of the former

Facing page: Winter Palace, St Petersburg

Russia's commercial banks are keen to win new clients

from individuals for a term of at least one year and forbidden to keep current and settlement accounts of legal entities and natural persons) have a current minimum of Ecu250,000 (Rb750 million), rising to Rb1 billion by 1999. Banks operating on the basis of 'credit co-operation', that is attracting resources from participants only and also placing them with participants, have a current minimum of Rb100 million and there are no plans to change that. Regulations on authorised capital structure require up to 10 per cent of capital in tangible assets (excluding buildings and premises), up to 1 per cent in intangibles, including securities issued by third persons, and the remaining 89 per cent in monetary funds (roubles and foreign currency).

The World Bank and the European Bank for Reconstruction and Development are providing some US$390 million to help build up a core group of 30 to 40 Russian commercial banks capable of acting as a catalyst for the wider development of the banking sector. The aim is to improve the quality of banking services and enable the core group to form the basis of a private clearing bank system. Technical assistance will also be provided to help the banks qualify as 'on-lenders' of World Bank and other international credit lines. The World Bank will provide US$200 million of the total, which will promote 'twinning' with western banks to modernise and standardise management and information systems. It will also be used to train Central Bank inspectors and create early warning mechanisms to detect problem banks.

The World Bank worked with the Central Bank to develop the International Standard Bank (ISB) programme to create a tier of banks that would be more capitalised, adhere to better banking practices and be more closely supervised than other banks. Banks are encouraged to become ISBs voluntarily and would be rewarded by various benefits. The aim is to gradually raise the level of soundness of the banking system, enable foreign companies to identify the best banks in Russia, and provide the public with the means of recognising the most appropriate banks for its specific needs. Eventually the Central Bank would have to force IBS standards on all banks.

Another development in early December 1994 was the announcement by seven leading Russian banks that they will pursue a common investment and credit policy to help develop the fragmented banking system. The new alliance, called the Reliability Club, consists of Sberbank, Agroprombank, Promstroybank, Tokobank, Mosbusinessbank, Vneshtorgbank and Vozrozhdeniye, whose combined assets as of 1 July 1994 amounted to about Rb60 trillion. The move by the banks, most of them former specialised state banks, came less than a month after three of the country's largest commercial banks, Stolichny, Imperial and Natsionainy Kredit, formed a similar alliance.

Vyacheslav Kornev, chairman of Sberbank, which has a near monopoly on household savings, said the coalition 'is a natural one since most of the seven banks already have stakes in each other. We have common interests and the alliance will, for instance, help us follow a common policy on interest rates'. He said members of the Reliability Club would also jointly finance projects designed to upgrade the Russian banking system, including several new clearing centres in co-operation with the World Bank and private western institutions.

Russian and western experts are working together to develop effective securities markets. Oddly enough, Russia's secondary markets, trading in the shares of newly privatised companies, came into being before primary markets where companies can issue shares to raise fresh funds. Developing the securities market is also an official government priority for 1995, in the hope of diverting an estimated Rb20,000 billion in domestic savings into productive investment and away from pyramid scams like the MMM fiasco.

Britain's Know-How Fund is currently helping several Russian companies launch share issues. The first was Red October, the Russian chocolate firm, which issued 3.5 million shares (one million for sale to international investors), and its 48-page prospectus is, in Russian terms, a model of disclosure which could raise the all-round level of transparency in future. Nine other companies will use British know-how to follow in Red October's pioneering path.

However, the giants of the nation's industry do not see Russia's equity markets as being large enough to raise the sort of capital they want. Gazprom, the huge gas concern, is selling 9 per cent of its stock through a placing arranged by UK merchant bank Kleinwort Benson. LUKoil, Russia's biggest privatised oil company, will sell about 15 per cent of its equity abroad and is now listed on

1957

III

THE CENTRAL AUTHORITIES

The fall of communism and the breakdown of central planning have left a vacuum at the heart of the Russian economic and financial system, and there is no professional civil service or tradition of the rule of law to fill the void. Laws and decrees have been approved but without clear means to implement them. Even official statistical data are generally deemed to be unreliable.

Elections in December 1993 saw just about 50 per cent of the electorate casting votes and there were substantial gains for the communists and ultra-nationalists. However, pro-reform and independent candidates are still exerting considerable influence on legislation, although Deputy Prime Minister Yegor Gaidar and Finance Minister Boris Fyodorov resigned after the elections, leaving radical reformers thin on the ground. The Cabinet of Prime Minister Viktor Chernomyrdin is largely made up of moderate conservatives, some with experience in Soviet industry and agriculture. President Yeltsin himself was left in a more powerful position by the new constitution and has alternated between seeming to try to rule by decree and doing nothing at all.

In the financial sector, the Central Bank is filling the vacuum by creating its own regulations or 'normative' acts. However, since the 'Law On the Central Bank of Russia' lays out the bank's terms of reference in a very general way (see Exhibit 3.1) the bank seems to have acquired or claimed the right to set the limits of its competence independently; in other words it assumes a quasi-legislative role in banking. Some private bankers claim that normative acts and bank instructions are ceasing to define existing laws and have started to substitute them. On the one hand, they say, Russian banking legislation provokes the Central Bank to fulfil a legislative role that should be completely alien to it, and on the other hand, commercial banks and credit institutions gain the ability to read what they wish into the laws.

There is a consensus that financial sector reform is urgent and several bills and decrees (including an updated Central Bank law) were making their slow, disputed way through the state Duma at the end of 1994. However, banking reform alone is not a panacea, but should take place within more general economic reforms that are still lacking. The two-tiered banking system is already in place, with the Central Bank at the first level and the commercial banks and other credit institutions at the second, but the law still needs to fix that structure as well as the proper composition of each level. All Russian commercial banks must be seen as equal in law and with equal rights to establish relations with the Central Bank and other authorities.

Russian bankers believe there is no organisation in the world that has the same mixture of functions as the Central Bank of Russia and tend to believe the concentration of these functions in one place is undesirable. Banking legislation should redistribute these functions between the Central Bank and other state organisations, they say. Other institutions have at best indirect influence over the banks. The Finance Ministry issues licences for non-banking financial institutions. The ministry's tax policy unit and, above all, its tax inspectorate, are in charge of combating tax evasion, and have investigated banks from time to time on such matters. An exchange control inspectorate also exists, but does not seem very active.

Facing page: Space monument, Moscow

tant effect on the liquidity supplied to the economy and differences of timing results in what is called the balance sheet float. If credits are made before offsetting debts, the banking system will provide liquidity to the economy; if the reverse happens liquidity is withdrawn. Hence, an efficient payments system tries to balance the timing of credits and debits to achieve a neutral effect on liquidity. The Central Bank's accounting practices for payments affect the liquidity of the whole commercial banking system.

Exhibit 3.3

Monthly interest rates, %

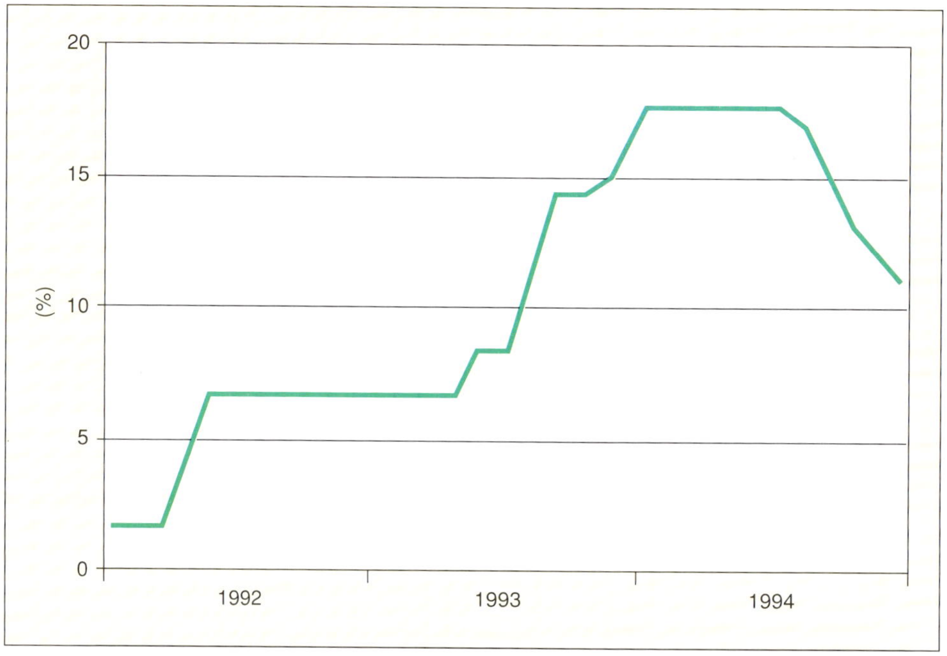

Source: Central Bank.

Exhibit 3.4

Interest rates

Annualised rates on short-term loans between commercial banks, week of 2 December 1994

Days	*% Bid*	*Change*	*% Offer*	*Change*
1	68.64	−21.36	85.87	−24.19
3	81.70	−29.01	103.00	−21.00
7	105.70	−17.30	120.00	−14.33
14	118.14	−12.56	134.22	−6.51
21	130.17	+0.04	104.29	−41.49
30	138.67	+8.49	153.00	+0.21
60	139.25	+3.50	159.38	+0.38
90	150.57	+2.07	167.78	−0.58

Source: Moscow Times.

If the Central Bank of Russia credits the account of a bank receiving funds before it debits the account of the bank paying funds, a debit float is created and, in effect, increases the reserves of the commercial banking system, increasing the bank's lending capacity. On the other hand, if the Central Bank debits the account of the payer before crediting the account of the receiver, credit float is created, commercial bank reserves are decreased and hence so is lending capacity.

The main payment instrument in Russia is the payment order. The Central Bank debits the account of a commercial bank originating the payment order. Some payments orders take weeks to reach the Central Bank and the offsetting debit is not made until then. In this way the Russian banking system accumulates a large credit float because of current accounting practices and inefficiencies that result in long clearing times for payment instruments. The accounting practices start with the Central Bank and are carried forward by the commercial banks, resulting in reductions in commercial bank reserves and a withdrawal of liquidity from the economy. The systematic debiting of payments before crediting is the direct result of the Central Bank's policies.

The Central Bank also takes part in the payments system as a provider of interbank payment services and its role as a kind of clearing house is particularly important given the early stage of Russia's market-based payments system. It has a network of offices and processing facilities which could tie the economy together and holds accounts for commercial banks, which could be used for interbank settlement. A Central Bank steering committee is working with the IMF and the World Bank to evaluate potential reforms to the Russian payments system. Meanwhile a group of the larger commercial banks, dissatisfied with Central Bank performance in this area, are looking to organise their own joint clearing facilities. The Central Bank, however, has a clear supervisory role to play in the payments system and clearing houses.

Advanced banking systems have a large value transfer system to deal with large payments, providing same day settlement with finality and increasing efficiency while reducing risk. A same day settlement system for large rouble payments would encourage the development of money markets and help the Central Bank control the money supply. Markets for short-term funds exist on some exchanges, and chiefly in the over-the-counter market, but limitations in interbank settlement have stunted market development. Minimum maturities for interbank funds and large corporate deposits are measured in weeks, (see Exhibits 3.3 and 3.4) because it could take several days or more to settle a transaction using traditional payment methods when the parties are located in the same city and much longer when they are located in different Russian regions.

An active interbank market will eventually be the main vehicle used by banks to manage their reserves with the Central Bank, and equilibrium between the supply of and demand for bank reserves will be governed by the price of the reserves which banks lend to and buy from each other. The price will probably be an overnight rate, which could be an important monetary indicator to the Central Bank, showing the state of the market. By buying or selling government securities the Central Bank will be able to add or subtract reserves in the banking system, affecting the overnight rate for interbank funds. But the further development of the interbank and government securities market will be possible only with a large rouble transfer system. Such a system would have to be operated by the Central Bank in real-time, minimising delay between the initiation of a payment and its final settlement. This also implies a burden for the Central Bank, which would have to guarantee the finality of all payments it agrees to settle.

Settlement of payments happens on a gross or net basis. In gross settlement the total amount of each individual payment is transferred; in net settlement the banks exchanging payments offset the amounts they are due to pay to and receive from each other to produce a single net debit or credit position for all banks involved, across all payments subject to the netting. The banks taking part in the netting will transfer only the necessary monetary value to settle net obligations, obviously much less than the total gross obligations. The offsetting of payable and receivable amounts can be bilateral or multilateral, but the latter is the basis for the settlements resulting from transactions on most financial exchanges and clearing houses in Russia. There are benefits and risks involved.

Netting economises on the balances that need to be maintained to settle payments flows, and

Exhibit 4.3

Documents necessary for documentation

Document		*Resident banks with no non-residents*	*Joint banking ventures with non-residents*	*Banks wholly owned by non-residents*	*Foreign banks' affiliates*
Application with a request to register the Charter and to issue a licence		✔	✔	✔	✔
Statutory documents: – Charter of the bank – Statutory Agreement –subscription list of participants (partners/shareholders) with a commitment to pay up their contribution to the authorised capital within one year – minutes of meeting of the founding members		✔	✔	✔	
List of partners/shareholders of the bank		✔	✔	✔	
Auditor's report on the financial status of partners/shareholders (not required when the stake is paid up front)		✔	✔		
Feasibility study (economic justification) for creation of the bank		✔	✔	✔	✔
Statement of accounts of legal entities and natural persons – would-be clients, with references to other banks they had used before		✔	✔		
Copy of the payment order certifying payment to the budget of the registration fee		✔	✔	✔	✔
Data on top managers' qualifications and professional skills		✔	✔	✔	✔
Participants: resident natural persons	Statement of income		✔	✔	
Participants: non-resident legal entities (all documents should be legalised at the Russian consulate complete with a certified Russian-language translation)	Decision of participant's ruling body to participate in the bank's creation		✔	✔	✔
	Charter or other document certifying status of a participant with financial statements for three preceding years		✔	✔	✔
	Written approval of the competent authority of the participant's home country for opening a bank/affiliate in the Russian Federation		✔	✔	✔
	Unconditional commitment to bear liability for affiliate's debts				✔
Participants: non-resident natural persons (all documents should be legalised at the Russian consulate complete with a certified Russian-language translation)	Attestment by prime-rate foreign bank of individual's solvency		✔	✔	✔
	References of no less than two foreign legal entities or natural persons with recognised creditworthiness		✔	✔	✔

Source: Central Bank.

calls itself a universal bank, Rosselkhozbank still behaves like a branch of government whose job is to hand out official funds.

Promstroybank was founded at the start of 1992 when its Soviet predecessor of the same name was shut down. Many regional offices of the Soviet bank broke away to become separate banks, such as Promstroi St Petersburg. Today, Promstroi has six regional and 32 smaller branches. Its Moscow headquarters has one-third of its total staff (2,500) and accounts for over 70 per cent of its loans. It is also a majority owner of 12 other banks, once its branches. The principal shareholders are large state-owned companies in industry and construction, while about 20 per cent is held by private business. About half its loans are still funded by directed credit programmes, including those for the conversion of military industry and official investment projects. However, Promstroybank is making great efforts to distance itself from directed credit and attract more private funds destined for private borrowers.

A GROWING SECTOR

State enterprises are the main shareholders in many commercial banks, and as these companies are converted to joint stock companies under privatisation, there is a sort of parallel privatisation process in the banks themselves. The state natural gas company, Gazprom, set up Imperial Bank, Tokobank was founded by oil interests, AvtoVAZbank was once a branch of the Lada automobile concern, but these banks are flourishing as diversified commercial banks. Other banks, set up to perform financial services for a state company or group of companies, are also seeing their shareholders privatised. In such banks the shareholders, the lenders and the borrowers come from the same closed circle, but even these institutions are starting to stretch themselves and reach for new business.

Most of the sector is made up by banks that opened their doors after Mikhail Gorbachev paved the way for independent banks in 1988. The largest of the new banks is Inkombank, and they include such front runners as Credo Bank, Stolichny, Menatep and Most-Bank. Their original clients were the new breed of traders. They made advances and took an astonishing range of goods as collateral. As their clients increasingly traded abroad, the banks began to get to know such areas as currency exchange and international correspondent accounts. They learned fast and some of them learned well. Some of the banks, about 20 or so, have put on financial muscle and know-how, but such things as checking accounts as used in the West are unknown.

RATINGS AND PERFORMANCE

There is something of a vogue in Russia for producing lists of domestic banks, according to varied criteria. Several Russian banks claim in their advertising to be among the top 10 or 20 in terms of capital, assets, deposits, loans or some meaningful ratio. There are generally problems with the figures. The supposed worth of assets could have been arrived at by the government, which is generally agreed to be an unreliable source, or by management assigning an arbitrary value. Loan figures for some of the former specialised banks are clouded by very large credits that might never be repaid. Profits rest on such things as how the accountants have factored in inflation. There are also tax and legal factors behind understated amounts of capitalisation. The lists seem to have something in common: most of the top 10 are former specialised banks and the majority of the top 20 have the weight of big industries behind them.

The World Bank's ratings (see Exhibit 4.4), as of 1 January 1993 put Rosselkhozbank on top in terms of assets, followed by Sberbank, Mosbisnessbank, Promstroybank and Moscow Industrial. Next comes Tokobank, with the power of oil money behind it, and Unicombank, followed by the first non-Moscow bank in the top 10, Promstroybank of St Petersburg (which broke away from the old Promstroybank to become an independent institution). The independents Credo Bank and Inkombank make up the rest of the leading 10 in terms of assets. The World Bank's top 20 had assets totalling Rb6,542 billion (the top 100 had assets of Rb9,809 billion), and

Exhibit 4.6

Top 100 Russian banks

Rank (Prev. Rank)	Name	Assets	% chg	Capital	Net deposits	Loans	% chg	Profit	% chg
1. (5)	Sberbank of Russia	20,641,606	1,072	1,658,342	8,684,353	8,573,376	722	400,000	408
2. (1)	Vneshtorgbank of Russia	14,460,010	69	1,762725	NA	958,911	172	204,742	3,658
3. (NA)	Agroprombank of Russia (Moscow)	14,161,582	NA	1,076,316	604,610	7,650,762	NA	NA	NA
4. (6)	Inkombank	3,984,451	281	906,904	109,725	1,655,757	2,967	86,511	634
5. (4)	Mosbusinessbank	3,640,704	177	196,277	102,399	463,441	258	209,758	447
6. (3)	International Moscow Bank	3,483,045	115	235,722	NA	340,115	506	28,511	99
7. (7)	Promstroybank of Russia (Moscow)	3,171,928	249	115,177	194,084	699,532	277	123,789	413
8. (10)	Moscow Industrial Bank	3,114,793	406	199,250	37,588	491,863	304	229,364	777
9. (8)	Imperial	2,383,033	270	267,054	2,920	135,870	765	15,547	107
10. (11)	Unicombank	2,356,140	366	149,735	152,365	584,787	269	143,451	424
11. (NA)	International Financial Company	2,165,782	NA	75,992	NA	74,709	NA	12,945	NA
12. (33)	Russian Credit	2,009,345	1,068	36,541	10,718	64,822	284	15,229	2,810
13. (9)	Tokobank	1,962,540	251	440,267	368,683	854,799	656	10,034	112
14. (NA)	ONEXIM Bank	1,780,286	NA	102,181	NA	69,068	NA	466	NA
15. (18)	Moscow Inter-Regional Commercial Bank	1,750,027	445	71,893	154,219	820,832	694	73,994	290
16. (15)	Menatep	1,553,407	347	43,154	32,681	278,614	151	6,556	85
17. (13)	Promstroybank (St Petersburg)	1,537,699	309	103,741	53,636	260,968	289	100,826	447
18. (19)	Vozrozhdeniye	1,520,037	437	66,992	101,248	505,161	378	47,533	321
19. (25)	Petrochemical Bank (Neftekhimbank)	1,178,691	404	193,420	24,083	223,149	779	48,447	1,139
20. (54)	Avtobank	1,154,053	960	89,778	71,731	123,151	592	54,659	600
21. (12)	Credo Bank	1,081,775	207	59,210	40,543	115,123	297	27,292	306
22. (16)	Zapsibcombank	1,026,993	238	36,139	120,986	209,304	248	13,281	90
23. (21?)	AvtoVAZbank	1,025,381	303	80,629	156,442	263,352	412	239	NA
24. (26)	Yenisei	1,014,339	371	145,912	55,036	365,480	383	21,371	242
25. (23)	Stolichny	1,003,148	322	70,413	15,370	74,913	400	9,627	187
26. (27)	Kuzbassprombank	984,714	369	24,744	189,566	339,983	302	22,052	191
27. (108)	Alfa-Bank	957,477	1,769	41,053	2,821	53,183	588	31,240	977
28. (100)	Credprombank	906,776	1,477	65,124	58,760	210,645	448	37,256	909
29. (NA)	National Credit	822,957	NA	52,104	27,425	394,960	NA	9,442	NA
30. (70)	Tveruniversalbank	796,190	818	31,502	60,680	195,338	407	16,045	449
31. (24)	Chelindbank	782,591	258	108,673	66,257	209,645	224	56,105	292
32. (22)	Bashprombank	781,051	238	105,293	120,220	277,503	260	29,692	187
33. (143)	Yakutzolotobank	780,667	2,672	NA	NA	NA	NA	NA	NA
34. (50)	Kubinbank	763,915	602	42,250	82,353	393,117	362	22	NA
35. (84)	Sakhabank	755,126	972	77,868	24,455	372,957	548	23,950	1,071
36. (72)	Yakutagroprombank	753,444	807	120,323	14,993	464,274	745	6,453	984
37. (104)	Industria-Service	719,933	1,237	12,758	14,661	87,672	308	498	−18
38. (39)	Chelyabcomzembank	712,698	444	2,541	11,820	269,112	290	1,208	−74
39. (28)	Bashkiria	683,439	288	35,408	26,459	324,310	296	3,082	643
40. (20)	Electrobank	674,401	195	53,779	47,911	427,840	156	7,059	−37
41. (35)	Agroprombank (Volgograd)	669,963	400	65,507	22,148	324,138	430	12,966	236
42. (31)	Mezhcombank	667,743	341	66,806	109,855	163,059	507	29,247	416
43. (38)	Srednevolzhsky Bank	665,644	405	26,376	91,102	334,025	387	NA	NA
44. (32)	St Petersburg	664,521	348	50,099	12,237	166,858	341	58,416	438
45. (NA)	Bashcreditbank	661,464	NA	55,977	56,539	235,146	NA	62,778	NA
46. (42)	Permcombank	656,836	429	33,284	71,395	154,555	378	5,755	219
47. (NA)	Orgbank	650,419	NA	13,994	14,107	NA	NA	8,615	NA
48. (106)	Mytishchinsky Bank	641,235	1,156	49,878	101,258	211,234	995	8,653	299
49. (53)	Promstroybank (Nizhny Novgorod)	632,726	509	106,709	20,885	180,541	309	73,786	607
50. (45)	Komibank	556,666	388	NA	NA	NA	NA	NA	NA

Compiled by Rating.

Exhibit 4.6 (continued)

Top 100 Russian banks

Rank (Prev. Rank)	Name	Assets	% chg.	Capital	Net deposits	Loans	% chg.	Profit	% chg.
51. (29)	Narodny Bank	541,052	230	43,216	9,417	211,030	NA	29,592	NA
52. (49)	Promstroybank (Rostov-on-Don)	523,458	409	28,358	34,292	198,051	400	18,920	271
53. (34)	Promstroybank (Yekaterinburg)	520,391	290	41,014	58,311	136,458	225	22,164	253
54. (30)	Conversbank	515,659	225	25,500	23,709	126,125	413	8,077	146
55. (17)	Yugorsky Bank	501,473	122	24,687	236,565	181,240	899	NA	NA
56. (47)	Promstroybank (Arkhangelsk)	493,987	358	42,655	18,866	223,730	567	4,812	114
57. (77)	Most-Bank	490,494	583	38,485	20,179	156,948	992	20,191	603
58. (51)	Complexbank	480,894	379	29,250	9,612	235,289	370	NA	NA
59. (55)	Vostsibcombank	473,035	396	49,441	42,848	182,057	413	54,676	1,039
60. (36)	Agroprombank (Rostov-on-Don)	449,763	271	25,080	18,617	185,186	266	14,034	584
61. (NA)	Eurofinance	448,732	NA	27,738	NA	139,186	NA	4,705	NA
62. (46)	Samaraagrobank	440,905	310	13,940	47,950	157,700	243	644	−89
63. (90)	Vostokinvestbank	435,355	642	NA	37,104	NA	NA	−12,680	NA
64. (62)	Zapaduralbank	433,996	405	20,875	49,316	99,800	303	10,389	319
65. (60)	Promstroybank (Kazan)	427,360	385	16,704	74,698	226,078	395	19,622	273
66. (NA)	Sibtorgbank	422,908	NA	14,704	61,419	174,400	NA	10,957	NA
67. (61)	Dalnevostochny	422,875	384	27,504	23,855	115,940	335	20,497	433
68. (97)	Mosstroybank	420,848	420	14,995	30,650	145,471	575	23,918	540
69. (79)	Mosstroyeconombank	420,384	501	34,038	80,711	223,583	545	27,116	281
70. (73)	Lefortovsky	419,910	453	10,587	14,113	47,123	247	16,907	580
71. (37)	Neftegazstroybank	417,329	253	17,059	23,910	249,743	222	5,912	80
72. (14)	Promstroybank (Omsk)	414,730	89	44,502	29,655	84,045	259	28,583	373
73. (NA)	Promstroybank (Khabarovsk)	411,020	NA	8,952	46,182	179,292	NA	NA	NA
74. (40)	Kuzbassotsbank	404,670	2,639	33,709	57,829	158,322	277	1,733	26
75. (44)	Eurasia	383,841	266	8,939	23,946	119,444	233	9,835	211
76. (NA)	Promstroybank (Blagoveshchensk)	383,361	NA	27,735	10,996	115,258	NA	14,088	NA
77. (75)	Promstroybank (Tomsk)	383,027	431	24,095	20,000	113,964	432	13,908	434
78. (69)	LadaBank	380,545	386	NA	NA	NA	NA	NA	NA
79. (59)	Kubanbank	376,035	338	17,261	91,042	155,860	440	22,818	388
80. (127)	Promradiechbank	371,788	996	5,219	22,856	126,347	820	2,994	214
81. (99)	RNCB (Russian National Commerce Bank)	370,091	595	25,299	12,876	120,958	801	19,529	441
82. (NA)	Yakimanka	369,749	NA	1,054	1,607	26,218	NA	858	NA
83. (57)	Altaicreditprombank	367,974	316	88,871	41	297,570	527	NA	NA
84. (67)	Vostok	364,518	362	23,419	121,394	146,880	382	92	NA
85. (123)	Business	357,989	898	12,030	11,360	70,985	349	16,273	469
86. (48)	Siberian Bank	355,911	274	19,242	69,382	118,867	242	875	21
87. (41)	Sotsinvestbank	341,787	205	23,788	54,490	103,034	234	10,456	200
88. (NA)	Montazhspetsbank	339,255	NA	8,452	2,976	23,050	NA	8,402	NA
89. (56)	Kolyma Bank	334,546	283	NA	NA	NA	NA	NA	NA
90. (63)	SCB-Bank	333,758	313	NA	NA	NA	NA	NA	NA
91. (58)	Gazprombank	331,906	297	1,049	30,858	79,666	239	10,259	428
92. (NA)	Promstroybank (Murmansk)	330,184	NA	14,917	84	108,914	NA	NA	NA
93. (82)	Aviabank	325,645	414	5,629	28,072	68,195	221	1,474	65
94. (NA)	Frunzensky	324,691	NA	15,982	867	36,104	NA	12,059	NA
95. (NA)	GLORIAbank	319,508	NA	11,869	NA	NA	NA	NA	NA
96. (102)	Delovaya Rossiya	314,766	534	21,155	3,567	101,875	601	13,145	496
97. (NA)	Prezentcombank	308,253	NA	16,281	1,250	38,946	NA	1,767	NA
98. (150)	Petrovsky Bank	305,865	1,168	17,739	38,517	76,808	1,102	816	125
99. (126)	Resurs-Bank	301,393	795	26,475	4,417	79,778	396	8,399	293
100. (NA)	Gorny Altai	301,182	NA	94,417	63,345	112,955	NA	NA	NA

that 70 per cent of banking turnover is in Moscow. These factors are the result of the old Soviet policy of concentrating expertise in Moscow and the unhappy reality that there are few people trained to run banks in the Russian provinces.

The Moscow commercial bank, GLORIAbank and the consulting firm PAKK analysed the 1 January 1994 balance sheet of 1,424 commercial banks (see Exhibits 4.7(a), 4.7(b) and 4.7(c)) and rated them according to balance, capital, equity, and various balance sheet ratios. The results showed that eight Russian banks had assets of more than Rb1 trillion, and their combined assets accounted for over 17 per cent of commercial banks' total assets. Another 45 banks had assets of between Rb200 billion and Rb1 trillion, or 45 per cent of the total assets of the sample group. Some 270 banks had assets somewhere between Rb20 and Rb2,000 billion, or 25 per cent of the total assets. Finally, 1,101 banks had assets of under Rb20 billion, or 13 per cent of the total assets of the sample group of banks. It will come as no surprise to learn that the top eight were Vneshtorgbank, Mosbusinessbank, International Moscow Bank, Promstroybank of Russia, Inkombank, Moscow Industrial Bank, Russian Credit and Imperial.

However, in terms of capital, while the leader was the same, Russian Credit came second, National Credit third, Tokobank fourth and Oneksim Bank (a newcomer to the lists) fifth. These five had equity of more than Rb25 billion and accounted for 36 per cent of the total equity of the sample. Sixty-two banks had equity of between Rb3 and Rb25 billion, or 19 per cent of the total, 198 banks had equity of Rb1 to Rb3 billion and 1,158 banks had less than Rb1 billion.

In terms of capital, the leading bank remained the same, followed by Imperial, Tokobank, Inkombank, International Moscow Bank and Mosbusinessbank, which all had capital of more than Rb100 billion, or 35 per cent of the total. Sixty-four banks had capital of between Rb10 and Rb100 billion, or 34 per cent of the total. Some 222 banks had between Rb2 and Rb10 billion, while 1,130 banks had less than Rb2 billion.

Given the game of musical chairs played by the members of the list when the criterion changed, the researchers sorted out a group of 160 banks with assets amounting to more than Rb20 billion, capital of Rb2 billion and equity of Rb1 billion. Few banks turned out to have profits larger than Rb10 billion, while the profits/assets ratio was approximately the same for all banks in the smaller sample.

In a rating of the lending capacity of the Moscow region banks, the respected *Delovie Lyudi* magazine, using data from several sources, listed high capacity lenders in three groups and awarded the top capacity rating to Agroprombank, Mosbusinessbank, Moscow Industrial Bank, Promstroybank of Russia, Sberbank, Vneshtorgbank, and Vozrozhdeniye. The second rank of high capacity lenders was led by Imperial and included Inkombank, Tokobank and Unicombank. A third group included Most-Bank, Russian Credit and Stolichny.

Finally, the bank ratings published by the *Moscow Times* (see Exhibit 4.8) in December 1994 use profits-to-assets ratio as a measuring rod and break down Russia's top banks into three groups, the members of which are almost identical to the high capacity lenders in *Delovie Lyudi's* groupings.

Given the fierce competition in the sector, it is not surprising to find that Moscow's biggest and most persistent advertisers are banks, which announce their virtues via hoarding, newspaper, magazine and TV. Some banks have even offered up to 1,000 per cent on rouble deposits and around 65 per cent for dollars. The faster inflation galloped, the more business they did, but such rates will surely drive these banks out of business eventually. However, a handful of Russian banks have emerged as acceptable international counterparties that find their way into most of the lists and stand out from the multitude of the mediocre or the downright bucket shops. The better banks are usually audited by one of the big six accounting firms, but also report quarterly to the Central Bank in what is known as Broadly Accepted Accounting Standards (BAAS), a transitional system. The World Bank and the European Bank for Reconstruction and Development (EBRD) spent two years selecting a group of Russian banks for their Financial Institutions Development Project (FIDP). These are not apparently always the best banks, but they are judged to be good enough and important enough to benefit from a twinning arrangement with one or more western banks.

Facing page: Moscow remains the centre of Russian banking

Exhibit 4.7(a)

Top five Russian commercial banks by balance

Bank	*Balance (Rb bn)*	*Capital (Rb bn)*	*Equity (Rb mn)*
Vneshtorgbank of Russia	10,803	653	339,175
Mosbusinessbank	3,118	106	1,800
International Moscow	2,757	142	275
Promstroybank of Russia	1,972	96	6,000
Inkombank Moscow	1,812	151	6,391

Exhibit 4.7(b)

Top five Russian commercial banks by equity

Bank	*Equity (Rb mn)*	*Balance (Rb bn)*	*Capital (Rb bn)*
Vneshtorgbank of Russia	339,175	10,803	653
Russian Credit	67,247	1,341	53
National Credit	29,833	282	10
Tokobank	25,600	967	311
Oneksim-Bank	25,000	420	49

Exhibit 4.7(c)

Top five Russian commercial banks by capital

Bank	*Capital (Rb mn)*	*Balance (Rb bn)*	*Equity (Rb mn)*
Vneshtorgbank of Russia	653	10,803	339,175
Imperial	336	1,002	775
Tokobank	311	967	25,600
Inkombank Moscow	151	1,812	6,391
International Moscow Bank	142	2,757	275

Grants of US$4.5 million each over three years will go toward the cost of hiring the foreign bank as a consultant, with the Russian institution making up any cost difference.

So far the World Bank has been remarkably coy about issuing a list of the chosen banks. However, one admitted candidate is Inkombank, which has short-listed ABN-Amro, Westdeutsche Landesbank, and Banco Bilbao Vizcaya as potential twins. Another candidate, Mosbusinessbank, is looking at Deutsche Bank, NatWest, Bank of America and BBV.

The World Bank's FIDP auditors criticised some banks for the number of loans made to their own shareholders, 'connected lending', in banking terminology. FIDP proposed limits of 25 per cent for single borrowers and only 10 per cent for shareholders. Inkombank was set up in 1988 with shareholders that include the oil and gas pipelines operator Transneft and the Association of Aircraft Manufacturers (Sokol); however, it claims not to have lent more than the statutory 10 per cent of its own funds to any client.

DialogBank chose not to apply for the FIDP. It is a relatively small bank but, along with its

Exhibit 4.8

Bank Ratings

Figures are in billions of roubles; R=rank, P/A=Profits-to-assets ratio, as of 30 November 1994

	Assets	*Capital*	*R*	*Profit*	*R*	*P/A*
A3 Banks						
AgropromRos	14,161	1,076.0	3	–	–	–
VneshtorgRos	14,460	1,762.0	1	204.0	4	0.0141
Mosbusinessbank	3,640	1,96.0	5	209.0	3	0.0576
MosIndusrialBk	3,114	1,99.0	4	229.0	2	0.0736
PromstroybkRos	3,171	1,15.0	6	123.0	5	0.0390
SberbankRos	20,641	16,58.0	2	400.0	1	0.0193
A2 Banks						
Avtobank	1,154	89.0	6	54.0	3	0.0473
Vozrozhdeniye	1,520	66.0	7	47.0	4	0.0312
Imperial	2,383	267.0	3	15.0	6	0.0065
Inkombank	3,984	906.0	1	88.0	2	0.0217
MezhMosBank	3,483	235.0	4	28.0	5	0.0081
Orgbank	650	13.0	8	8.6	8	0.0132
Tokobank	1,962	440.0	2	10.0	7	0.0051
Unicombank	2,365	149.0	5	143.0	1	0.0608
A1 Banks						
Alfa-Bank	957	41.0	6	31.0	1	0.0326
Vita	297	6.4	11	8.7	9	0.0292
Konversbank	515	25.0	8	8.1	10	0.0156
Credo Bank	1,081	59.0	3	27.0	4	0.0252
Lefortovsky	419	10.0	10	16.0	6	0.0402
Mezhcombank	667	66.0	2	29.0	2	0.0437
Most-Bank	490	38.0	7	20.0	5	0.0411
MytishkomBk	–	–	–	–	–	–
Narodny	541	43.0	5	29.0	2	0.0548
Natsionalny Kredit	822	52.0	4	9.4	8	0.0114
Neftegazstroybank	417	17.0	9	5.9	11	0.0141
ONEXIM Bank	–	–	–	–	–	–
Promradtekhbank	371	5.2	12	2.9	12	0.0080
Stolichny	1,003	70	1	9.6	7	0.0095

Source: Moscow Times, December 1994.

brokerage arm Troika Dialog, is involved in some of Russia's most rapidly developing markets. One foreign banker calls it 'the best-run bank in Russia'. It offers commercial services to around 1,000 clients, including some solvent Russian enterprises, foreign companies and foreign embassies in Moscow. It might well claim to be the most automated bank in eastern Europe and aims to service 20,000 clients at each of its Russian branches.

There is considerable insistence among Russian bankers that economic growth must be ensured to stabilise the country's financial system and its currency. But there is also a very important feedback on growth from the financial system. Grigory Yavlinsky, one of the authors of the

СССР
РЕСПУБЛИК

'500 Day-Plan', which favoured gradualism rather than shock therapy (implemented in 1992) for the Russian economy, points out that in present-day Russian conditions, it will be impossible to attain growth and structural adjustment if the proper policies in the 'real economy' are not accompanied by adequate measures in the financial sector. Banks, says Yavlinsky, do not just create money, they also ensure the necessary allocation of real resources in the economy.

The commercial banks provide only short-term loans; indeed little else can be expected in an economy where annual inflation is usually measured in four digits. Real interest rates have risen considerably, but still remain negative most of the time. Yavlinsky maintains that the banks gain high profits in three basic ways: first, short-term loans (terms ranging from one to three months) to which a compounded interest rate is applied. Second, deposit interest rates are naturally lower than lending rates, and the banking system enjoys a legal monopoly on settlements among industrial enterprises and therefore merely needs to lend with a margin over interest paid on settlement accounts of the enterprises. The widespread use of interfirm credit can be attributed in part to the desire of enterprises to avoid what Yavlinsky describes as 'this *de-facto* taxation of money on their accounts'. Third, he adds, most large banks combine rouble and dollar loans, thereby raising the effective interest rate. Enterprises in need of rouble funds are, in some cases, offered bank loans of up to 50 per cent denominated in US dollars. For instance, during the three months of summer 1993, when the dollar–rouble exchange rate had stabilised and the lending rate stood at about 200 per cent, this implied an effective 200 per cent annual interest rate on the dollar part of the loan.

These devices serve all possible goals, other than the main one of reallocating resources efficiently and creatively. Yavlinsky, who left the state Duma to found Russia's leading think-tank EPIcentre (Centre for Economic and Political Research) in 1990, has urged the government to develop a system of state and private banks offering long-term credits. Long-term credits are currently provided by the Central Bank and distributed by the commercial banks (directed credits), which makes them political in nature and cannot assure effective feasibility studies or a system of monitoring. A system of state and private banks, acting with state support and co-ordinating activities with the World Bank, EBRD and any other international institutions interested in helping finance Russia's long-term restructuring, could provide what is currently lacking, he says.

But, if long-term projects are ultimately to be financed by private sources, rather than budget deficits, personal savings must be vigorously promoted.

Sberbank has been, and to a large extent still is, in a monopoly situation in the small personal savings field and its deposit interest rates are 'ridiculously low'. If the money it accumulates is to be channelled into long-term investment projects, its interest rates can hardly be expected to rise much. Yavlinsky, a potential presidential candidate next time round, reminds the authorities that special savings deposits, repaid in products such as automobiles, were tried out in the latter years of the Soviet Union and suffered a loss of credibility when the state defaulted on them. They could be reintroduced with full state guarantees, he suggests. Additionally, he points out that Russian experience in the 1920s could be utilised as a means of stabilising the currency and promoting savings. At that time a new 'parallel' currency was introduced, fully backed by liquid reserves, precious metals and hard currencies. The more stable monetary units in Russia's fledgling market economy are the US dollar and the Deutschmark, but it would be more expedient to have a national currency which would be stable internationally and fully convertible. The new money, injected slowly and cautiously to maintain a fixed exchange rate between it and a basket of hard currencies, would by virtue of its stability, gradually squeeze out all local soft currencies, including the Russian rouble. 'This goal', Yavlinsky says, 'took less than two years to be achieved in full in Soviet Russia in the 1920s.'

Given the near total absence of financing from private sources for long-term projects in Russia, something clearly needs to be done. Since nothing approaching an answer to the problem has come from the government or the Central Bank, many bankers feel Yavlinsky's proposals should at least be debated. Certainly there is a consensus that saving must be promoted in a creative and vigorous way and that the domestic currency, whatever it may be called eventually, must be made stable and fully convertible.

THE INTERBANK MARKET

The better banks are able to refinance themselves in the interbank market, whose rates are less steep than those of the Central Bank; but those able to shop in that market are few. Mosbusinessbank has '30 or 40 banks that we can deal with comfortably'. Sberbank is a major contributor to the interbank market, putting about a third of its Rb7.9 billion balance into interbank loans. Foreign banks remain wary of Russian risk, placing some short-term interbank deposits with a handful of banks. Bank Austria was experimenting with three-month deposits of between US$2 million and US$4 million 'to test how reliable the banks are'. International Moscow Bank, a joint venture, is lending to Russian banks, but 'we don't rush in with one-year deposits'. If Citibank did need to place deposits locally, 'There are, hypothetically, about five banks we would be comfortable dealing with in small size – up to one month.'

The interbank market still depends on pieces of paper, which means that only the Moscow region is liquid. Even there, the spread between bid and offer can be tens of percentage points and there is no realistic benchmark rate. Banks without a Moscow operation must look elsewhere. The government's main instruments of monetary policy is the rate it charges for credits from the central credit board, which banks then lend to specified companies. But banks regard this as a political rather than a market rate and most have distanced themselves from such directed credits with their thin 3 per cent margin. Banks denied access to the interbank market have to turn to the Central Bank's monthly credit auctions, where it offers at least 15 per cent of the total centralised credit, or the Central Bank's seven-day discount window, where rates are about 20 per cent higher.

The interbank marker remains the cheapest source of funds, aside from customer deposits. Some Russian banks have started to offer promissory notes or commercial paper as an alternative, but the foreign banks are not enthusiastic, since existing legislation does not seem to back such instruments. In fact the only legal basis for the notes claimed so far is that they were accepted as long as 60 years ago by Soviet commissars. Nonetheless, Mosbusinessbank was preparing an issue of rouble promissory notes in mid-1994. Promissory notes have been suggested as the solution to inter-company debt – one of Russia's biggest problems. Most companies are caught in a chain of payment arrears, whose gross totals about Rb1 trillion. The chain stretches from the government – behind on many payments – because tax revenues are 70 per cent below budget and it is short of cash, down through the companies of all sizes. Although the laws have been written, neither the enforcement of payments nor bankruptcy have been tested in the courts.

Along with the bond and currency markets, the interbank market underpins the Russian financial system. While the market indices are not widely understood, they are significant as interbank transactions are closely connected with crediting and deposit transactions and the situation on the interbank market often shapes the interest rates set by banks on deposits, settlement accounts and market loans. Interbank loans and deposits constitute an alternative way for banks to draw cash resources. Monitoring has revealed that changes in the interest offered on deposits and interbank credits in 1994 coincided with deposit rates, repeating medium-term fluctuations in interbank credit rates after a certain time lag. This could help forecast how interest rates on deposits are likely to change in the near future.

Interbank and commercial credits can be seen by banks as rival options for the investment of free funds. In developed nations, interbank market rates such as Libor are employed to determine the rates on commercial credits. This is done by adding a few percentage points to the Libor rate, depending on the guarantees available, the borrowers credit rating, history and other factors. As the risk of defaults on commercial credits is higher, they tend to be more expensive than interbank credits, so the level of interbank credit rates constitutes the limit below which rates on credits to end-borrowers cannot fall. Of course, this is only true if a bank wants to make a profit, rather than simply supporting a shareholder with financial injections.

One of the general indicators on the Moscow money market is the IBC (Interbank Credit Rate). Indices of this sort include the Mibid (Moscow Interbank Bid), Mibor (Moscow Interbank Offered Rate), and Instar (Interbank Short-Term Actual Rate). The Mibid/Mibor rates, computed by the Information Consortium with Central Bank participation, are an average of declared bank rates on IBCs sought and offered. The Mibor is viewed as the stated prime lending rate.

In advanced financial systems, stated rates are close to or identical with actual rates, that is a bank tries to keep to the rates it has itself announced. However, in Russia, a bank does not necessarily agree to perform a transaction at the originally quoted price and this is not seen as a violation of business ethics. The volatile conditions on the Russian financial market often result in actual rates varying greatly from those initially declared, so the latter do not mirror the real state of affairs on the IBC market with any accuracy. Additionally, the practical use of the Mibid/Mibor rates is hindered by the substantial absolute margin between the IBC rates offered by lenders and sought by borrowers. The Mibid/Mibor rates are calculated based on the IBC quotations of larger banks, which excludes the medium-sized banking operations that actually determine the situation in the interbank market. But a developed IBC market without some equivalent of Mibid/Mibor rates would probably be impossible. There is, however, much room for improvement.

The Interbank Finance House computes Instar on the basis of actual transactions as the average weighted rate on credits of each lending term. The index is objective, but the method of calculation has flaws. Many banks covered by Instar computing do not attract or float IBCs on a large scale. The volume of business is crucial for determining average rates and the Instar rate mostly reflects the policy of the authorised banks on the IBC market. Experts are critical of the statistical filtration of deals, whose interest rates contrast sharply with the norm. When Instar is calculated, the multitude of small transactions makes a greater impact on the resulting average than several major deals with combined value which outweighs that of the smaller transactions.

Since September 1994, the Central Bank has employed Miacr (the Moscow Interbank Actual Rate), which is computed as 'the average weighted rate based on the amounts of actual credit transactions by commercial banks' – in other words, the rate on credits actually drawn. However, there is a feeling that it is wrong to accentuate actual credit rates at the expense of the rates at which loans are attracted. No data has been published on the banks covered by the calculations or the computing methods. Finally, in August 1994, the Financial Information Agency began daily calculations and reports of its own Moscow IBC market index, which is the average weighted lenders' and borrowers' rates in actual transactions. Calculations are based on the rates and turnovers of the larger banks operating on the interbank market. For a bank to be included it has to remain above the established minimum weekly turnover limit for four weeks. If gross turnover slips below the limit, the bank is excluded from the coverage four weeks later.

Clear deviant rates on individual transactions are offset by means of statistical methods, including the classical theory of exceptions. The index can be used to work out the profitability of the interbank market as well as the parameters of transactions with other financial assets. All existing indicators have their drawbacks and there is scope for improvement not only in computer techniques but also by finding a way to obtain information from some of the larger banks unwilling to share data about their business.

BANKS AND THE HARD CURRENCY MARKET

A number of Russian banks have made enormous profits by moving in and out of hard currency at the appropriate time, taking advantage of the Central Bank's abrupt twists and turns in interest rate policy. After price controls were lifted in January 1992, the discount rate stayed around the 100 per cent mark for about 18 months. Meanwhile inflation was running at over 1,000 per cent. The gainers were banks, such as Promstroybank, which handled billions in directed credits to handpicked industrial clients, with the 3 per cent margin. Sberbank sucked in the national savings at such a rate that some claim it is the most profitable bank in the world. It paid only 30 per cent at the time, but there was little choice for people wanting to save surplus cash. Some of the newer

Improved economic conditions have boosted demand for housing in the Moscow region commercial banks joined the profits spree. Former specialised banks obtained government money at 80 per cent annually, lent funds to a commercial bank at 130 per cent, and the commercial bank lent to clients with an appropriate mark-up. The prices of the goods sold by the client would rise to cover these costs in a few short months and everyone was remarkably happy.

Things changed in 1993 when the then Finance Minister Boris Fyodorov persuaded the Central Bank to hike discount rates to around 200 per cent. At that time the rouble seemed to be holding its value and holders of rouble assets were making money by lending to each other. One bank said it had about 90 per cent of its capital on the interbank market and others probably came close to that. The large profits on such insider business did bring back some flight capital, which helped support the currency and keep the merry-go-round moving. But few businesses could afford to borrow money at the prevailing rates. In the summer of 1994, a cut in interest rates to around 130 per cent and a Central Bank decree that it would not purchase roubles sent the rouble plummeting, even though monthly interest rates had come down into the single digit range. The banks looked for alternative routes to profit.

Improved economic conditions boosted the demand for housing and office space in the Moscow region and some banks lent for construction or for the import of goods in wide demand. Some, such as Inkombank, began attempting to challenge Sberbank's near monopoly on savings by offering better interest rates.

According to a report by the EPIcentre think-tank, the hard currency market situation was stable until September 1994, but rouble depreciation amounted to 6.3 per cent over the previous months. The rouble's depreciation was quicker than the level of interest rates on short-term interbank credits and arbitrage transactions became profitable in September. These typically involved the receipt of a rouble credit, its conversion into dollars, and then conversion of dollars to roubles and repayment of the rouble credit. Money on the rouble market was moving into hard currency and creating a demand for the dollar.

The Central Bank announced in September that it would change its priorities. Previously it had sought to neutralise dramatic changes in the dollar/rouble exchange rate by intervening in the market. Now it said the number one priority was the need to protect the competitiveness of domestic commodities and encourage exporters. This seemed to mean promoting depreciation of the rouble against the dollar, compared to actual inflation rates. It said its second priority would be to approximately co-ordinate rouble depreciation and inflation. EPIcentre thought these priorities were contradictory.

A storm broke on the hard currency market in the last 10 days of September and early October. The rouble dropped on 22 September by 5.4 per cent, on 28 September by 6.26 per cent, and on 5 October by 5.25 per cent. EPIcentre believes the gap between dollar supply and demand was 'increased artificially', in expectation of a hard currency intervention by the Central Bank, which would have needed to inject only a small amount of hard currency to prevent a dramatic increase in the exchange rate. 'Evidently the major commercial banks began to speculate on the fall of the rouble rate, while the Bank of Russia voluntarily withdrew, demonstratively refusing to take part in the sales and stressing that it still controls the hard currency market and is simply allowing the market to find a new balance.' EPIcentre believes the Central Bank officials lost their nerve. On 1 July 1994 the bank's hard currency reserves amounted to US$6–7 billion and with its hard currency interventions in August and September totalling US$2.5 billion, this high reserve loss made the bank nervous.

The hard currency reserves of commercial banks were growing more rapidly than those of the Central Bank; in fact the bank itself estimated them at around US$13–15 billion in August. After the autumn interventions the situation changed even more in favour of the commercial banks. One effect of the rouble's fall was to make imports more expensive and exports more competitive, but another was to spur inflation once again in September and October.

An even greater storm lay ahead. On 11 October 1994 the rouble had depreciated by 845 points (27.43 per cent during one trading session). Before that date there had been only four such drops during the entire existence of the Moscow Interbank Currency Exchange (Micex), with three of them occurring during the announcement and start of the shock therapy reforms: November 1991 to January 1992. The official rouble rate is determined by the rate of the Micex, but rouble depreciation did not just affect the hard currency market. In a number of stores and shops goods are priced in US dollars, although payment can be made only in roubles, and imports during 1992–94 rose sharply as a percentage of Russia's retail turnover. Hence, exchange rate dynamics influence inflation, interest rates, and the people's standard of living.

EPIcentre says the January 1994 upsurge in hard currency demand stemmed from several factors, including a protracted containment of the exchange rate in the summer and autumn of 1993, the rise in January inflation and the start of the new financial year. The Central Bank made efforts to control leaps in the rouble rate, accounting for 52 per cent of the hard currency supply (nearly US$1.2 billion). From February hard currency demand began to contract and the exchange rate stabilised somewhat, its decreases lagging behind inflation rates. In the spring the Moscow government brought in a tax on hard currency transactions in Moscow and such transactions became less profitable. Speculators seemed to lose interest in hard currency transactions. and, on the whole, the Micex was serving only compulsory currency sales by exporters. All remaining currency transactions were carried out on the interbank market. In June, the Central Bank bought, for the first time in 1994, a little more currency than it actually sold.

The Central Bank was curbing the fall of the rouble by reducing its own hard currency reserves, but failed to complement the loss of its reserves by buying currency on the exchange, EPIcentre points out. It acquired hard currency from the Ministry of Finance, mainly credits from the IMF, so there was a growing potential for the rouble rate to be overestimated. In the second quarter of 1994, money supply growth rates increased. Because of a contraction of inflation, interest rates in Russia became positive in real terms, while the rouble depreciated more slowly than inflation. The population's investments in commercial banks and other financial companies grew sharply and the volume of transactions with state treasury bonds rose considerably, while high interest rates were maintained in the interbank credit market. The diversion of money into speculative rouble transactions slowed consumer inflation and made interest rates even higher in real terms. It became clear that this could not continue, as the maintenance of high interest rates for private investors would have ended in a wave of bankruptcies. Nor was it profitable for the state to pay exorbitant interest on its own obligations.

The economic situation began changing in June and a wave of private investor bankruptcies started at the beginning of July. Public interest in hard currency cash quickened as people sought to protect their savings from inflation. As a rule, when the rouble's fall is fast, the population and the financial sector invests in dollars; when the rouble declines slowly, the size of such investments is reduced. In 1992 average monthly purchases of hard currency increased 50-fold, in 1993 they went up 40-fold. By 1994 purchase volumes had risen to US$1.3 billion a month, and rose only 1.4 times in the first seven months of the year. However, in the August–September period, there was a dramatic change: purchase volume virtually doubled to US$2.8 billion.

In September three trends were observed: an accelerated depreciation of the rouble, inflationary growth which reduced real interest rate levels, and a reduction in bank deposit interest rates. The interbank credit market reference rate, which had fallen from 120 per cent to 103 per cent in August, bounced back to 115 per cent by 3 October and there were abrupt increases in the rates for short-term credits (with one-day credits soaring from 40 per cent to 92 per cent). Interest in state treasury bonds, usually popular with the banks, began to fall rapidly. People got rid of their bonds, bond prices fell, and an initial distribution auction of the 20th issue of state treasury bonds flopped. Despite a total growth in bond yields of 45 percentage points (up to 165 per cent annual interest), less than half the issue was placed. Dollar demand did not contract and the Central Bank's reserves were drying up, but the government and the Central Bank did nothing very much to change the situation.

Over the 21 September to 7 October period, the yield from investments in hard currency totalled almost 700 per cent annual interest, EPIcentre calculates. Naturally such a fantastic yield attracted a lot of participants to the hard currency market. All rouble resources were mobilised for hard currency speculation. At the beginning of October, rates on 1–3-day credits reached up to 1,000 per cent on some registered transactions. On 11 October dollar demand exceeded supply 14-fold. The rouble dropped to over 3,000 to the dollar and could have dropped further if the Central Bank had not hastily intervened with money and persuasion, convincing the commercial banks that enough was enough. The banks promptly stopped trading, reduced purchase applications and increased the hard currency supply.

The collapse of the rouble on the Micex made all Russians 30 per cent poorer, reducing the average salary from the equivalent of US$62 to around US$48, and 11 October became 'Black Tuesday'. There was thunder and lightning from President Yeltsin, who threatened to expose and punish the guilty parties. The Central Bank's interventions finally took the rouble back to pre-crisis levels, theoretically restoring the value of Russian salaries, but prices did not come down when the rouble rose again. Importers struggled to repay hard currency loans raised to finance imports, because price hikes meant they could not sell their goods quickly. Even the exporters soon realised that they too lived and shopped in Russia. Small businesses and banks that speculated in foreign exchange and did not move out fast enough when the Central Bank finally came to the rouble's rescue were undoubtedly in trouble.

Everyone had a theory about who was to blame. Anatoly Chubais, then chairman of the state Property Committee, blamed 'seasonal factors', Prime Minister Viktor Chernomyrdin blamed 'foreign exchange dealers', and claimed the rouble collapse was not 'a reflection of the actual state of the Russian economy'. But emergency stabilisation measures, including an increase in the Central Bank's refinance rate to 170 per cent and a decision to float another issue of treasury bills demonstrated that the economy had indeed been hit by Black Tuesday. President Yeltsin talked of 'political sabotage', pointing a finger at the opposition; others blamed the Central Bank for not regulating the activities of the banks properly; some exonerated the Central Bank and the Finance Ministry, blaming the government itself, because the Central Bank's decision to stop intervening in the market could not have been taken without the prior approval of the president or the prime minister. Naturally, the commercial banks were blamed, particularly those trading on the Micex, and the directors of state companies who bought dollars to protect their money from inflation came in for criticism, as did exporters who stood to gain from further falls in the rouble

EPIcentre had its own explanation, which both involved and exculpated the commercial banks. 'We are convinced that the actions of the commercial banks in all four onslaughts on the rouble and the silent demonstrative permission of the Bank of Russia to allow the rouble to depreciate were co-ordinated', it said. 'We cannot see anything criminal in the acts of the commercial banks (this is how economic subjects should operate on the market) and believe that the Bank of Russia should be held responsible for making strategic and tactical blunders, as should the government for stubbornly refusing to admit to even temporary defeat in its anti-inflation drive and for consequently failing to do anything to avert the negative developments on Russia's hard currency market.'

The rouble depreciation assumed serious political proportions. Both Central Bank chairman Viktor Geraschenko and acting Minister of Finance Sergei Dubinin were forced out by the president. But 1994 was to close without the state Duma approving Yeltsin's choice of Tatyana Paramonova as Geraschenko's successor at the Central Bank and she functioned as acting chairman pending approval, which the Duma said would be forthcoming. By November 1994 the refinance rate had reached 180 per cent and the rouble was depreciating more slowly under the watchful eye of the Central Bank, striving to make arbitrage transactions unprofitable. By the end of the year the rouble stood in the region of 2,300 to the dollar. Annual inflation was thought to be about 207 per cent.

There is little doubt that several of the better banks trading on the Micex came out of the market at the right time and made very high profits indeed. Western diplomats, brokers and businessmen thought the panic would not have a lasting effect on investor confidence. Several thought that Russia's incoherent and punishing tax system is a larger disincentive to investors than the currency crash of Black Tuesday.

THE FINANCIAL–INDUSTRIAL GROUPS

During the 1989 to 1991 period, major state industrial companies had extra cash on their hands with which they set up their own banks. Those days are over. Economic conditions, particularly high inflation, have been very unfavourable for production but extremely profitable for lending. Today, many of the banks created under perestroika and after have matured quickly, diversified their holdings, expanded their share base, and liberated themselves from the control of the companies that set them up. The rules in Russia's emerging market economy are laid down by financial structures which have gradually started to divide their parents among themselves.

Since the current economic climate is unfavourable for small business, capital from Russian banks is being channelled into the large industrial enterprises, shares of which can still be bought up fairly cheaply. In 1994, observers noted the formation of 'unofficial' but powerful financial–industrial groups known by the Russian acronym FPG. According to President Yeltin's decree On the Role of Financial–Industrial Groups and the Procedure for Forming Them, an FPG is any organisation that includes both industrial enterprises and financial entities, which has been set up under the provisions of that decree, which resulted from the lobbying of state industry directors anxious to extract resources out of the financial sector and into industry.

By the end of 1994, only three FPGs had been registered officially: Sokol in Voronezh, Dragotsennosti Urala in Yekaterinburg, and Ruskhim in Moscow. None had done anything with their new status. Russia's other financial–industrial structures are not in any hurry to register because the decree introduced restrictions on shareholding by FPGs in non-banking enterprises, including the buying of shares in companies undergoing privatisation. Banks found a way around the restrictions by forming 'investment companies', and so have no motive to register as FPGs, which would give the government extra information about their activities. In addition, the unofficial FPGs worry that the government might pressure them to invest in unprofitable ventures.

Unofficially, the leading non-registered FPGs are considered to be Inkombank, with its network of financial, investment and insurance subsidiaries; Alfa-Bank, which controls one of Russia's largest investment funds; Bioprocess, which holds shares in nearly 100 firms in oil and chemicals; Tveruniversal, Menatep and others. Such putative FPGs, usually consisting of major Moscow banks and industrial companies throughout Russia, are said by some to be holding Russia together economically. But they now find the opportunities at home too limited.

The unofficial FPGs have let it be known that Yeltsin's decree is already out of date, since it does not meet their economic needs. A new draft law on FPGs was prepared and sent to the upper chamber, the Federation Council, after having been submitted to leading bankers for evaluation. Legislators say it is intended to stimulate a new round of formation and structuring of FPGs in Russia, increasing their power and presence.

As some of the FPGs have property in the former Soviet republics, several Russian officials have insisted that the other countries of the Commonwealth of Independent States adopt similar laws, guaranteeing that FPGs property will not be renationalised. In the CIS countries, FPGs are a new idea and the Russian groups should overwhelm in economic terms any FPGs that might arise in the CIS countries. Indeed the thought is occurring that the Russian FPGs might well be instrumental in restoring a unified economy over the territory of the former Soviet Union. Experts say that Russian banks already control the re-export of Russian raw materials from the Baltic states and that they are making inroads into other economic spheres. Groups in Russia, the Ukraine, Belarus and Kazakhstan who are lobbying for a so-called Economic Union on the old Soviet territory are actively discussing the organisation of FPGs and lobbying for legislation to cover their activities. Legislation similar to the latest Russian version was introduced during 1994 in the legislatures of the Ukraine, Belarus and Kazakhstan.

THE ASSOCIATION OF RUSSIAN BANKS

The history of Russian commercial banking is very short, covering little more than five years, and in 1988 there were only two dozen banks registered. In March 1991, there were 65, all of which attended the first congress of commercial banks, where they founded the Association of Russian Banks (ARB) and elected a 27-strong council to run it. In May 1992 a second congress was held and the new association announced that it had a total of 470 members. One year later the number grew to 612. By the time the fourth congress came round in April 1994 there were 784 members and by the end of that year the number swelled to at least 860, including commercial banks, regional banking associations, financial companies and other related organisations. Some 51 per cent of the members have been in the business three or four years.

Geographically, the ARB covers all Russia's economic regions, although the ratio of ARB members to the total number of banks in those regions is different. ARB banks are mostly in the Volga-Vyatka area (over 44 per cent of all commercial banks); in the Northern, North West and North Caucasian regions ARB members represent less than 30 per cent and members have 2,240 branches and subsidiaries. Forty-one branches function in the other former Soviet republics. Sberbank, the savings bank of Russia, is also a member of the ARB, with more than 31,000 branches and offices.

So far, the ARB has recruited over one-third of the existing banks as members. Most, but not all, of the larger banks belong, among them Most-Bank, Inkombank, AvtoVAZbank, Technobank, International Moscow Bank, Credo Bank, Stolichny Bank and Forum Bank, all of which have representatives on the council. Several foreign banks and organisations in Russia have joined, including Bank Austria AG, Banque Société Générale and Price Waterhouse. In general, the association represents and lobbies for the interests of the commercial banks on all fronts and is quite prepared to take on the Central Bank and government departments when necessary.

Its policies generally reflect majority opinion among members or the positions taken by the more powerful banks. Hence, it can be vociferous about the need for information services, computer networks and management training; it wants bankers protected from the criminal classes, and urges legislation ranging from deposit insurance and clear bankruptcy rules to Central Bank reform. It does not object 'in principle' to the presence of foreign banks in the Russian market, but considers 'their wide presence premature'.

In its forecasts for the future the ARB sees more growth in the sector, noting that 'there are 100 applications by new banks waiting to be registered at the Central Bank, and this is as it should be'. The larger banks, especially those in Moscow, will expand their networks into the provinces, but the association also forecasts bankruptcies and the absorption of smaller banks by the financial giants. It foresees some 'collision of interests' between national and foreign banks.

The ARB president is Sergei Egorov and the association published its first directory of banks in 1994, in Russian and English. Its address is: Bldg. 2, 4B Sadovaya, Moscow 103379. Telephone (095) 209-1643 and 209-1683. Fax: (095) 209-1643.

A CROSS-SECTION OF THE COMMERCIAL BANKS

Baltiyskiy Bank, St Petersburg

Chairman: Andrey Lovyagin. Founded by the largest transport companies of the North-West regions. Authorised funds in early 1994 totalled Rb9.8 billion. Its currency balance was Rb160.7 billion and its profits stood at R3.4 billion. It provides the whole range of banking services in roubles and hard currencies and has set up correspondent relationships with many Russian and foreign banks. It has been a Swift member since 1993 and has five branches in various parts of the country. It will open four more branches in the near future.

Credo Bank, Moscow

President: Yuri Agapov. Founded in 1989. Authorised capital in 1993 totalled Rb23.1 billion, up from Rb9.1 billion the previous year. Revenues Rb80.054 billion, up from Rb7.893 billion. Profit

Rb29.594 billion, up from Rb2.957 billion. Credo Bank is in the process of shifting to international banking and accountancy standards, and is training staff and building up authorised capital, while seeking to attract more foreign investment clients. It plans to issue new types of securities, such as bonds, savings and deposit certificates and promissory notes. It will invest more in insurance, trusts, mutual funds, pension funds and leasing, as well as exploring the real estate market. Credo will expand its sales of Barclays' international money orders nationwide, expand its branch network both inside and outside Russia, issue new types of plastic cards, install cash terminals and cash machines. Credo Bank has diverse correspondent banks at home and abroad. It has 27 subsidiaries in Russian industrial and financial centres. The bank has opened over 20,000 accounts for Russian and foreign enterprises as well as over 25,000 accounts for Russian citizens and foreigners. It has 1,475 shareholders, issues the Credo Card-Visa card and uses the Swift international network.

DialogBank, Moscow

President: Peter Derby. Founded 1989 and licensed for all commercial banking operations, both domestically and internationally. Total assets of Rb239.3 billion in July 1994. Net income Rb5.480 billion. A conservative bank which emphasises service and safety. Places great emphasis on automation and banking technology. Offers services in any currency. Corporate services include current (DDA) accounts, investment accounts, foreign exchange against the Russian rouble, as well as other CIS currencies and the US dollar, deposits, trade finance services, vault and cash operations, custodial services for stocks and bonds, funds transfer, treasury bill (GKO) and MinFin (Taiga) bond trading, lending and corporate finance advisory services. Full network of correspondent banks in Russia, the CIS and the rest of the world. About to introduce CrownNet, a state-of-the-art corporate cash management system that allows clients to perform most banking transactions from their own offices. Issues Eurocard/Mastercard and DialogBank debit card, deals with all major travellers cheques and Eurocheques and is to install ATMs in Moscow that will dispense both Russian roubles and US dollars. Services special requirements of investors. Founder member and shareholder of the Micex, Russia's largest currency exchange. One of the first banks to go on-line with Swift and uses Reuters services. One of a select few banks with the right to trade Ministry of Finance rouble denominated gold-backed certificates. The 10 shareholders are Russian and American companies. Also owns Troika Dialog, which trades in Russian equities and was a leader in privatisation voucher trading.

ELBIM Bank, Moscow

Chairman: Sergei Morozov. Registered in 1990 as a commercial bank for assistance to the development of advanced technologies and investments in the electric power industry, biotechnology and medicine. Licensed in 1992 for all commercial bank activities. There are 150 shareholders, among them aviation, nuclear power, industrial and foreign interests. ELBIM Bank manages customers' accounts in roubles and hard currency, grants various banking facilities to Russian and foreign citizens and to organisations. Being a member of the Europay International system, ELBIM issues Eurocard/MasterCard as well as its own ELBIM Bank Debit Card co-branding with Cirrus-Maestro (under the licence) which can be used both within Russian and abroad. At the start of 1995, the bank's capital came to Rb80 billion and its profits to Rb22.5 billion. Some ratings put the bank among Russia's top 20 in terms of its reliability. It has branches in Moscow and several other cities and has opened a representative office in London. ELBIM Bank has been developing modern banking technologies leading to Russian settlement system optimisation, introducing a new IMD cheque-based payment facility of its own devising.

Fisist Bank, Moscow

President: Mikhail Petrovich Gladilin. Founded in 1989 as one of the first commercial banks in Russia, Finist became a joint stock company in 1991. The shareholders are 219 companies and organisations, most of them in the private sector. By mid-1994, Finist Bank's authorised capital had grown from Rb250 million to Rb1 billion, turnover from Rb30 billion to Rb3.2 trillion, profit from Rb91.9 million to over Rb20 billion. The bank's shares have been listed in Russia and it is the co-owner of several industrial and commercial enterprises. It has correspondent banks in the CIS, Europe and the United States and 20 branches in Russia, Armenia and Moldova. It plans to raise authorised capital to Rb3 billion, open new branches and widen its range of services in roubles and hard currency. It will also develop its international transactions and co-operation with foreign financial institutions, as well as carrying out joint projects with foreign investors.

GLORIAbank, Moscow

Chairman: Dmitry Anatolyevich Chernev. Founded in 1992 and its hard currency licence granted in 1993. Mainly active in interbank crediting and offers a wide range of services. Speeding up settlements with Russian, CIS and foreign partners. Some securities operations. In 1994, its authorised fund had grown from Rb25 million to Rb1.5 billion, and 1993 profits came to Rb8.7 billion. Main shareholders are in industry and exports. It has three branches in Moscow, one in Novy Urengoy and an affiliate in Kirov. Aims to raise authorised capital to the equivalent of US$10 million, introduce the GLORIA STB card, provide services for members of MasterCard/Eurocard and holders of travellers cheques. Also wants to issue Visa cards, use Swift services, open six new Moscow branches, two currency exchange offices, and establish new regional branches. Plans to open a clearing house for Loro accounts of other banks and create a single information and operational infrastructure for all Moscow, plus a centre of financial analysis and strategic research.

Inkombank, Moscow

President: Vladimir Pavlovich Vinogradov. Inkombank was registered in 1988 and received its licence in 1991. The main shareholders are very large industrial and foreign trade concerns. The bank is said to be among the 1,000 largest banks in the world. Its assets total Rb18 trillion, which place it eighth in Russia, according to some ratings. It covers 20 per cent of the Russian hard currency market and serves about 25 per cent of total company international payments. Its correspondent network consists of 300 banks in Russia and the CIS, plus 49 banks in America, Europe and South-East Asia. The bank offers all kinds of commercial banking services and participates in Visa International and Europay International. It intends to sell Thomas Cook travellers cheques. In 1993, its profits rose sharply from Rb5.418 billion to Rb34.688 billion. It serves more than 25,000 corporate and one million individual clients, has 31 branches in Russia, one in Cyprus and offices in Germany and Switzerland.

International Moscow Bank, Moscow

Chairman: Vladislav Sudakov. Registered in 1989 as a joint venture, the first of its kind in the Russian Federation. Shareholders include Bayerische Vereinsbank, Vneshekonombank of Russia, Kansallis-Osake-Pankki, Holding International, Creditanstalt–Bankverein, Promstroybank of Russia, and Sberbank. In 1994, the authorised fund consisted wholly of hard currency (US$80 million). Capital increased from US$100.6 million to US$117.2 million. Gross income rose from US$128.8 million to US$143.9 million. The bank was one of the first to start operations in the international financial market and it had a network of 655 leading banks in 90 countries in 1994. More than 200 Russian banks arrange payments through correspondent accounts in IMB. It has a very large volume of credit lines opened with foreign state agencies for export credits. It opened its first branch in St Petersburg in 1993. Some 80 per cent of its clients are Russian exporting companies.

Cathedral of the Assumption and Cathedral of St Michael Archangel, inside Kremlin, Moscow

Kirovsotsbank, Kirov

Chairman: Valentina Dmitrievna Yentaltseva. Founded in 1990 on the basis of the former Soviet Zhilsotsbank, this is the first non-state bank in Kirov. The shareholders are 109 provincial light industrial and construction companies along with 700 individual shareholders. Authorised capital grew Rb12 million to Rb1.1 billion, turnover from Rb22.5 billion to over Rb1.1 trillion in 1994. There are now over 2,500 clients. The bank has six subsidiaries and plans to open five more. Staff are trained in Britain, Germany and Austria. The bank aims to boost its authorised fund to Rb3 billion, increase its branch network, extend correspondent contacts and diversify rouble and hard currency services.

Mezhcombank, Moscow

Chairman: Sergei K. Ovsiannikov. Mezhcombank began operations in 1990, combining a comprehensive range of services with international specialisation. In June 1994, its assets came to Rb667.7 billion, soaring from just over Rb292.2 billion six months previously. In 1992, the bank occupied sixth place in the national reliability rating, and some listings placed it among the top 10 banks in Moscow and the top 30 in Russia. Its clients include major export-import companies, joint ventures and foreign firms such as McDonalds Moscow, Coca-Cola, Philips and Novotel. It has a correspondent network of over 100 foreign banks and 20 in the territory of the former Soviet republics of Ukraine, Belarus, Kazakhstan, Latvia and Estonia. It is also a member of Swift, Reuters and Micex. It occupies a leading position in the emerging cheque market and in 1993 launched the Mezhcombank debit card for payroll payments. It is a licensee for Eurocard/ Mastercard. The bank was among the first 24 institutions licensed to act as primary dealers in government short-term bonds and is also an authorised dealer in gold certificates issued by the Ministry of Finance. Mezhcombank has a network of branches across Russia in seven major cities. It is soon to open its first foreign office.

NBD Bank, Nizhny Novgorod

Chairman: Boris Brevnov. NBD, or Nizhegorodsky Bankirsky Dom, was licensed in 1992 with authorised capital of Rb600 million. The main founders are 59 large industrial enterprises of the Nizhny Novgorod region. Priority areas of business are to assist in the conversion of military enterprises to consumer product manufacturing. The bank has been placing a second share issue to increase its capital to Rb6 billion. Its main customers are about 2,000 regional companies. NBD received a credit from the European Bank for Reconstruction and Development (EBRD) to channel credits to small businesses in the area. It has correspondent relations with 11 foreign banks and has four branches in the region. The bank plans to join Swift and Reuters and open new branches in the near future.

Promstroybank of Russia, Moscow

Chairman: Yakov Dubenetsky. Promstroybank of Russia was registered in 1991, taking the place of the old Soviet Promstroybank, which was set up as a specialised bank in 1922. Some 889 companies in industry and construction and over 2,600 private individuals are the shareholders. In 1993 it decided to establish a holding group, the only one in the banking sector, and the system now includes 12 affiliate banks and some 119 branches. The bank offers clients a full range of domestic and international services. Its clients include major industrial companies, medium-sized and small private firms, joint ventures and thousands of private customers. It provides an extensive clearing network in Russia, the CIS, the Baltic countries and abroad, offering speedy settlement operations. Promstroybank had total assets of over Rb2 trillion and made a profit of Rb125.456 billion in 1993. In 1994 its authorised capital was increased to Rb40 billion. The bank provides foreign trade guarantees and related consultancy services. It has over 120 correspondent banks abroad and boasts modern telecommunications which permit real-time transactions. It is a user of the Reuters system.

Rostovsotsbank, Rostov-on-the Don

Chairman: Valentina Yashkova. Rostovsotsbank was established in 1990, based on the regional branch of the old Soviet Zhilsotsbank. There were 57 founders in such industries as meat, pharmaceuticals and insurance. Current shareholders comprise 202 companies and organisations and 1,101 individuals. In 1994 the bank's capital came to Rb1.2 billion. It is a universal bank, but grants priority to customers in industry and services. It has a hard currency licence and maintains correspondent relations with 10 banks in seven countries. The bank has invested capital in the St Petersburg Stock Exchange, the Don Exchange and the Rostov interbank hard currency exchange, as well as in insurance and other interests. It has six branches and one representative office and plans to increase its authorised capital to Rb2 billion, expand services to individual clients and broaden correspondent relations with Russian and CIS banks.

Sberbank, Moscow

President: Oleg Yashin. Sberbank was founded by the Central Bank of the Russian Federation, which holds 45 per cent of its fixed capital. Its shareholders include 8,000 companies and 200,000 individuals. Sberbank is the successor of the former Soviet savings bank, but is not a joint stock company and operates as a commercial bank, offering a wide range of banking services, such as allocation of money by way of negotiable instruments, deposits and investment accounts, non-cash settlements, credits to companies and individual clients, and foreign currency operations. At the beginning of 1994, its authorised capital amounted to Rb100 billion, and its profits came to Rb931.7 billion. Licensed in 1994, the bank still attracts 90 per cent of Russia's household savings. It was a founder of AvtoVAZbank, International Moscow Bank, Vneshtorgbank of Russia, and housing and foreign trade bodies, has correspondent banks in London, Frankfurt, Paris, New York and other cities, and, according to its latest figures, its system consists of 38,834 separate units, including 78 banks, 2,380 branches, 30,563 subsidiaries and 5,813 agencies. Sberbank seeks to perfect its current system and include new banking services, advancing its technical facilities and international ties.

Tekobank, Petrozavodsk, Republic of Karelia

President: Andrey Nezhelsky. Registered by the Soviet Gosbank in 1989 and re-registered by the Russian Central Bank in 1991. Shareholders are 140 regional companies and 1,995 individuals. Authorised fund amounts to over Rb1.8 billion and the shareholders have decided to increase that to Rb10 billion in the short term. In late 1991 the bank was licensed for hard currency operations and set up correspondent contacts abroad with French, German and Finnish banks. It has invested in 23 regional affiliates and has branches in Moscow, St Petersburg, Murmansk, Petrozavodsk, Taganrog and six other cities.

Tokobank, Moscow

President: Victor Yakunin. Founded in 1989 as a joint stock company commercial bank by a number of ministries and government bodies of the USSR, Tokobank was licensed in 1990. Current shareholders are 663 companies and individuals, including foreigners. Provides credit in roubles and hard currency to basic branches of industry (primarily metals, oil and gas, conversion of defence industries), and makes settlements inside and outside the country. By the start of 1994 its authorised fund had grown from Rb27 million to Rb312 billion and it boasted 12,000 clients (including 2,000 currency clients). It has a credit line from the US Eximbank, a number of leading western insurance companies accept Tokobank letters of credit as state guaranteed documents, and it has co-operated closely with the World Bank, the International Finance Corporation and the European Bank for Reconstruction and Development in several projects. It has 245 correspondent banks, 189 of them abroad, and is one of the leading clearing centres in hard currency for Russian and CIS banks. It is a founder of the Micex and the Russian Bank for Projects and Finance, a shareholder of Ost-West Handelsbank (Frankfurt) and of the Russian-Turkish Yapy-Yokobank. It also has a controlling share of Kronbank of Moscow. The bank has 16 branches in major industrial centres, is a member of Swift, and employs Reuters Dealing and Midas systems. It plans to increase the authorised fund to Rb8 billion and expand its branch network.

Vozrozhdeniye (V.Bank), Moscow

Chairman: Dmitri L. Orlov. Founded in 1990 as a commercial bank by various companies and established in 1991 as a universal bank, V.Bank saw its total assets soar from Rb78.903 billion at the start of 1993 to Rb579.307 billion one year later. It now has 54 branches and 30 affiliates. The bank offers universal banking, treasury, corporate and project financing to more than 45,000 foreign and domestic customers. V.Bank is an authorised dealer in government short-term non-coupon bonds and Ministry of Finance gold certificates, and it operates in all major currencies. Correspondent relations have been established with 67 foreign banks and 13 in the CIS area. It offers to assist international companies to optimise their efforts in Russian markets. Plans to join the Sprint system and open new offices.

V
BANKING SERVICES

Russia has no tradition of commercial banking as known in the West. In pre-Revolutionary times, the development of a capitalist credit system started with the founding of the Imperial State Bank in 1896. Until the abolition of serfdom, Russia's government banks behaved like savings banks, and until the mid-1980s, even the Imperial State Bank depended for its funds mainly on deposits and current accounts, on which it paid interest, complemented by treasury funds. Its disposable profits were classed as a source of budget revenue. By 1914, the State Bank network included 10 offices in major cities and 127 branches. The simplest transactions were completed by the local treasuries, of which there were 791. All credits issued by subsidiaries, however small the credit might be, were approved by the board of the State Bank, which made operations very slow indeed. The Finance Ministry was the direct manager of the bank and had the right to dispose of most of the funds. As in the Soviet system, there were credits directed to favoured clients at low or no interest rates at all. Debts were sometimes written off and there seemed little distinction between loans and subsidies. Russia by now had a widespread if underdeveloped credit system.

The 1917 Revolution put an end to any further development of banking in Russia and the sector took a different turn into monobanking, in which the Soviet Gosbank handed out part of the government's budget to special channel banks which distributed it as soft credit to chosen industries and economic sectors. The only contact with the public was provided by the official savings bank, whose many branches took in all household savings and used them to finance government deficits. The government, however, did guarantee the savings deposits. That was the only form of banking experienced by Russians for 70 years, until shortly before the break-up of the Soviet Union.

UNIVERSAL BANKS

All banking services in Russia are comparatively new, but the explosive growth of the commercial banks has made such services available very quickly indeed. The better Russian banks now offer the full range of commercial bank services and strive to be as 'universal' as possible in that regard. Interest rates on deposits can vary from one bank to the next and are often rather low, but the competition is tending to force them slightly higher. Interest rates on borrowing are usually rather high, sometimes exorbitant. All the institutions that called themselves 'banks' handle deposit accounts, current accounts and the like. Better banks offer foreign exchange facilities, investment banking services (especially in the government bond market), debit and credit cards, as well as a range of corporate services.

Since banks are licensed to provide general services, there are no merchant banks as such, and the best-known, dedicated investment bank is DialogBank's subsidiary Troika Dialog, although other universal banks (Mezhcombank among them) do provide investment services. At present there seems to be no one providing factoring facilities. Leasing is also in its infancy in Russia, with Promstroybank being the only institution with a leasing department by the end of 1994. Vneshtorgbank, a former specialised bank, which once had a virtual monopoly on trade financing, still does the bulk of business in that area, but is being challenged by several of the big-

Facing page: Interior of Hermitage, Winter Palace, St Petersburg ger commercial banks, some of which have already made considerable profits in that sector.

Long-term financing for industrial and infrastructure projects or mergers and acquisitions is out of the question for most commercial banks. Even the top institutions lack the capital and experience to put large-scale financial packages together and are more at home funding projects in light industry. Such needs have been met from the government's budget via directed credits and occasionally with multilateral funding.

Russian banks are Janus-faced institutions. For rouble operations they use one part of the organisation and for hard currency operations another, duplicate department. Each bank is really two banks and clients must visit both to keep track of their assets. There are two balance sheets, one in roubles, the other in hard currency. This situation dates from a time when the rouble was not internally convertible and, since a bank's hard currency assets could not be set down in roubles, the Central Bank required two different sets of reports.

RETAIL BANKING

Many banks are modernising branches and developing retail services to attract new clients. Since Russia remains for the most part a society without cheques, the biggest retail development has been in plastic money. Stolichny Bank pioneered plastic cards in Russia and in 1993 the domestic and international companies battled for a place in the market. At present the market leaders are trying to join forces to reduce the existing chaos. There were in 1994 seven incompatible systems for processing debits through ATMs. A consortium of banks that led the field formed the United Payments System (UPS) to rationalise standards. The group is installing ATMs to accept not only their own STB cards, but also the Union Card, their largest competitor. There are still five other systems outside the UPS awaiting integration.

According to research by Credo Bank, the percentage of different plastic payment systems on the world market differs markedly from Russian distribution (see Exhibit 5.1). In world terms, the leader is Visa International, with 50 per cent of the market, followed by Europay International with 30 per cent, American Express with 18 per cent and Diners Club and JCB with lesser percentages. In contrast, the Russian leader is American Express, with 47 per cent of the market, followed by Visa International with 27 per cent, Europay International with 19 per cent, and Diners Club and JCB with minority shares. 'Against the background of the competition between Visa International and Europay International, the best results have been achieved by American Express, pursuing an independent policy of investments in the Russian market', the bank's report said. However, it was the competition between the first two companies that to a large extent has determined the development of the credit card market in Russia.

A new phase in the plastic money market started after Credo Bank joined Visa International in 1990 and became the first commercial bank to issue Visa cards in Russia in September 1991. Then other banks implemented similar Visa card issuance programmes. Today the most active banks of the 17 members of the Visa International payment system include Credo Bank, Inkombank, Most-Bank, Mosbusinessbank and Menatep Bank. There are also 27 Russian members of Europay International.

In November 1992, Credo Bank established with Intourservice (which had serviced payments on international cards issued by Russian banks) a joint stock company called United Card Service, with Credo Bank's president Yuri V. Agapov as chairman. The new company took over Intourservice's plastic payments role. There ensued a struggle among the Russian banks for control of UCS. Foreign stockholders sold their shares and the company became the joint property of Credo Bank (51 per cent) and Most-Bank (49 per cent). In consequence, Credo Bank acquired the agency rights and became a leading acquirer bank for all international payments systems. It is now the sole clearing bank on Russian territory for Visa, Europay, DCI and JCB systems.

This resulted in there being two domestic processing centres in Russia: the UCS and Card-center (see Exhibit 5.2) the first holding an exclusive position in Visa, Diners Club and JCB, while the second shared the Europay card system. Meanwhile, Most-Bank is constructing its own processing centre together with Credit Mutuel Bank. This, to be called Multicard, will process Visa and Europay systems. Meanwhile, American Express (Russia) Ltd services mainly American Express cards.

DEBIT VERSUS CREDIT

The Central Bank of Russia has as yet no nation-wide programme of organisation and development of plastic money in roubles. Credo Bank points out that the initiative has been left to the commercial banks and 'that any national card will have its own way of development in the absence of an accepted standard'. The most popular cards circulated in Russia are:

- STB Card of the Stolichny Bank. Some 50,000 cards were issued. The total number of banks issuing STB is about 120. The cards are accepted for payment in 1,800 different points in Moscow, 300 in St Petersburg, and also in Lipetsk, Chelyabinsk and Riga. The estimated cost of the project was US$5 million.
- Union Card, a joint development of Inkombank and Avtobank. Some 20,000 cards were issued. There are now about 400 banks that have joined the system. The cards are accepted for payment in 300 different points. This was a completely domestic development.
- OLBI Card. Project development of the National Credit Bank. The cards are accepted in the chain of stores of the same name.
- ORTEX card. Property of the Ortcard International financial company. These cards are used as deposit instruments and there is also a store for servicing.
- Most-Card. An internal development of Most-Bank. It is purely a rouble card and accepted at large Moscow stores. They are not competitors for STB and Union Card and are only issued to customers of the bank.

In addition to these, in 1993 Mezhcombank launched its debit card scheme, tailored as a cash card for payroll payments. The bank was also accepted as a principal licensee for Eurocard Mastercard.

The Credo Bank report stresses that much remains to be done if the plastic card market is to be properly developed. What is lacking is an all-Russian plastic money programme, it said. The infrastructure set up by the commercial banks must be expanded and either uniform standards or an interface of interaction for different payment systems should be chosen. The bank believes that regional processing centres should be established and automation introduced into the settlements process. It will be necessary to 'carry out continuous explanatory work among the general public on the advantages of credit card holding and the ease of use, as well as developing a legal basis for protecting card holders against the malicious actions of other persons'.

Russian banks offering plastic money are mostly using debit cards. Credit cards are granted only to 'top grade clients', whose reputation is well known and beyond doubt. The banks 'will be ready to work with credit cards when we are in possession of the credit history of our customers and a mechanism of interbank information exchange regarding customers' reliability appears', Credo Bank said.

According to current calculations, about 300,000 Russian companies and individuals hold plastic cards, but only about 15 per cent of them hold Russian cards. Since hard currency payment on Russian territory is officially forbidden, plastic money is sure to become more popular in future. It is easier to pay by plastic card than to convert hard currency and risk losing out due to fluctuations in the exchange rate. To obtain a debit card, a client simply opens an account at an issuing bank and operates within the limits of his balance. To obtain a credit card he must not only pay several thousand dollars (see Exhibit 5.3), but present documents, including some proof of his earnings. Debit cards are understandably more popular in Russia.

CARD TECHNOLOGY

Cards are generally divided into magnetic or microchip products. Magnetic cards require

Exhibit 5.1

World and Russian plastic payment system

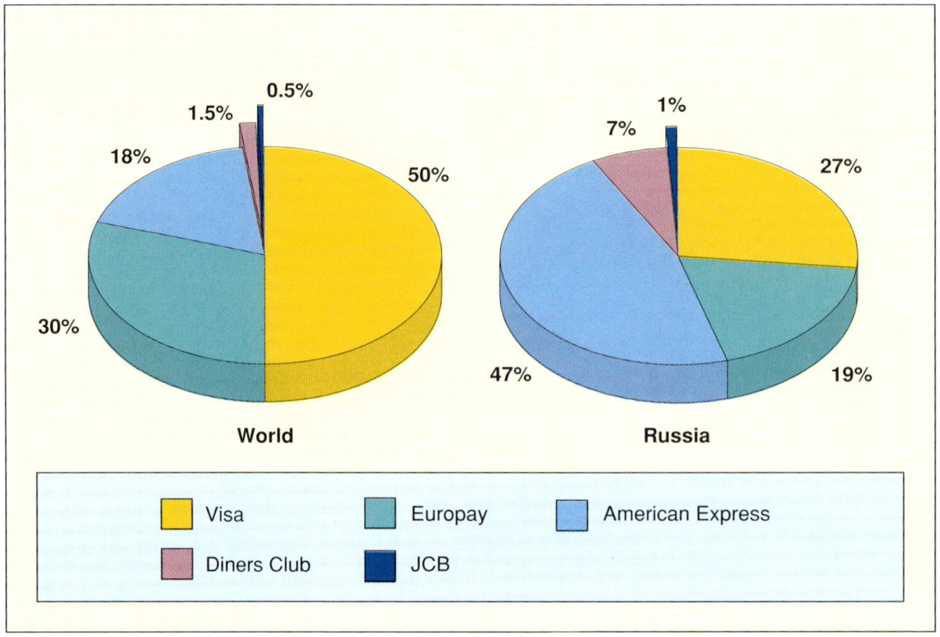

Source: Credo Bank.

Exhibit 5.2

Russian card processing centres

Data	*UCA*	*CardCenter*
Equity capital	US$1 million	US$3,300 million
1993 turnover	US$170 million	US$10 million
Number of stockholders	2	14
International payment systems	Europay International, Visa	
	Diners Club International, JCB	Europay International
Russian payments systems	STB, Union Card	–
Hardware support	VAP, Pcs, Nowell	EM, Sequoia
Software support	Cardwoman	TP-II, GEN
Number of trading businesses	340	500

Source: Credo Bank.

diversified, high quality and relatively inexpensive means of communication. But making payments with these cards takes time. With microchip cards, all necessary information is included on the card's chip and this considerably increases the speed at which payments can be made and reduces the likelihood of errors. Surpassing the balance limit and theft are practically impossible with microchip cards and they are almost impossible to fake. Visa and Europay have been working on a standard chip to replace magnetic cards. Currently, microchip smart cards in Russia are issued by Optimum Bank, Tveruniversalbank and the Siberian Trade Bank. But a number of others have

Exhibit 5.3

Russian banks fees on issuing and servicing international credit cards

Issuing bank	*Card*	*Card type*	*Cost of card*	*Fee for issuing and annual charge*	*Commission fee on cash forwarding (%)*
Sberbank	Eurocard/MasterCard	credit	Dm13,000	–	5
Moscow MBB	MBB-Visa	salary/debit/corp	–/US$2,085/US$3,085	–/US$85/US$85	2
Inkombank	Incombank-Visa	salary/settlement/corp	*/US$2,05/–	US$50	–
Credo Bank	Credo Card-Visa	salary/debit corp/D/corp	US$275/US$2,525/US$13,025	US$25	free
Most-Bank	Visa/	standard/business/gold	US$3,050/US$5,080/US$10,120	US$50/US$80/US$12	1.5
	EuroCard/MasterCard	classic/business/gold	US$3,050/US$5,080/US$10,120	US$50/US$80/US$12	1.5
DialogBank	DialogBank EuroCard/MasterCard	blue/silver	US$1,500/US$3,000	–	3
Optimum	Visa Gold	settlement	US$2,200	US$20	1
Elbim Bank	EuroCard/MasterCard Gold	settlement	US$20,100	US$10	–
Credit-Moscow	EuroCard/MasterCard	settlement/credit	US$2,580/US$2,580+deposit	US$30	0.6 (min US$3)
East-European Investment Bank	American Express	corp/settlement	US$20,500	US$50	–
Russian Credit	Visa (of all Russian bank issuers)	–	–	–	1.9
	EuroCard/MasterCard all Russian bank issuers)	–	–	–	4
Menatep	EuroCard/MasterCard of Most-Bank	–	–	–	3
Stolichny	EuroCard/MasterCard of Most-Bank	–	–	–	2
Mytishchi Commercial Bank	Credo Card (Visa)	–	–	–	free
	EuroCard/MasterCard of Most-Bank	–	–	–	3

* Balance must be returned to US$250 each month

shown interest in the technology. Both Sberbank and Promstroybank signed contracts in 1993 with international manufacturers for a supply of non-cash payment systems using smart cards. Other contracts have been signed by Bashprombank in Ufa, Moscow's Fram-bank, while the St Petersburg Bank and the Northern Trade Bank have displayed some interest in the new technology. The group of card issuers, United Payments System, wants to create an automated system to register corporate tax payments based on the same technology.

The best-known plastic cards in the world are available in Russia. Visa cardholders can withdraw cash at 20 Russian banks and their branches. Cash forwarding on domestically- issued American Express and Diners Card is more difficult since only about five banks operate with them, but the service is available at the Russian Credit Bank, Sberbank and Credo Bank. Almost all banks which run credit card operations can forward cash on foreign-issued cards. The Stolichny and Menatep banks accept foreign-issued Visa cards, but do not provide services for holders of Visa cards issued by Inkombank or Credo Bank. Elbim Bank issues Eurocard/MasterCard and an Elbim Bank Debit Card which can be used within Russia.

The fear is frequently expressed that Russia is becoming a museum for outdated foreign technologies, especially where the magnetic card is concerned. But, since the infrastructure for magnetic cards does not exist on a wide scale in Russia, the country could clearly switch to smart cards with relative ease. In Russia and the CIS, the introduction of magnetic cards has been slow.

Poor communications across the vast expanses of the country did not help, nor did the high initial cost of introducing the cards. But almost all the banks in Russia currently offer clients magnetic debit cards. In practice, each transaction involves the payee contacting the bank to check and subsequently alter the account balance and, given the poor communications, this means withdrawing cash can take a very long time for a relatively simple transaction.

Smart cards store the holder's balance, which is altered with each purchase, on the card. However, they cost about five times as much as magnetic cards to produce. But the saving would come later in terms of the cost of the communications network needed to support magnetic cards. Stolichny Bank reported that it spent US$12 million to introduce its magnetic card service. Some Russian firms are manufacturing equipment to process smart card transactions, which costs much less than its western counterparts. Vostok Bank uses smart cards manufactured by Skan-Tek of Russia. The single card permits transactions in any currency to be carried out.

OBSTACLES TO MASS INTRODUCTION

For some time to come only Russians who travel abroad will be able to take full advantage of plastic credit cards. The transition to a wide use of such cards is obviously best done in a stable economic environment, but with high inflation, a reduction in real income and state revenues and a slump in industrial activity, their widespread introduction becomes more difficult. Since the time when only a few currency shops and Intourist accepted credit cards, little has changed in the way in which they are perceived and the way in which they are introduced. Individual banks collect sufficient resources to handle hard currency cards such as Visa or Mastercard, or even rouble cards which are less widely accepted. Those who actually use the cards are usually bank employees and the small number of clients with large incomes. They remain for the majority unaffordable, due to their high cost and the size of the initial deposit.

There is also the traditional barrier for Russians. They are used to paying cash for goods and services and the tradition of many generations will slow the development of a credit card system in Russia.

AUTOMATED TELLER MACHINES (ATMS)

The advantages of making settlements by cards as opposed to cash are clear enough. However, the widespread introduction of credit and debit cards has been hampered by the lack of a related infrastructure and legislation, as well as by the fact that the majority of banks target mainly corporate clients. Virtually the only bank which works actively with small clients is Sberbank. However, Sberbank is not free from problems. Since its regional network handles clients through their local branches, which store all the information on the account balance, the client can be largely tied to the branch at which he opened his account. In addition, Sberbank itself experiences difficulties in receiving information promptly, because it is not always possible to arrange constant communications among the various branches and divisions.

Solutions to the problem are being marketed in Russia, based on IBM, Olivetti, Bull and SAMIC technologies, but one of the leading firms is the Russian IBS company, a systems integrator and distributor of specialised banking equipment, whose main partner is, not surprisingly, Sberbank. The automated system at Sberbank is one of the largest projects in Russian retail banking in recent years. At the core of the system is the Delta-Bank automated banking retail system, developed in the late 1980s by the Kiev company, Delta Systems, and IBS. Under this system payments are made using magnetic cards issued by the bank itself. The Delta-Bank system, developed to solve communications problems between branches and clients, helps reduce the volume of cash operations made and ensures constant access to information on account balances, expanding the range of services available to the client. All information on client balances is stored in a single database at the bank's headquarters. Clients access information using a plastic card and can perform transactions at any of the bank's branches.

An extended banking network allows clients to pay by card in shops, restaurants and for petrol. In effect, the network is expanded by automated teller machines serving cardholders. The ATM works round the clock and lets clients withdraw cash, make bank transfers, forward payments, and access information on their account. ATMs not only automate the bank's cash operations, but also the accounting, financial management and economic planning. A feature of the system is its ability to re-evaluate the balance quickly following a change in interest rates to some other factor affecting the account. The database has four ways of protecting information stored, including encoding and compressing. It issues each cardholder with a personal identification number (PIN).

IBS is installing the system, complete with ATMs, around Moscow, producing the cards required and training Sberbank staff. Two branches of the Moscow division, the Kolomensky and Meshchansky offices, managing a total of over one million accounts, have been fully automated, as have branches in eight other Russian regions. Two other Moscow divisions are in the process of being automated. In February 1994, the first two Moscow branches began using teller cash dispensers (TCDs) supplied by De La Rue Systems, and clients no longer had to queue up twice, once at the clerk's desk and once at the cashier's desk.

The TCD can process notes of six different denominations simultaneously and automatically discards any with defects. It can store as much as Rb150 million and acts as a safe that cannot be opened without special equipment. More than 20 of these machines were operating at Sberbank and several other banks by the end of 1994. Contracts had been signed for several others. IBS has also introduced the currency exchange teller, made by Sigma of Italy. The first was installed at the Stolichny at the GUM department store in February and serves hundreds of clients each day. Another 10 were bought by Sberbank and other banks. The Sigma works up to 20 different currencies simultaneously and alters exchange and commission rates automatically. It has a built-in forgery detector, designed in Germany.

DialogBank is one of the institutions committed to installing ATMs in Moscow in the near future.

ELBIM BANK'S CHEQUE SYSTEM

While several bankers think that Russia would be well advised to skip from cash to plastic money and forget the use of cheques altogether, some believe that cheques could play a crucial role in the financial system. One such advocate is Elbim Bank's chairman Sergei Morozov, who asserts that his bank has designed a new type of cheque, which would speed up settlements in roubles or hard currency and be virtually forgery-proof (see Exhibit 5.4).

Morozov has pushed Elbim cheques in a variety of published articles. Russia, he says, needs to introduce a convertible payments facility. Foreign banks show little interest in a weak, inconvertible Russian rouble and few foreign banks maintain a foreign currency Loro account with a Russian bank. 'The inconvertible Russian rouble has no future at all', Morozov says. His solution to the problem is a universal payment facility, the international multi-currency debit (pre-paid) cheque (IMCD), which Elbim started to introduce in 1994. The IMCD cheques may or may not have a fixed denomination. Printed in France, they incorporate between 12 and 17 protection devices and can be used like plastic cards, except that they can only be used once. They can also be used without payment authorisation.

IMCD cheques can be used for payment transactions between individuals and as a payment facility in places where plastic cards are not accepted, because of the unavailability of telecommunications channels for authorisation or the high rates charged for the use of such channels. At present the developing Russian economy requires large amounts of banknotes with a high face value, and delayed settlements cause an increasing demand for bank notes whose production implies increasing costs. Since plastic cardholders need to draw money from automated telling machines, plastic cannot significantly cut down on the amount of physical cash in the system. Russia, he reminds us, has suffered a great deal of bank note forgery.

IMCD cheques can be issued in any currency, including roubles, at existing exchange rates

Elbim Bank cheques

One US cent

10 US cents

One US dollar

10 US dollars

100 US dollars

Open cheque

and they can be used to pay for goods and services. This is clearly more convenient than changing roubles for hard currency or vice versa at an exchange office before being able to make a purchase. To accept the cheques a retailer would only need to sign an agreement with the issuing bank and commission (about 3.5 per cent of the face value of fixed denomination cheques) would be paid not by the customer but by the company accepting the cheque. Hence accepting these cheques would be less expensive than accepting plastic cards in Russia, where the charge is currently higher. The user of the cheque would pay a 2 per cent commission only if he decided to change the cheque into currency.

The cheques with fixed denominations will be in US dollars, while cheques without fixed denominations can be in any foreign currency or in roubles. Cheques without fixed denominations would be made out at a bank, with the bank charging US$5 for each cheque, irrespective of its amount. They can be bearer cheques, payable to specified individuals, or order cheques. The fixed denomination cheques have the size of one-dollar bills so that they can be used in ATMs throughout the world.

'The cheques should be accepted in any country in the current open economic environment', Morozov says. 'They could be used to reduce the amount of money in circulation and they would greatly reduce the costs of money printing. Forgery would be difficult and Elbim Bank alone would pay for any damage inflicted by forgery, which will compel us to continually seek better ways of protecting the cheques.'

Morozov points out that cash is involved in only about 2 per cent of transaction settlements in Germany and Switzerland, and only 10 per cent in the United States. In Russia cash is involved in up to 40 per cent of transaction settlements. 'The introduction of non-monetary payment facilities is now of great importance for Russia', he says. 'Ideally, the Central Bank should handle only non-cash roubles, while all transactions could be settled with the aid of IMCD cheques. In any case, the use of the cheques would allow us gradually to reduce the amount of cash in circulation in Russia to at least the German or Swiss levels.' Plastic cards cannot help because they can hardly become widespread in Russia. 'On the other hand, the IMCD cheques have been specially developed to help solve this problem.'

RELATED SERVICES

If Russian banking is in its infancy, related services such as insurance and pension funds have barely been placed into the cradle. There are about 200 insurance companies in Russia, but most of them are rather small and have sparked no interest from foreign investors. Russian bankers seemed surprised when asked to discuss the insurance sector. 'It is of no importance at all', one said. 'It will be a very long time before insurance becomes a significant business in Russia', was another opinion. The insurance sector offers few options, aside from life and accident insurance, but among future growth areas will be property insurance.

There are 600 registered private pension funds, but only 30 were active in any way in 1994. A total of around US$180 million had been taken in by the funds. Again, there was little interest in the banking sector, but both the Russian army and the state-owned railways were reported to be having discussions with European private pension fund specialists. Commentators thought that state employees would not take kindly to seeing their official pension funds privatised and that the time is not yet ripe for private pension funds in Russia. The active private funds seem to be tied closely to individual companies and some may even be controlled by those companies, some observers thought.

There were some 800 commodity exchanges across Russia in 1990, most small and very few efficient. The Moscow Commodities Exchange, also the scene of some active privatisation voucher trading between 1992 and 1994, is reckoned to be the best of the three in Moscow. Russia's best stock exchange is generally agreed to be in Vladivostok, while Moscow has the Moscow International and Moscow Central exchanges. The capital also has the Moscow Interbank Currency Exchange, which is much busier and has handled much business in government bonds. Indeed the Micex is thought by many to be the best-developed of Russia's exchanges.

VI
BANK OPERATIONS

TRAINING AND STAFF DEVELOPMENT

Most Russian banks were founded fairly recently, grew rapidly and did not pay much attention to the type of person they employed. Today that attitude has gone for good and a carefully worked out, long-term personnel management policy is a priority for the better banks. It is generally recognised that getting Russian banks ready to operate in a free market environment requires different measures to those used in the former Soviet banking system. Massive training and retraining programmes are necessary for management, marketing, controlling risk, ensuring financial stability and performance, and even performing basic banking operations.

Often, the mentality and attitude of bank employees is seen as being as important as their professional qualifications. This is because the traditional Soviet values, which placed personal safety and a secure position ahead of the company's well-being, tend to hinder the proper development of Russian banks. The right attitude is cultivated in several institutions by carefully selecting employees, training them and creating an atmosphere which promotes the values shared by western bankers. The theory is that there are two goals – a minimum and a maximum. The lesser goal is to train competent, conscientious clerks with enough skill and knowledge to perform their duties, while the greater goal is to train western-style managers.

The institutional, legal and regulatory framework in which the banking system functions are still evolving. The situation really has no parallel and the usual methods of training for an established system just do not apply. Structuring a loan or a credit contract takes place with a legal context, but corporate law is not well articulated in Russia and training should concern itself with the evolving nature of the system and of contracts themselves. Mostly, banking personnel are unprepared to carry out the activities their new roles require. Training – even basic training – has become urgent. A programme of core skills has been introduced at some banks to permit bankers to take part effectively with foreign technical experts in the development of institutions and financial markets.

In theory, bank employees should master a range of professional and communications skills. In reality, banking practices differ from bank to bank. Commercial banks can choose between various ways of improving personnel skills. Some send their employees to Russian training centres, some send them abroad, or organise on-the-job training. There are international assistance programmes, including one run by the World Bank and the EBRD for twinning Russian banks with western counterparts, which will be expected to help train staff and managers. Some have made use of their correspondent banks abroad to train managers. Specific training programmes can last anything between 10 and 18 months.

Western governments and institutions have provided different forms of training for Russian bankers. Most of this has been through short courses that offer exposure to a different banking culture rather than intensive training. But the magnitude of the needs demands a training programme with greater consistency and depth. The World Bank recommended the formation of banking institutes similar to those in Poland and Hungary. A number of initiatives have already been made including the setting up of the Moscow Banking School, with the support of the European Bank Training Network and the European Commission.

Since credit is at the heart of banking and is the area of greatest risk, the elaboration of credit programmes is a priority. The banks also need to develop strategic, tactical and financial planning skills to guide the way in which they are managed.

The criteria used to assess training programmes include the total expenditure on training, the length of time dedicated to it and the number of employees and managers in training. In many banks promotion will depend on the individual employees' involvement and performance in training programmes. Banks try to define programme goals and the particular priorities for each employee. It is thought desirable that bank employees should have a good knowledge of business ethics, communication skills and the ability to smooth ruffled and unsatisfied clients. Clients are polled regularly in some banks about their satisfaction with services and the polls can serve as an incentive to employees wanting to improve themselves.

Developing professional ethics presupposes a change to European standards and the active participation of employees in the training sessions, through discussions and management games. These provide the constant feedback to allow employees to assess their progress. Some computer programs are used, such as Etiket, developed by the Liberal Arts Technology agency, and videos record and play back training sessions. The hope is to establish in employees a distinction between appropriate and inappropriate behaviour, and in some banks 'behaviour codes' have been adopted. It is recommended by psychologists hired to help design training programmes that managers be taught psychological self-training techniques, how to avoid conflicts, the proper use of business ethics, and group psychology. Western management techniques are also taught. It is pointed out that the results of training will depend upon whether or not it reflects the policy implemented by top management or is merely theoretical. But if the goals are clear and the teachers good, the results should be noticeable, bankers say.

Competition among Russian banks is fierce and likely to grow as they fight among themselves; later they will compete with foreign banks for a piece of the available market. The factors that make a bank attractive to clients include the quality and diversity of its services, rates of interest on loans and accounts, bank charges, the range of financial instruments, the speed of settlements, the bank's reliability and reputation and the personal treatment meted out to clients by clerks and management. There is little in the way of a tradition of service in Russia, and increasing the efficiency of personnel-management programmes will not only help introduce new technology, but also improve the quality of the human factor in bank services.

Russian banks now face many personnel problems, some of which are connected to the development of banking legislation and the introduction of new financial methods. The high demand for banking services and the growing number of private savers make these problems critical. The situation is complicated even more when banks switch to international accounting standards, develop telecommunications or introduce new payments systems. Almost every Russian bank targets a particular market and develops its own strategy and management rules and, hence its own requirements for training and management.

BANKING TECHNOLOGY

Russian banking experts still argue over questions such as whether a bank should develop an in-house banking solution or buy a ready-made system. They debate the advantages of Russian or foreign-made systems and about what kind of platform should be used to develop banking systems. As recently as 1992, when almost all banks used personal computers (not even hooked up into a network) the belief was that PC networks were a stopgap, a temporary choice forced by the need to get work done and make money quickly. It was said that the future lay in the high-duty Unix systems, but banks did not have the money to buy them nor the staff to operate them. In 1994, most banks used the same systems they had thought to be temporary, indeed those systems are now regarded as permanent solutions in some banking institutions.

Exhibit 6.1

Leading dealers in banking solutions in Russia

Company	*Package*	*Marketing and promotion*	*Independent estimate*	*Overall rating*
Diasoft	10	9	9	28
R-Style	9	10	8	27
Programbank	9	8	9	26
Inversiya	9	7	8	24
Asoft	8	7	8	23

Source: Delovie Lyudi.

The consensus now seems to be that western experience need not necessarily be copied slavishly. Russian banks have skipped the mainframe phase of development altogether and, starting from scratch, they can choose computers guided by the nature of the tasks in hand and by the financial costs. And if the job can be done by a cheap PC, why not do it that way? Some have learned that if a PC network is professionally configured it can be used to tackle sophisticated assignments, particularly bank accounting. All that is needed is quality hardware and a sensible network topology. The amount of data processed by banks has not grown as fast as once believed and those who predicted a breakdown of database management systems (DBMS) based on PCs have been proved wrong. Even large institutions like Credo Bank, Inkombank and the Siberian Merchant Bank do not handle such large volumes of data as cannot be processed by an ordinary local area network (LAN).

Since the amount of information processed is not growing very rapidly, and LAN equipment has gained and is gaining in capacity, even the capabilities of existing networks are sufficient for the overwhelming majority of banks. However, there is a software problem on the horizon, most experts will admit. The PC-based DBMS, such as Clipper or Clarion, may sometimes fail to cope with large quantities of information, but disaster is not close. Banking solutions developed with BTrieve tools have appeared, devoid of many of the drawbacks of the older DBMS. In addition, some DBMS suppliers, such as Oracle and others, have produced versions operating in the Netware environment.

Different banks are taking different approaches to computer-aided banking, usually depending on their geographical location, size and main activities. The competition among the 600 or so Moscow banks has compelled them to introduce a wide range of computerised banking solutions. As the demand grows, the suppliers of banking solutions are coming up with more attractive offers. There are about 100 such banking solutions available in Russia, but only about 20 show real demand. The leaders are Diasoft, R-Style, Programbank, Inversiya and ASOFT (see Exhibit 6.1).

Although Russia's commercial banks differ greatly from each other, they have a set of common problems. They all need to computerise transactions, hard currency accounting, and private account handling, as well as reporting, analysis planning and audit procedures. Large banks need to computerise communications with their branches. Computerised interbank transfers will also be important. Finding the appropriate solutions will speed up clearing. Therefore, the most advanced banks are now making sure that their systems are compatible.

The frequent changes in Russian legislation and new accounting and reporting procedures mean computerised banking solutions must adapt easily to new requirements. But in the current situation, important characteristics are reliability and prevention of unauthorised access. It is helpful if solutions are easy to operate and have a friendly interface with other system users.

Diasoft offers its Diasoft Bank system, which allows banks to computerise accounts and meet all the usual requirements. It offers hot line support, provides personnel training and upgrades the system when necessary. Diasoft Bank is based on the Clarion system and costs around US$40,000. R-Style has a banking system costing around US$15,000, which is written in the SI and Assembler languages for use with IBM-compatible computer networks with a unified database. The main advantage of the system, called RS Bank, is that it operates in real-time mode. Programbank, another supplier, offers a Clipper-based system which allows for rapid adjustments to changes in Russia's banking legislation, now installed at 360 banks. Other market leaders include Inkombank's Sadko system, and AO LIM's Tula.

Many suppliers have now realised that establishing a unified banking and clearing system will not be possible without close co-operation among them, especially in view of the growing number of banks introducing plastic cards and ATMs. It has been estimated that a large Moscow bank could spend between US$200,000 and US$1 million on a computerised banking system, and there are 150 such banks in the capital with hard currency trading licences. When purchasing systems, buyers will visit all of the main hardware suppliers in Moscow. Unfortunately, few suppliers of tried and tested banking software are based in the capital. The buyers work with little knowledge of the computer industry and must make judgements from several competing sales claims. Some cannot tell the difference between doing business with a hardware manufacturer and a banking solutions supplier and there are few systems integration specialists in Moscow. The buyers often forget that a modern banking system requires a modern bank for it to work properly and fail to grasp how thoroughly they would have to reorganise their whole business in order to make use of it.

The centre of any banking system is the General Ledger, which monitors all the bank's activities. In one recent project, the introduction of a significant-sized banking system was held up while various interest groups within the bank resisted demands to release all of their information to be included in the General Ledger. In some institutions control over the computer system implies power. It is hardly surprising that some banks have bought the wrong solutions and, in other cases, have not been aware of the months of work needed to get them working properly. The fact is that there is a huge gulf between the way Russian banks operate and what western applications were designed to do. Russia, for instance, has a completely different clearing system and different accounting standards and there are many ways in which banking practice differs from that in the US and Europe. Russian banks use a multiple cashier and queuing system alien to the West (a client queues up once to deal with a cashier and again to get his money). In some banks the client will go to yet another cashier if he wants hard currency rather than roubles. Banking applications have to take this sort of thing into account.

Many of the more widely-used western banking packages are now fairly old and were written in second or third generation computer languages, so making changes within these applications to suit the Russian context can take large amounts of programming. Indeed, the Vneshtorgbank automation department has gone on record as saying that there is not a single integrated banking package suitable for the bank. One compromise adopted by some banks is to commission programmers to write a system from scratch. While such systems work, they are fairly simple and some do not support double entry bookkeeping. Others make it possible to amend accounts without a transaction being registered, thus giving anyone in the bank undetectable access to everyone's money.

The software industry simply has not kept pace with the rapid development of the banking sector as a whole. Few banks have the experience of a US partner to count on. DialogBank's US partners were able to advise on what the technological foundations of the bank should be. But that knowledge is not exclusive and can be made available if banks look beyond the Moscow hardware firms to the big international consultancies.

AUTOMATION AND THE CENTRAL BANK

The Central Bank has not set the best example. Potentially it represents a huge contract for someone. It acts as the clearing centre for commercial banks and, if its monopoly survives, it will need a very large system to automate its operations. In 1991 the bank invited proposals from Bull, Digital,

IBM, Unisys, Olivetti, Coopers and Lybrand, and the Sema Group. At the time it had 43 mainframes or minicomputer-based centres and 80 administrative units needing PC LANs. It estimated that it would have to spend US$300 million to acquire hardware, software and telecommunications equipment to modernise the system it had. It did not have the money.

Since 1991 it has invited various suppliers to set up clearing systems in different administrative areas, such as Moscow, St Petersburg and Irkutsk. Several large suppliers – including Digital and IBM – have installations at various Central Bank affiliates. The systems were to be supplied at a discount on a pilot basis. Some of these systems have completely different architectures. In 1993, a Digital-based clearing system started up in one of the Moscow districts after a six-month pilot period and is being used by the Central Bank and 15 commercial banks. Unisys supplied a clearing system for north-west Moscow, which has the capacity to handle one million transactions a day. In 1993, Unisys won a US$5 million contract with the Central Bank's St Petersburg division to install a regional clearing system for north-west Russia.

After years of fairly barren negotiations with foreign companies, the Central Bank seemed to be turning to Russian suppliers in 1994. Lanit, a Moscow-based joint venture, which has installed a Novell network and won a number of small automation contracts with the bank, was taken on board as a supplier. Other locals jostling for Central Bank contracts are Jet Infosystems and Elko Technologies.

Sberbank, still largely state-controlled, is working with several firms. In 1994 it signed a contract with Unisys said to be worth an eight figure sum. UK-based ICL has installed a system in Moscow for the savings bank which handles all the foreign exchange business and is gunning for Sberbank contracts in other cities. Intermicro Business Systems (IBS) has installed ATM systems for four Sberbank districts and a total of 18 branches have bought the system.

PROGRESS IN THE COMMERCIAL BANKS

DialogBank, the Russian-American owned commercial bank, used input from the US partners in selecting and planning its computer system, and that made it easier for the bank to buy and customise packages than it is for most commercial banks. The bank's main business is providing a full commercial banking service to corporations. In its early days it used a locally developed system called C-Bank and an international fund transfer package called MicroCash Register, developed by a New York bank with whom DialogBank has ties. In 1992, the bank became a member of Swift and bought two MicroVAX computers and ST400 interface software from Swift. Since July 1993, it has used a locally developed accounting package designed by the Russian firm Diasoft.

In 1993 DialogBank conducted a thorough overhaul of its information systems in order to keep up with its business growth. The bank decided to retain Coopers and Lybrand, the UK-based accountancy group which has a world reputation for computer system selection. Coopers drew up a seven-supplier shortlist and finally settled on an integrated solution from the Irish firm ACT Kindle, based around a General Ledger, with modules for foreign exchange, lending, report-writing, financial returns, settlements and branch management. There are five branches linked on-line by leased lines. ACT Kindle is mainly a back office solution and the bank hopes to develop front office applications built around a single database. It is also looking at its operating systems options. Its current central processor runs on Hewlett-Packard hardware.

Conversbank is one of the larger Russian commercial banks with about 4,000 customers and eight branches. It began its search for automation in the belief that information technology is a tool for making a bank function better, not for transforming it into something different. The first question asked was: What problems do we need to solve? Most Russian banks are really two banks in one, with one half dealing in roubles and the other in foreign currency, but Conversbank wanted one bank and one balance sheet. In others words, division of the bank should be by function, not by currency. Simply adding the results of the two halves together makes it very hard to evaluate resources and liquidity, a bank official pointed out. 'Until western banks can take an objective look at Russian partners, none will offer the kind of credit lines or

General Staff Headquarters, St Petersburg

bilateral ties which are crucial if the Russian bank is eventually to emerge into international respectability', he said.

Conversbank chose to be a universal bank. In order to offer a range of services it implemented a clear division between back and front office functions. There were no suitable systems in Russia, so the bank examined and tested the world's best-known integrated banking packages. Finally, it chose a French application called SAMIC V2. The Russian economy was in turmoil and the bank wanted a package that was flexible enough to be constantly adjusted. Specialists spent two weeks in Paris testing the systems and running simulated Russian applications. SAMIC V2 runs on the proprietary IBM AS/400 mini computer.

Vneshtorgbank is Russia's largest in terms of turnover and has the most foreign trade experience. Its customers include the Russian government, foreign companies, embassies and hundreds of Russia's largest firms. Once the state foreign trade bank, it is now a universal bank offering a full range of commercial and retail services. Vneshtorgbank also employed Coopers and Lybrand to advise on decisions before a contract was signed and to help plan the bank's information technology strategy. The bank found that 'there is no such thing as an off-the-shelf banking product that can be used in Russia'. It eventually put together a package of many parts that met its need for flexibility.

The Vneshtorgbank system is based around four main software modules for General Ledger and front office system, a foreign exchange dealing system, a document management application and a Swift product. Existing, proven applications were an important part of the mix. Two were Wang applications: Safe, which runs the bank's international fund transfer operations, and the Doka document management system. The system the bank bought is a client server solution based on the HP 9000 series model T500 corporate business servers, including a full disaster recovery site at one of the bank's locations. Hewlett-Packard will also connect several of the sites into a private ×25 network.

The Moscow Interbank Currency Exchange (Micex) has been called 'the most important private sector financial institution in the Russian Federation'. Its daily exchange sessions are used by the Central Bank to set the official US dollar–rouble rate and are used as a benchmark by every Russian commercial bank. At the end of 1993, more than US$1 billion dollars were bought and sold on the Micex every week. The exchange is a joint stock company owned by 32 commercial banks, the Association of Russian Banks, and the Moscow city government. It also trades in Deutschmarks and CIS currencies, and the Ministry of Finance uses it to auction short-term (three and six month) government obligations. It is beginning to trade shares, futures and options.

With all this business, it would be catastrophic if the Micex computer system were to go down. In 1993, Micex decided to make the transition from a locally developed PC LAN-based trading system with a maximum capacity of 30 users to a system able to support simultaneous currency and securities trading across the whole of Russia. Micex needed a system which would enable it to go from being an auction house to a major financial institution and which could support hundreds of users simultaneously. The system had to be open enough for banks and exchanges across Russia to access it, and it had to have the capacity and flexibility to expand activities into the securities market. Micex bought a three-tiered solution, based almost completely on Hewlett-Packard technology. An HP twin processor – Emeralds – formed the core of the system connected to a gateway consisting of two H20 Unix servers. The gateway feeds into the Micex local network of HP Vectra PCs and connects the exchange to all its partners across the country. There is a million-client depository for securities trading.

Very few suppliers in Russia were able to provide the system's integration services and the long-term technical support necessary for this kind of on-line system. The Micex now has a special four-hour support agreement with Hewlett-Packard Moscow. The Micex trading system was installed by Swedish systems integrator CMA, with whom the exchange had a good working relationship. It was a trading system and system router supplied by Financial Market Software Consultants (FMSC) of Australia and is used at currency exchanges in the Far East.

BANKING SOFTWARE

The first banking programs in Russia were designed to work with fairly primitive computers, but the situation soon changed with the advent of network technology. Now the most widely used programs are 'A Kiev Day of Operations', and 'A Tula Day of Operations', both of which are accepted as standard programs and passed around through the influence of the Central Bank. However, the Kiev company is reported to have gone out of business and the rights for the program have gone to other firms, such as Unity Bars and Moscow's ATB. Only one of the three Tula program producers, LIM, remains in business.

The Moscow companies have done well over the past few years. Programbank, Inversiya and Asoft, once known as the 'big three' of program design, have been joined, even overtaken, by Diasoft, while R-Style's RS-Bank program has become widely known. For the banks, these five are the leading developers of banking systems. But the locally developed programs contain some defects. Thirty banks recently polled on their satisfaction with these products made it clear they were not entirely convinced, in fact two-thirds said they were not very satisfied. More specific complaints were that the functions are not sufficiently automated; they had to be adapted, and they did not suit the individual bank's real requirements. A number of errors, especially in hard currency transactions, were noted. Around 60 per cent of the defects named were technical and can hardly be eliminated from the automation systems.

The banks are apparently ready for advanced computer technology and some are unlikely to wait around for Russian versions to be invented. A market for Unix banking products has been evident since the end of 1992, mostly among the large banks which encountered practical problems in using DOS-based systems with advanced banking structures. An IBM partner, IVK Systems, reports that at the beginning of 1994 more than 10 copies of well-known foreign banking systems had been installed in the CIS, in powerful AS/400 series computers. The Midas package, developed by the British firm BIS, was installed at Tokobank, the International Moscow Bank, the International Investment Bank and the Moscow branch of the Bank of Austria. The Kapiti package, developed by the same company was installed at the Russian–Asian bank, the Irkutsk branch of the Central Bank, Zabaikalzolotobank, Irkutskkomsotsbank and the Minsk-based Belvneshekonombank.

Meanwhile, the Paba package, designed by the German company Actis, was set up at Stolichny Bank, the Samico package, developed by the same firm, was adapted and translated into Russian by Conversbank, and the IBIS/AS package from the British firm IBIS was installed at Evrofinance Bank.

Some banks got few benefits from their foreign systems. One reason was the specific accounting rules followed in Russia, which differ somewhat from International Accounting Standards. Another problem was the low standard of the Central Bank's cash settlement centres, to which banks mostly go because there are no other widespread settlement systems. The banking practices in Russia are frequently primitive and western packages are often not used to their full potential. Legislation is constantly changing which means regular changes have to be made to programs. When back-dated laws are introduced, problems could be insoluble. In short, western programs are alien and unsuited to the Russian banking system under present conditions, and many banks must supplement them with Russian packages.

Stolichny Bank continues to use individual modules of Programbank's system, Tokobank uses Asoft's system and, immediately after installing its Samic system Conversbank bought a program from R-Style. There is also the price factor: the cost of installing Russian software can be in the region of US$10,000 to US$20,000. The cost of the program package alone of any western system goes to US$500,000 or more. They are also expensive to install and carry language and terminology problems. If a bank buys an automation system from a western company it has to use the company's experts to install it. Each expert could cost over US$1,000 a day.

The shortcomings of western and Russian systems have led many to obtain specially customised western systems. These are not widely available, but have had some success among the

Russian banks. The first systems of this kind were designed by the St Petersburg company NEST, using the Informix banking system based on Unix in 1991, by Prok using the Rdb banking system based on VAX VMS in 1992, and by Fors using the Oracle banking system in the same year. Another firm, Server, used an Informix banking system based on UNIX, and ASOFT produced a magnetic card processing system using an Ingres banking system based on Unix in 1993. Advanced banking systems appeared on the market in 1994, known as Unix systems, designed by the five leading Russian suppliers.

ACCOUNTING PROBLEMS

As Russia moves toward a market system, its accounts and accounting practices are expected to change, drawing slowly and gradually closer to western standards. Many companies, particularly the banks, want to have accounts that meet International Accounting Standards (IAS) in order to attract western investors. The joint project between the World Bank and the EBRD to support certain Russian financial institutions requires as a first step for a participating bank an audit of financial statements prepared in accordance with International Accounting Standards. Some of the larger Russian banks now have their balance sheets audited by one of the international accounting companies.

It is often not possible for a Russian bank to make all the disclosures required by IAS due to the limited accounting and management information available. The full impact of accruals, related party transactions, market value of securities, maturities of assets and liabilities, contingencies and commitments, including off-balance sheet items cannot always be determined and so cannot be adjusted or disclosed in financial statements. Russian banks in general need to expand substantially their accounting and management information systems with the view to a transition to IAS style financial statements.

Russian banks have not traditionally prepared financial statements on an accrual basis. Under the accruals method, revenue expected from an asset is allocated on a rational basis over the term of the loan. The revenue may not actually be paid to a bank holding the loan during a period, but should be accrued even though the interest may be paid in a lump sum at the end of the term of the loan. An IAS financial statement for a Russian bank would require a calculation of interest accruals for all interest-bearing assets and liabilities at the year-end closing date. Some other items subject to accrual are commissions on long-term loans, premiums and discounts on investment securities to be held to maturity.

Under the principle of prudence, unrealised losses should be provided for and unrealised gains generally excluded unless the gain is certain. The largest impact of the concept of prudence for Russian banks would be in the area of loan loss provision. IAS requires that when it is likely that a loan will not be repaid in full, a provision for the expected loss should be made in the financial statements. The losses specifically identified and potential unspecific losses which experience shows are present in a particular loan portfolio are recognised as an expense, charged against income and deducted from the total carrying amount of loans and advances as provision for losses. Any accrued interest on the loans, if previously booked, is also provided for. In Russia one of the main objections to provisions is that they are not tax deductible. Few Russian banks make loan loss provisions in the statutory books, as the IAS requires.

The IAS standard on financial reporting in hyperinflationary economies defined hyperinflation and the Russian economy falls within that definition. In that context, Russian enterprises could structure their financial statements either in the currency of the country or in a convertible currency. In the first case, the effects of inflation must be accounted for using retail price indices. In the second case the usual choice is the US dollar. But a consistent policy must be adopted to convert from one currency to another and the rouble's evident instability makes that difficult.

Taxes on income are generally accounted for in a market economy as a tax expense when determining the net income of an enterprise. Income tax, therefore, would be presented under IAS as an expense and not a distribution of income. In Russia, the concept of retained earnings does not exist, all profits are utilised, in theory, or set aside for particular purposes through the creation of funds. Under IAS, it is necessary to disclose transactions and balances with related parties, such as loans advanced to shareholders or directors. In Russia this is not always done. Also, contingencies and events occurring after the balance sheet date require the disclosure of transactions that are currently not recognised as assets or liabilities, but which give rise to contingencies or commitments, such as a commitment to extend credit that is irrevocable for any reason, or contingencies arising from off-balance sheet items. Russian banks generally do not maintain specific records of off-balance sheet operations that provide the detail required by IAS.

Although some of the differences between Russian accounting and IAS appear minor, observers say they can make for major discrepancies. Since it is not possible to reconcile the two systems and many of the better banks are trying to use IAS, though forced to present accounts to the Central Bank and tax authorities in the Russian style, it is expected that there will be legislation sooner or later to phase out traditional Russian accounting and phase in IAS.

SECURITY OPERATIONS

While computer and many other banking operations can theoretically be made secure, Russian bankers have special problems in guarding not only cash but life and limb. The free market brought with it numerous opportunities for illegal enrichment and a tidal wave of crime threatened to submerge Russian life, particularly in the cities. The banks, which had grown and prospered when all other economic areas were shrinking, became natural targets for criminal gangs wanting a piece of the action and quite ready to kill to get it. Over a two year period, 1992–94, more than 15 senior bankers and some 20 junior bankers have been murdered by gangsters. Similar numbers of other businessmen have been killed or threatened. Now most bankers have bodyguards and some employ what amounts to a private army of security men. Yuri Agapov, president of Credo Bank, has at least three bodyguards accompanying him since the head of his St Petersburg branch was killed in 1993. Stolichny Bank president Aleksandr Smolensky is accompanied by a car full of armed men, Vladimir Gussinsky, president of Most-Bank, is reputed to have a squadron of security men guarding his bank and his family. The assassination of Nikolai Likachev, chairman of Rosselkhozbank, in December 1993 convinced most bankers of the need for protection, since his bank (Russia's second largest) was the only one lacking a big security force. Even the Central Bank annex, next to the Interior Ministry, was bombed by remote control. The ministries offer little help in general, not wanting to be seen to discriminate in favour of the rich.

The gangs are well armed – sophisticated weapons are easy to acquire from military installations since the breakup of the Soviet Union – and often use high-powered rifles with telescopic sights and grenade launchers. Gussinsky purchased an armoured car to travel about in and usually goes in a convoy of guard-packed automobiles. His small son never leaves the house without protection and an older son is at school outside Russia. While his bank has never suffered a Mafia attack, it was attacked by President Yeltsin's guards in December 1994, after his security cavalcade got mixed up with Yeltsin's in downtown Moscow. Yeltsin's men followed Gussinsky's guards back to the bank and crashed through the doors, beating security men and waving their weapons. The explanation was that the guards were mistaken for would-be attackers, and the very existence of such private armies makes similar incidents likely. Most-Bank has about 650 security men, including former policemen, and it spends about 5 per cent of its earnings on protecting itself.

Some banks extend their security protection to top clients. One client was threatened by a gang which tried to blow up his house and kidnap one of his family. Most-Bank's force carried out a joint operation with the police and 'force was used', Gussinsky said. In another case, a large store was under attack, the owner called his bank and five trained commandos arrived to deal with the gang. Off the record, bankers referred to cases where troublemakers had been 'done away with'. Some bank security departments have direct contacts with the Interior Ministry and the KGB.

Bankers have appealed to the president for protection on several occasions. They told him criminals 'are trying to spread their sphere of influence over commercial banks and have resorted to direct physical reprisals against those who don't give in to their threats and bribes'. They warned him that some of the largest banks are being targeted and complained that 'the law-enforcement bodies have actually taken no measures to investigate a series of contract murders, claiming that they were the results of settling scores between commercial banks'. The Interior Ministry calculates that 150 major criminal gangs now exist, with some 3,000 smaller ones under their wings, and that these gangs control 40,000 private and state-run businesses. A recent report claimed that '70 to 80 per cent of privatised enterprises and commercial banks have been forced to pay bandits'. More than 29,000 murders were committed in 1993, 27 per cent up on the previous year.

Presidential adviser Pyotr Filipov, who wrote the report, recommended that the president fight the gangs with élite units all over the country that remain independent of the police. Many killings are professional jobs committed by former mercenaries from the civil conflicts arising in the former Soviet Union. The *Moscow News* said the fee for killing a businessman can be in the region of US$15,000. Since the banks have suffered this type of attack more than any other sector of business, it is little wonder that bankers are taking drastic steps to protect themselves and their property in the face of official negligence. But these private armies are in effect substitutes for real law enforcement, vigilante bands that circumstances seem to have lent some legitimacy.

Some banks and other businesses, a minority, use similar persuasion to collect debts, without directly involving themselves. They use what they call a *krisha*, or 'roof', really an unofficial enforcer. Usually the client, if he is powerful, has his own 'roof'. Hence, banker and client do not meet to discuss the debt, their krishas sort the matter out and get paid from profits. The problem here is that the 'roofs' are probably criminals and at this stage of the proceedings banking and crime go hand in hand. It would hardly be surprising if sometimes the 'roof' falls in on the banker.

Developments in 1994, however, seemed to confirm that the government has finally woken up to the dangers faced by bankers and is ready to take some sort of steps to ensure their safety. Until this happens it will continue to turn a blind eye to the armoured cars and the private armies. Russia's top banks have already shown they can protect themselves and their clients, but they feel it would have been healthier if the state had fulfilled that task from the beginning.

VII

THE BOND MARKET

OPPORTUNITIES IN INVESTMENT BANKING

Today there is an urgent need to explore further ways of developing investment banking operations in Russia. There have been signs indicating that investment banking may grow quite rapidly in a number of fields. Currently it remains a largely vacant niche of the financial market, since existing Russian and foreign companies will be unable to supply the demand for high-quality investment banking services in the foreseeable future. Some bank securities departments have accumulated considerable experience in organising new types of operations in the financial market and achieved significant results. This should make it possible to consider a variety of opinions concerning the development of bank securities departments into larger and more powerful structures specialising in investment banking. In some banks, the existing management systems impede the development of new fields of investment banking in a number of ways. Very often, the bank's terms of employment make it difficult to attract sufficient numbers of managers capable of generating new investment banking operations and pursuing them efficiently. Therefore, the task of selecting the best options for the development of investment banking operations calls for a substantial analysis of a bank's management system and for efforts to find ways of attracting managers capable of designing and introducing new techniques.

THE STATE ROUBLE BOND MARKET

The transformation of state-owned enterprises into public stock companies has not yet resulted in large-scale stock sales in the open market, so most of the impetus promoting the development of the Russian securities market still derives from the issue of state bonds. Securities now actively circulating in the market are state long bonds (GDOs), issued in 1990–91, and state zero coupon short bonds (GKOs). In the autumn of 1994, the Russian government declared a strategy of moving toward considerably broader issuance of state securities, starting with treasury bills (GKVs), to finance the government's budget deficit.

STATE LONG BONDS (GDOS)

In 1990 and 1991, there were several types of long bonds issued in Russia, totalling in excess of Rb80 billion (at 1991 prices). Most of those bonds were not sold immediately because inflation was much higher than their interest rates. In 1992, the Central Bank of Russia divided all the long bonds into several classes and began to quote buying and selling rates daily for each class of bonds during the so-called 'special week'. Central Bank quotations ensured acceptable interest rates and made it possible to divide one large long-term loan into several liquid short-term loans floated throughout the Russian territory.

STATE SHORT BONDS (GKOS)

Apart from long bonds, the Russian Ministry of Finance began to float short zero coupon bonds (GKOs) in May 1993. GKOs are auctioned below par in paperless operations. The original par value of a short bond was Rb100,000; later it was increased to Rb1 million. Currently, GKOs are floated by primary dealers, which are mainly the 57 commercial banks authorised by the Central Bank. Auctions to float 3-month, 6-month and 12-month GKOs are held a few times every month. By November 1994, the total value of GKOs floated exceeded Rb7.5 trillion. In September the average daily volume of GKO secondary trading reached Rb85 billion (with two-hour trading sessions held every week-day). The Ministry of Finance has been working to restructure the state debt byissuing more bonds with longer maturities. The share of 6-month bonds in the total number of GKOs in circulation increased from 3.6 per cent in early 1994 to 23 per cent by 18 October that year.

A special infrastructure comprising a trading, depository and payments system for the GKO market has been established within the Moscow Interbank Currency Exchange (Micex). The trading system is a network of terminals in the Micex trading room. The terminals of the other two participants – the Central Bank of Russia and Mezhcombank – are linked with the trading system by optical-fibre telecommunications lines. The number of participants in GKO trading is expected to grow considerably in the near future.

The payments system requires that certain amounts of money are transferred into its accounts in advance, so full and timely payments for GKOs purchased are thereby guaranteed, and all purchases are completed on the following day. The Central Depository keeps records of the bonds held by end-investors and its information is checked against information from primary dealers' subdepositories by the Central Bank of Russia on a daily basis. GKO transactions are not only a way of making short- and medium-term investments, but also a means of conducting high-profit speculation, which makes the market attractive to many investors. In February 1994, the GKO market was opened to non-resident investors, but their investment is limited to 10 per cent of the amount invested by residents.

Dealers and investors have the right to make competitive bids, with firm prices specified, as well as non-competitive bids – in which case bonds are sold at weighted average prices of competitive bids. The volume of non-competitive bids ranges from 20 to 50 per cent, depending on the type of issue.

The GKO market offers a number of unique opportunities not yet found in any other area of Russia's financial market, since it combines the following major features: an efficient system of non-cash payments; guarantees of full and timely payments; the possibility of investing practically unlimited amounts of money; GKOs' absolute liquidity; relatively high yields on medium-term investments; and the possibility of gaining extremely high returns on short-term speculation.

The GKO market has excellent prospects. The Finance Ministry intends to increase GKO issues. There are plans to install telecommunications lines to link the market with five regional trading sites – St Petersburg, Rostov-on-Don, Vladivostok, Novosibirsk and Yekaterinburg – which will open the market to investors in all the key regions of Russia. Non-resident investors are also expected to show increased interest in GKOs.

The principal primary operators in the GKO market, which make large investments of their own funds and render broker services to end investors, are Sberbank, Vneshtorgbank, Promstroybank, the International Finance Company, Oneximbank, Agroprombank, the International Moscow Bank, Tokobank, Mosbusinessbank, Mezhcombank, Unicombank, AvtoVAZbank and Alpha-Bank. Some dealers participating in primary auctions invest hundreds of billions of roubles during a single session. Information about GKO holders is confidential.

GKO market services to end investors revolve mainly around purchases of GKOs during auctions or secondary trading sessions. Several primary dealers render consulting services to their clients regarding expected developments in the market, especially before trading sessions. Some dealers conclude agreements with end investors for trust management of their assets invested in GKOs.

Exhibit 7.1

Average spread over Bunds, %*

*The average spread of four Vnesheconombank Dm Eurobonds over the German 8% Bund, maturing 20 March 1997.
Source: Bloomberg.

Exhibit 7.3

Volume in three-month T-bills

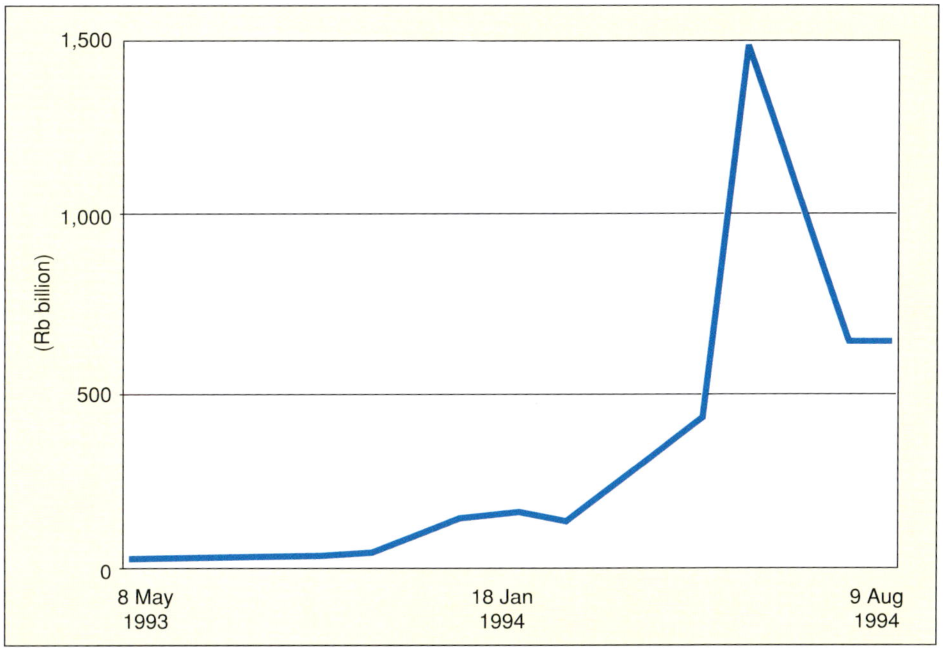

Source: Central Bank.

Exhibit 7.2

Volumes and yields of Russian Treasury BIlls (GKO) (primary market)

Issue Number	*Issue Date Maturity Date*	*Days Outstanding*	*Redemption*	*Min price*	*Max yield*	*Average price*	*Average yield*	*Discount rate*	*Total supply (bn roubles)*	*Total demand (bn roubles)*	*Amount issued (bn roubles)*
23001	26.10-25.10.95	364		22.56	529.55	25.53	450.00	170	200.00	274.00	60.00
22007(1)	27.10-0.8.03.95	132	redeemed	54.80	350.88	59.19	293.31	170	500.00	285.51	233.06
21023	1.11-1.02.95	92	redeemed	64.22	340.22	67.53	293.00	170	1,300.00	788.32	753.32
22008	8.11-10.05.95	183		48.18	330.03	49.89	308.20	170	400.00	380.00	206.10
22006(1)	16.11-14.02.95	90	redeemed	71.76	245.54	72.38	238.09	170	400.00	603.70	397.10
21024	22.11-15.02.95	85	redeemed	71.37	265.01	72.98	244.58	170	1,000.00	1,043.02	957.33
23001(2)	30.11-25.10.96	329		36.00	303.43	36.02	303.22	180	400.00	754.50	104.41
21025	6.12.94-1.03.95	85	redeemed	71.89	258.32	72.97	244.72	180	1,400.00	1,613.04	1,399.63
22009	13.12-14.06.95	183		49.00	319.38	50.49	300.90	180	600.00	726.20	457.60
21026	21.12-15.03.95	84	redeemed	67.00	329.26	68.74	303.94	180	1,700.00	1,662.16	1,606.10
23001(3)	27.12-25.10.95	302		30.00	433.86	30.77	418.43	180	200.00	149.16	52.82
21027	5.01-5.04.95	90		66.03	320.99	67.67	298.10	200	1,000.00	1,163.28	
21028	11.01-19.04.95			63.32	331.93	63.88	323.99	200	2,000.00	2,361.80	1,998.00
22008(2)	18.01-10.05.95	112		55.62	400.05	57.76	366.66	200	2,500.00	2,598.00	2,440.00
21029	24.01-12.04	77		70.56	304.27	70.89	299.44	200	1,000.00	806.70	278.50
21030	01.02-03.05	91		65.15	330.09	65.79	320.87	200	2,000.00	1,857.68	1,385.83
22010	08.02-09.08	182		46.80	350.73	47.61	339.47	200	800.00	1,135.98	770.47
21031	15.02-17.05.95	91		67.81	292.93	68.4	285.08	200	2,800.00	3,853.43	2,479.0
23001(4)	22.02-25.10.05	245		39.04	357.89	39.64	348.96	200	450.00	744.50	143.10
21032	1.03-7.06.95	98		69.51	251.34	70.19	243.35	200	2,200.00	3,420.00	1,282.00
22011	9.03-13.09.95	189		52.40	269.89	53.05	264.35	200	3,000.00	2,951.00	2,133.00
21033	15.03-21.06.95	98		71.00	234.04	71.33	230.31	200	3,000.00	3,835.00	2,400.00
23001(5)	22.03-25.10.95	217		53.22	227.46	53.76	222.58	200	500.00	1,000.00	252.81
22010	29.03-9.08	133		75.00	140.74	75.15	139.61	200	500.00	558.93	241.60
21001	18.05-17.08.93	91	redeemed	83.20	115.70	84.70	103.11	100	1.00	1.48	8.89
21002	15.06-21.09.93	98	redeemed	81.21	123.11	83.20	107.46	110	3.00	2.76	2.49
21003	20.07-19.10.93	91	redeemed	76.61	174.94	77.76	163.88	170	9.00	4.03	3.70
21004	17.08-16.11.93	91	redeemed	77.51	166.26	77.97	161.86	170	5.50	16.46	4.98
21005	21.09-21.12.93	91	redeemed	77.61	165.31	78.05	161.14	170	15.00	27.15	14.37
21006	19.10-18.01.94	91	redeemed	75.11	189.88	76.46	176.38	210	22.00	32.56	21.95
21007	16.11-15.02.94	91	redeemed	76.51	175.92	76.96	171.55	210	55.00	105.25	54.65
21008	21.12-15.03.94	84	redeemed	77.92	176.00	78.58	169.22	210	120.00	166.06	166.06
22001	22.12-22.06.94	182	redeemed	60.21	189.33	61.29	180.94	210	10.00	40.28	9.99
21009	18.01-19.04.94	91	redeemed	75.51	200.13	76.88	185.61	210	130.00	98.97	89.38
21010	15.02-17.05.94	91	redeemed	73.01	228.12	74.60	210.09	210	100.00	112.83	95.73
21011	15.03-21.06.94	98	redeemed	72.06	222.17	72.79	214.19	210	175.00	214.08	150.81
22002	16.03-21.09.94	189	redeemed	54.33	249.75	56.56	228.16	210	15.00	23.45	14.97
21012	19.04-19.07.94	91	redeemed	74.31	213.33	75.06	205.03	210	300.00	398.20	298.62
21013	17.05-16.08.94	91	redeemed	77.07	183.59	77.51	179.06	200	400.00	605.21	399.34
22003	18.05-08.11.94	174	redeemed	65.80	167.74	66.48	162.71	200	50.00	227.61	49.73
21014	21.06-20.09.94	91	redeemed	78.72	166.81	79.49	159.20	185	1,500.00	1,635.60	1,497.35
22004	22.06-13.21.94	174	redeemed	64.60	176.85	66.52	162.43	170	160.00	201.55	150.78
22005	12.07-10.01.95	182	redeemed	65.01	166.14	65.83	160.17	155	300.00	344.47	297.68
21015	19.07-18.10.94	91	redeemed	79.62	157.95	79.96	154.65	155	1,000.00	1,190.41	989.83
21016	02.08-01.11.94	91	redeemed	80.03	153.98	80.24	151.94	150	600.00	707.53	595.63
22006	09.08-14.02.95	189	redeemed	64.29	165.03	65.15	158.93	150	600.00	352.46	367.00
21017	16.08-22.11.94	98	redeemed	81.45	130.50	81.76	129.84	150	600.00	1,869.92	547.39
21018	06.09-06.12.94	91	redeemed	83.04	126.03	84.68	111.64	130	900.00	908.84	724.11
21019	20.09-21.12.94	92	redeemed	82.91	125.81	83.55	120.16	130	1,100.00	1,604.00	1,098.00
22007	21.09-08.03.95	168	redeemed	68.29	155.21	70.69	138.59	130	1,100.00	921.38	883.00
21020	06.10-04.01.95	90	redeemed	77.00	186.37	79.07	165.16	130	1,000.00	451.22	433.94
21021	13.10-11.01.9	90	redeemed	66.70	311.50	69.88	268.96	170	1,000.00	1,358.85	953.00
21022	18.10-18.01.95	92	redeemed	70.00	261.59	77.22	180.06	170	1,400.00	1,308.00	1,296.70

Source: Mezhcombank.

As the GKO market expands and grows more complex, vast opportunities will remain to conduct arbitrage transactions, moving assets from some bonds to others; and as financial institutions become increasingly specialised, it is reasonable to expect an expansion of trust operations involving GKOs. As more bidders are connected to remote terminals, this will expand the scale of broker operations. When operators are permitted to set their own prices for GKOs outside the electronic trading system, revenues in this market will grow substantially. Sales in GKOs in Russia's regions may also increase significantly. When non-resident investment account rules are liberalised, the GKO market may attract more foreign operators (see Exhibits 7.1 and 7.2). It is very likely that the market will gradually attract private investors.

Therefore, although the state has been increasing its debt considerably by floating GKOs, and some banks feel concern over the market's prospects – particularly that the state may fail to pay its debts – there are good reasons to believe that in the foreseeable future GKOs will remain very attractive and continue to be a major source of non-taxable income for many commercial banks.

STATE TREASURY BILLS (GKVS)

In 1994, the Ministry of Finance made two attempts to issue treasury securities to cover the state's debt to government-funded factories and commercial enterprises. The first attempt to organise secondary trading in those bills was blocked, as the bills were rejected by the banking community, so the entire issue was purchased by the Central Bank of Russia.

Treasury bills totalling Rb3 billion were sold in the secondary market in autumn 1994 (see Exhibit 7.3). This gave many financial institutions vast opportunities to conduct high-yield transactions involving such securities. In 1995, the government planned to issue treasury bills totalling dozens of trillions of roubles.

However, there are grave doubts concerning the adequacy of flotation and circulation techniques, so operators favouring well-balanced or conservative policies are unlikely to be active in this particular segment of the state bond market. Since their flotation and circulation have not been properly prepared, treasury bills will perform no better than gold certificates, at best. Gold certificates were issued by the Ministry of Finance in autumn 1993, but to date there is no secondary market for them.

DEVELOPMENT OF THE STATE CURRENCY BOND MARKET

EXTERNAL CURRENCY BONDS

At present there are external DM bonds of the USSR Vneshekonombank circulating in the Russian and foreign over-the-counter markets. Two loans of DM500 million each were to be redeemed on 8 February and 4 August 1995. Two other loans – DM750 million and DM500 million – were set to be redeemed on 29 March and 27 September 1996, respectively. A liquid secondary market for those bonds is maintained by a few Russian and foreign investment institutions. Operations involving state external currency bonds may become quite profitable, since the value of Russian debt is subject to considerable fluctuations. Opportunities to conduct profitable transactions involving these debt instruments are likely to remain in the future.

INTERNAL CURRENCY BOND MARKET

In addition to external loans, 3 per cent internal currency government bonds have been circulating quite actively in the market during 1994. These bonds, totalling US$7.8 billion, were floated by the Russian Ministry of Finance in May 1993 to restructure the debt to the owners of deposits blocked at the USSR Vneshekonombank in 1992, when the institution went bankrupt. The bonds are

printed securities with par values of US$1,000, US$10,000 and US$100,000. They are divided into five tranches with terms of 1, 2, 3, 10 and 15 years. Since the end of 1993, there has been an active over-the-counter market for these bonds and there is still a high demand for them among Russian and foreign investors.

The most active operators in currency bonds are Avtobank, the Alpha-Alliance bank, Vneshtorgbank, Alpha-Bank, Mosbusinessbank, the International Finance Company, the MFK-Moscow Partners Company, Inkombank, Tokobank, Optimum, Tveruniversalbank, Toribank, the Russian Finance Company, CSFB Morgan Grenfell, Indosuez Capital, Chemical Bank and the finance companies Tserikh, Hermes Capital Management and New Alliance Corporation. These financial institutions mainly purchase and sell bonds for themselves and sometimes for their clients.

Huge issues and long terms of currency loans indicate that the market will exist for a long time, but it will develop through a variety of stages. The initial stage was characterised by higher yields and revenues. Many operators made high profits in early 1994 and in the autumn of that year, when bond prices rose rapidly. There are reasons to believe that the currency bond market will remain attractive to Russian and foreign investors at least over the 1995–96 period and that operations in that market will yield high profits.

Repo transactions (sales conditioned on repurchases at fixed prices) have become widespread in the currency bond market. ING-Bank of Russia has been quite active in repo operations. It is possible to obtain currency assets in foreign money at lower rates than in Russia, so repo transactions yield an interest of 100 to 200 per cent annually on dollar loans. It is probably due to such transactions that dollar deposit rates in Russia have been getting closer to those in foreign banks. However, opportunities to conduct repo transactions will remain in the foreseeable future and the volume of such transactions among Russian banks will grow.

TRUST OPERATIONS

Trust management of rouble and hard currency assets has recently become widespread in Russia; interest in such management is rising continually, creating conditions for intensive development of a market for trust services. For a long time the development of such operations was held back by the absence of the institution of fiduciary ownership in Russian law. That institution was established early in 1994 by a first provisional enactment regulating trust operations.

Originally, trust operations were carried out by some newly established investment companies (some of the better known of these are GMM Trust Financial Services, Soviex Ltd, and Novik). Today, a few major commercial banks manage their clients' assets. It is impossible to give any approximation concerning the volumes of trust operations, but it would be no exaggeration to say that such operations are widespread.

Most banks managing their clients' funds convert currency assets into roubles, invest them in the internal money market, and then re-convert roubles gained into hard currency. This principle yields high profits when the dollar rises more slowly than interest rates in the internal money market. As a futures market develops, trust asset management will increasingly involve the use of options and futures both for speculation and for hedging against national currency devaluation.

During 1994, many companies have been willing to hold in trust not only roubles and foreign currency, but also state internal currency bonds. The bonds are sold in the market, in repo transactions or otherwise, the proceeds are invested in the usual way, and then the bonds are repurchased.

There has been a sharp increase in the number of proposals concerning portfolio investment of Russian residents' assets in foreign capital markets. Some foreign financial institutions have been quite active in offering asset management services. They include the investment banks Morgan Stanley, Merryll Lynch, Lehman Brothers, Smith Barney Shearson, and the commercial banks Citibank, the Bank of New York and the Bankers Trust Company. These and other financial institutions offer asset management services mainly to Russian commercial banks; they propose to

Facing page: St Basil's Cathedral, Moscow

invest their assets in bonds, stocks, and futures contracts in foreign money and capital markets. Many Russian banks use such services, transferring currency assets ranging from one or two million to many millions of dollars for portfolio management. In 1994, foreign investment banks were appreciably more active in offering asset management services to Russian credit institutions. Smaller finance companies are now entering the market. There have been unofficial reports that Hermes Capital Management of the United States is managing sizeable assets for Russian banks.

The legal framework for trust operations laid down by a special Presidential decree, is to be finalised in Russia's new Civil Code or by a special law. There is every reason to expect an intensive development of a trust services market in the near future. The concentration of capital by large commercial companies in Russia, the increasing need to enhance the efficiency of using temporarily surplus funds, combined with orientation at exceptionally high rates of return and the readiness to take risks, are good prerequisites for such a development. Also, the number of Russia's commercial banks and finance companies engaging in trust operations should increase in the near future.

There has been a considerable growth of interest in potential investment in the Russian market on the part of certain medium-sized and smaller foreign financial institutions. Asset management for foreign investors is likely to develop into a key type of investment banking operation in the Russian market. It is a known fact that some US investment banks are completing the establishment of investment funds for Russia. Companies that manage such funds may become leaders in the trust services market.

GROWING DEMAND FOR DEPOSITORY SERVICES

There is no obvious leader in Russia's market for depository services because that market is only now taking shape. One of the major depositories is the Vneshtorgbank of Russia, which has the natural monopoly on servicing the circulation of internal currency bonds. But, large as it is, Vneshtorgbank has been unable to ensure efficient circulation of those bonds as a centralised depository, so several commercial banks have had to be used to service currency bonds as paying agents. As a result, a few commercial banks have developed their own depository units and gained experience in depository services. The best-developed depositories are owned by major public incorporated commercial banks. As a rule, banks register the movement of their stock themselves, so many of them have built impressive depository and registration facilities. Depository service software packages have been designed and are now available in Russia.

Attempts to fulfil certain depository functions have been made by firms involved in privatisation of state-owned enterprises, but none of them has managed to build a far-flung efficient depository mechanism to date.

The undisputed leader in paperless depository handling of securities is the Moscow Interbank Currency Exchange (Micex), which has a unique centralised depository efficiently handling the entire trade in GKOs. But Micex has not established, and does not plan to establish, a depository for paper securities, which leaves open the niche for global depository services for the time being.

The demand for depository services is exceptionally high. An acute need for them is felt not only by Russian companies but also by foreign investors seeking to purchase Russian companies' stock. The absence of reliable transfer agents is probably one of the most powerful factors impeding foreign investment in Russian securities and the development of an internal secondary market for such securities. As a result, several foreign financial institutions have been exploring the possibility of organising depository services for investors in Russian company stock. For example, in 1994 the Bank of New York was engaged in preparations to issue American Depository Receipts (ADRs).

Over the past few years, considerable efforts have been made to explore depository operations (valuable recommendations on this subject have been prepared by a group of experts led by Mr A. A. Kozlov, chief of the securities department of the Central Bank). But even though the principles of depository activities have been sufficiently explored theoretically, the niche for depository services remains unoccupied and could be quite attractive to firms intending to engage in investment banking.

STOCKS ISSUED BY NEWLY INCORPORATED COMPANIES

Following the enactment of laws setting a legal framework for stock company operations in Russia, large primary issues of securities were organised by a few newly incorporated companies. The primary flotation of stock in the internal market raised large amounts of capital for firms intending to engage in investment activities (NIPEK, RINAKO, VPIK and some others). The failures of these companies to perform as expected subsequently affected the liquidity of their stock in the secondary market. When privatisation vouchers were put into circulation in 1992–94, many newly established voucher investment funds floated their stock, exchanging it for vouchers (including the First Voucher Investment Fund, MMM-Invest, Moskovskaya nedvizhimost, the Pyotr Velikiy association, Privatisation Programme, etc.). These funds collected huge amounts of vouchers, investing some of them into enterprises undergoing privatisation and selling the remainder in the secondary market.

Some recently established companies have been increasingly active in raising investor capital in the open market by issuing stock. The most active of these companies included AO MMM, the First Voucher Investment Fund, AO Suprimex, AO Telemarket, AO Olbi-Diplomat, AO Hermes-Centre, AO Hermes-planeta, AFT, AO Khopyor-invest, AO Holding Center, AO Doka-khleb and AO Bashkirsky benzin. Most of the issues were accompanied by impressive advertising campaigns. In their efforts to attract more investors, many companies paid high dividends on their shares or quoted regularly rising prices for their stock, which gave their shareholders considerable revenue for a while. Such operations have put some of these companies in a very difficult financial situation and undermined investors' confidence in this particular sector of the stock market.

TRADE IN COMMERCIAL BANK STOCK

Commercial banks have been quite active in issuing stock. By the start of 1994, 746 incorporated commercial banks were registered in Russia (about 37 per cent of the total number of banks). Many commercial banks tried to increase their capital by floating their stock in the open market.

In 1993, there were 1,245 issues of stock totalling Rb972 billion. Commercial banks' shares are noted for high liquidity and circulate extensively in the secondary market. They are listed by many stock exchanges in Russia. Banks uphold their shares, quoting firm buying and selling prices. The largest amounts of shares have been issued by Sberbank, Promstroybank, Tveruniversalbank, AvtoVAZbank, Mosbusinessbank, Inkombank, Neftekhimbank, Imperial, Menatep, Yugorsky, St Petersburg, and Vozrozhdenie.

ENTERPRISES UNDERGOING PRIVATISATION

In recent years, the stock market has been obtaining its main impetus from the stock of enterprises undergoing privatisation. Over 86,000 state-owned enterprises have changed their form of ownership. Large and medium-sized enterprises were mainly converted into joint stock companies. More than 11,300 enterprises were privatised in this way in 1993, with the state retaining a controlling interest in 305 of them (1.4 per cent of the total).

As their form of ownership was changed, their value was assessed on the basis of their low book value at pre-1992 prices, so the assets of the enterprises privatised in January to October 1993 exceeded Rb753 billion. The average value of enterprises privatised were as follows: Rb12 million for enterprises formerly owned by municipal authorities; Rb16 million for enterprises formerly owned by territorial authorities; and Rb54 million for former federally owned enterprises. As enterprises were converted into stock companies, their employees were offered three options of preferential terms. More than three-quarters of the newly incorporated enterprises selected option two, which gave controlling interest to their staff.

From 1 October 1992 to 1 July 1993, privatisation involved the use of privatisation vouchers. Some 150 million vouchers were issued, one for every citizen of Russia. These vouchers were intended to be exchanged for shares of enterprises undergoing privatisation at special voucher auctions. Trade in privatisation vouchers became Russia's first high-liquidity sector of the money market, which brought into being many new operators and promoted the development of the market infrastructure. Large amounts of privatisation vouchers changed hands at stock exchanges and in the over-the-counter market.

Voucher privatisation mainly restructured ownership (converting state ownership to other forms) and led to a formal change of owners, but did nothing to alter managerial and funding mechanisms. On 1 July 1994, the vouchers were no longer valid and the stock of enterprises undergoing privatisation began to be sold for money. The value of many shares is obviously lower than the pro-rata real value of companies' assets, so there is great profit to be made from purchasing those shares and reselling them to interested investors.

By mid-1994, Russia had a secondary market for high-liquidity shares of 30–40 major companies, with a far-flung infrastructure. During 1994, the number considerably increased of former state-owned enterprises that had implemented effective privatisation programmes and this ensured some degree of liquidity for their shares in the secondary market. Such firms included the production companies ZIL, Izhorsky Zavod, AO KamAz, LUKoil (its subsidiaries Langepasneftegas, Uraineftegas, and Kogalymneftegas), Komineft, Surgutneftegas, Yuganskeftegas, Norilsky Nikel, RAO EES Rossli, Permavia, Rostelcom, and AVVA.

In the spring and the summer of 1994, a notable increase was observed in the trade in shares of Russian enterprises undergoing privatisation. Those shares were actively purchased by a few major foreign investors, including CSFB, Brunswick, and Salomon. Large latent investments in enterprises undergoing privatisation were channelled through various offshore companies. Foreign investors were especially interested in the stock of companies in the oil and extraction industries.

The shares of several Russian companies, mainly oil companies, began to be quoted in the international financial markets. In 1994, there developed a number of financial institutions that became quite active in secondary stock trading in Russia. Operations involving the stock of enterprises undergoing privatisation brought exceptional profits in the spring and summer of 1994. Profits will remain high in the foreseeable future, but stock operations are extremely unstable and could cause significant losses (several operators suffered huge losses in the autumn of 1994 when the market was overheated).

CORPORATE SECURITIES

One possible source of funds for reorganisation of enterprises undergoing privatisation, many of which are facing grave financial difficulties, is to organise new issues of their shares and promote secondary trading in those shares. So far, these opportunities have been all but ignored. In the initial phase, the demand of former state-owned enterprises for assistance in organising primary flotation of their securities will exceed the supply of such services, which will open great opportunities for investment banking companies. Some of the major operators in the privatisation voucher market (Brok Service, Rinako Plus, Tserikh, Intrust, Consult-Invest, Olma and Grant) have close links with enterprises undergoing privatisation that are potential issuers of shares. But attempts made by these operators to issue shares have been few and far between. Commercial banks usually issue and organise circulation of their shares themselves, one reason being the absence of adequate asset management services rendered by competent specialised financial institutions.

THE DEVELOPMENT OF A FUTURES MARKET

A great potential for the development of investment banking is inherent in futures trade. Option and futures contracts for foreign currency were traded quite actively in Russia in 1994. Futures contracts for foreign currency became widespread in trade among commercial banks, but so far such contracts are not very common in over-the-counter interbank trade. Large volumes of futures instruments were purchased and sold at the Moscow Commodity Exchange and the Moscow Central Stock Exchange some time ago. But trading in futures contracts at the two exchanges was suspended in October 1994, due to inadequate development of trading techniques.

Substantial preparations for futures trading are being made by the Moscow Interbank Currency Exchange. There is every reason to believe that in 1995 Russia will have a well-organised market for terminal contracts. Initially, trade will be conducted in options and futures for foreign currency and GKOs. A futures market section of the Micex has been working on standards and regulations for futures market operators since the summer of 1994. Russia has few experts with any experience in futures market operations, so companies that manage to employ such people will be in a position to make monopoly profits for futures transactions for a few months. Futures trading may become a key element of investment banking over the next couple of years, and active use of futures instruments may expand asset management opportunities.

DEMAND FOR MERGER-RELATED SERVICES

Further political stabilisation in Russia should enhance the interest of foreign companies in direct investment into the Russian economy through the establishment of joint ventures or the acquisition of enterprises. The need to reorganise the management and performance of former state-owned enterprises, especially of those reduced to ruin by financial difficulties, creates the prerequisites for the development of a market for investment consulting and merger-related services. It is very difficult to say exactly when that market will develop or to define specific stages in its development, but it is a safe guess that the demand for such services will be high in 1995–96. Merger-related services may become another major field of investment banking activities.

Shares of GUM department store were some of the first to appear on the equity market

VIII
THE EQUITY MARKET

A BRIEF HISTORY

Russia's equity market simply did not exist before 1993 – for the very good reason that there was nothing much to buy. In that year shares of the large GUM department store, Moscow's Cosmos Hotel, and various commercial banks made their appearance, although none of them were of real interest to foreign investors. Voucher privatisation injected some life into the market and the first real run was created by the privatisation in April and May of 1993 of the dilapidated Minsk Hotel, a choice piece of real estate in the heart of Moscow.

The process gathered pace and in early 1994 Surgutneftegaz, the oil and gas company, trading at well below its valuation, was the first company to draw foreign interest, followed shortly afterwards by the Russian United Energy System (RUES). Oil and gas companies, or firms involved in infrastructure, attracted considerable attention, attracting about 78 per cent of total western portfolio investment (see Exhibit 8.1). In May there was a huge explosion of interest in vouchers with buyers such as Credit Suisse acquiring enormous quantities. By the late spring of 1994, the key players – such as CS First Boston and Salomon Brothers – were in place with the money, the experience and expertise to communicate the telling argument that Russian stocks were trading at a fraction of the cost of comparable companies in other emerging markets.

A young CS First Boston executive – Boris Jordan – is commonly credited with the original vision of Russia as the last and biggest emerging market. He was 26 years old when the institution took the decision to push Russia to the forefront of investors' awareness. Russia, it said, was cheap. If a firm's voucher value was, say, US$3 million and it occupied this much land and extracted this much oil, it had to be a bargain – and there were many such firms. Some called Jordan 'Moses leading the rabble into the promised land'. The message attracted hot money, often from hedge funds or from brokers with clients not bound by the usual restraints. Great as the risks might seem, the rewards had to be greater (see Exhibit 8.2).

Soon buyers were diversifying away from oil and gas into telecommunications and trade, with Rostelecom, St Petersburg Telecom and the Far East Shipping Company (FESCO) the main attractions, as western investors flocked to buy vouchers (bearer securities that traded for cash) to exchange for stock. Interest grew among Russian and US brokers. Investment banks were besieged by a flood of potential investors. Suddenly it was a roaring bull market, driven by western hedge funds which invested US$1.5 billion.

Despite the limited financial information available on Russian companies, western investors continued to buy Russian equities because of the enormous discounts at which they were trading. With valuations based on eastern European companies, they were trading at over 90 per cent discounts. Brokers such as Grants, Russian Broker House, CANCO, Olma, Renaca-Plus, Trinfico and Brunswick, backed by Swiss/Swedish money and run by former Russian and foreign employees of the state Property Agency (GKI) – which oversaw voucher privatisation – were swamped with business (see Exhibit 8.3).

At the same time, some US$8 billion of so-called 'taiga' bonds were issued by Vneshtorg-

Exhibit 8.1

Share prices of Russian oil companies

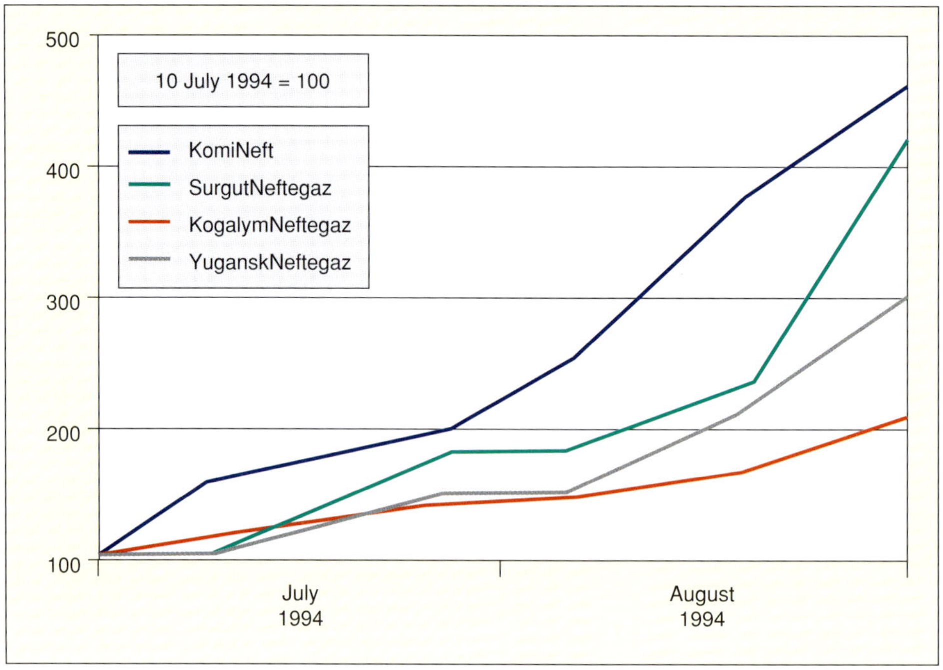

Source: Moscow Times.

Exhibit 8.2

Indicative enterprise* valuations of Russian companies, March 1994, US$

Telecommunications	*Unit*	*north America*	*western Europe*	*Russia*
Telecommunications	Access line	1,637	848	69.97
Electricity	Megawatt	372,000	650,000	2,260
Oil	Barrel of proven reserves	7.06	3.58	0.17
Tobacco	Cigarettes	5.16	4.07	2.42
Cement	Tonnes	144	162	1.92

*Valuation per unit of production = market capitalisation of leading companies in sector divided by volume of production

Source: CS First Boston.

bank, the successor of the old foreign trade bank, Vneshekonombank, to compensate for the latter's deposits, frozen when it was made bankrupt. They are to be redeemed in five tranches, the final one being in 2008. There was an important repayment date on 16 May, when US$650 million of the bonds were honoured. That and the yield reflecting the risk (some 1100–1400 basic points over US treasuries and 500–600 over Vneshekonombank bonds) stimulated brisk trading.

From May 1994, the voucher market went wild, suffering brusque fluctuations. First world investors crowded the market, stretching the existing information infrastructure to breaking point. Meanwhile, Alpha Capital linked up with Salomon Brothers and became one of the first Russian

Exhibit 8.3

Profitability of voucher investments in privatised enterprises*

Company	*Face value (Rb)*	*Shares per voucher*	*Average market value of a share***	*Acual value of invested voucher*
Rostelecom	12.5	9	US$6.5	US$58.5
UES of Russia	500	3	Rb50,400	Rb151,200
Komineft	100	9	US$19	US$71
Surgutneftegaz	250	15	US$30	US$450
LUKoil	125	7	US$37	US$259
Yuganskneftegaz	200	18	US$60	US$1,080
Noyabrskneftegaz	200	4	Rb35,000	Rb140,000
Purneftegaz	40	13	Rb24,150	Rb13,950
Norilsk Nikel	250	5	US$5.4	US$27
Far-East Shipping Company	1,000	3	Rb86,000	Rb258,000
Bratsk Aluminium Plant	200	6	US$13	US$84

*Based on exchange trading and quotations from leading brokers at the end of September, 1994

** The average market value is estimated in US dollars if the company's shares are quoted in dollars on the stock market

Source: Delovie Lyudi.

The Russian market has been attracting significant foreign interest

entities to act as a merchant bank, going out into the regions to identify opportunities.

There was no clear legal basis for the market and where there were laws there seemed to be few means of enforcement. Vouchers were bought for cash, mainly at Moscow's Russian Raw Materials and Commodities Exchange (RTSB), an enormously imposing three-storey former post office where membership cost around three US dollars. The surrounding streets were jammed with cars and armoured trucks. One dealer remembers that 'to buy vouchers you needed a lot of paper'. At that time the rouble's exchange rate was 2,000 to the dollar and the largest Russian note circulating was the equivalent of US$25. 'So, US$1 million in vouchers needed 40,000 pieces of paper for 40,000 vouchers and the cash had to be counted by scanner and verified by the seller and you had to deliver it and physically take the vouchers and check them', he said. 'People lugged millions in cash under armed guard and did business right under a big bust of Lenin.'

Russia was ill-prepared for all these million-dollar orders from institutional clients, 'but acquiring vouchers in person was cheaper than doing it over the wires', so the US dollars poured in. On some days Moscow ran out of cash: 'The banks had no more 50-rouble notes and on several occasions, because of the large injection of dollars into the Russian economy, it was not always possible to know when a voucher auction was taking place, because some people bribed officials to conceal the information. Those were hectic, nerve-wracking days, but a lot of fun', the dealer said.

In the summer of 1994, major western and Russian brokers and their clients moved into the secondary market and by then Morgan Grenfell was the new broker on the block. In July, August and September there was a mad rush to buy stocks as voucher privatisation came to an end. An estimated US$500 million per month from June to August flowed into the stock market, falling to US$40 million per month from September to December. In August some 52 million vouchers (of the 144 million issued) awaited shredding in the offices of the Cash Union. The market finally ran out of steam in October as the rouble fell and investors took profits *en masse*. Prices sank and the market itself fell heavily (see Exhibits 8.4(a) and (b)). By the end of 1994 western demand had pushed market capitalisation to US$30 billion from US$2 billion at the end of 1993. Between 10 per cent and 15 per cent of the top 20 Russian blue chip companies were held in western portfolios. Although the market never had the infrastructure to go from a standing start to boom time conditions, growing faster than the economy as a whole, somehow it survived without proper regulation and lacking even reliable telecommunications.

INDICES AVAILABLE

The two indices which investors began tracking in 1994, the AK&M index and the Moscow Times Index showed great volatility throughout the year. The AK&M cumulative index rose 8.3 times from the end of 1993 to the end of 1994, the AK&M industrial index grew by 15.5 times and the AK&M bank index increased by 2.3 times. The Moscow Times Index was introduced during the bull market, with its base prices calculated at the peak of the market. This index fell to 93 in US dollar terms from September to December 1994 (See Exhibit 8.5). Two independent information agencies began providing Russian stock indices: AK&M and Skate Press. AK&M is the first company to widely publish a Russian stock index. It introduced a cumulative index (50 companies included), bank index (10 banks included) and industrial index (29 industrial companies) in September 1993 (see Exhibit 8.6). The cumulative index includes stocks in both industry specific indices in addition to companies in the retail, transportation, service and communication sectors. The base date of indices is 1 September 1993 when indices were valued at 1.000 (one).

The Moscow Times Index was introduced in September 1994. It is prepared by Skate Press, an independent Russian information agency. The index is a capitalisation-weighted index designed to provide investors with a means of tracking the performance of the stocks of the top 30 Russian companies (see Exhibit 8.7). The Moscow Times, which is the most widely read English language daily in Russia, selected an advisory board which oversees the index and the criteria for inclusion. A company must meet all of the following criteria for inclusion in the index:

Exhibit 8.4(a)

The Russian Stock Market, ROS Index

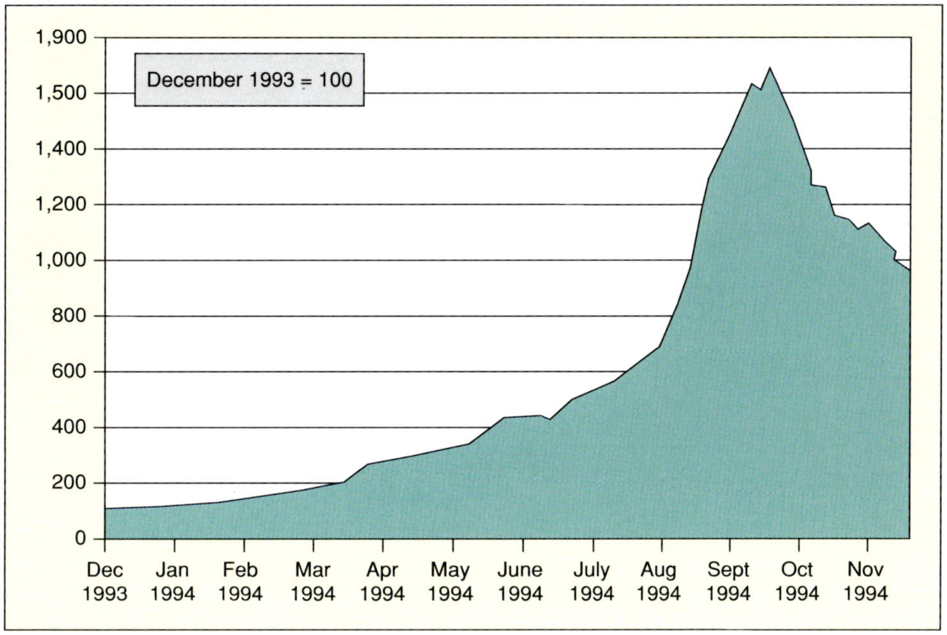

Source: Bloomberg.

Exhibit 8.4(b)

Rouble/US dollar trading, August 1993–November 1994

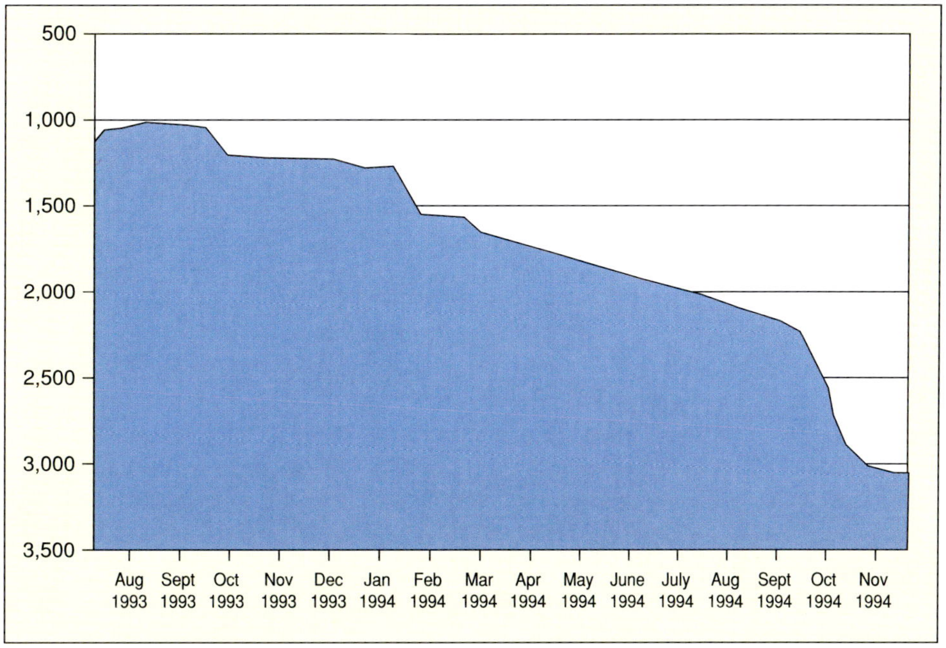

Source: Bloomberg.

Exhibit 8.5

Moscow Times Index

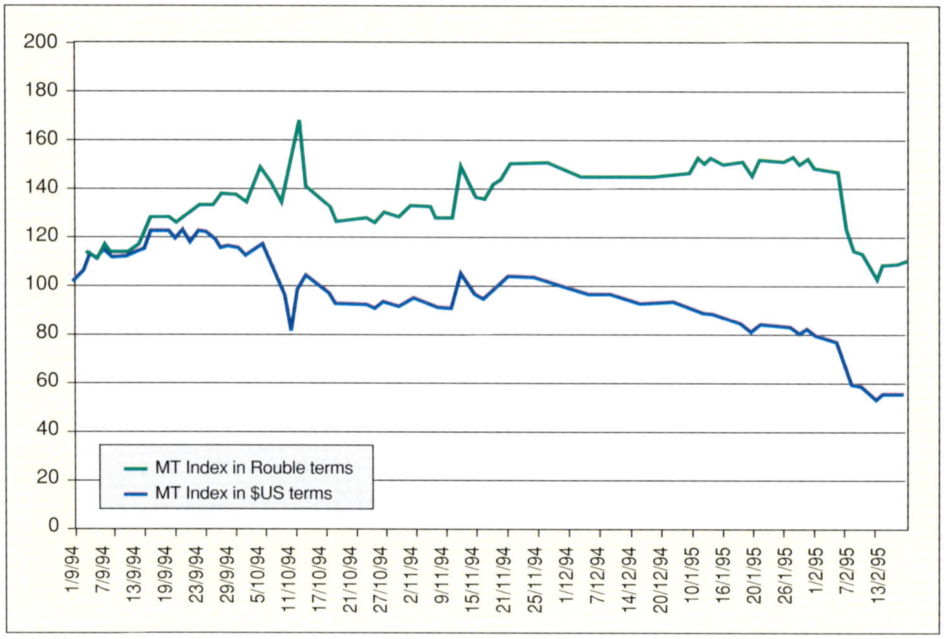

Source: Moscow Times.

- it must be among the top Russian companies in terms of market capitalisation (currently 30 companies);
- at least 25 per cent of all the shares issued must be publicly available for investment and must not be in the hands of a single party or parties acting in concert;
- three separate market-makers, who must be licensed, financial market participants, must provide a price for the individual stock and each market-maker must provide an independent bid/offer for the stock on a daily basis;
- securities that do not trade during at least one out of 60 days may be excluded

Accumulating accurate price information on Russian equities is difficult. Brokers/dealers frequently quote indicative prices in the local press and on their Reuters pages. AK&M and Skate Press often receive indicative prices which they use to calculate their respective indices. As a result, the indices may undervalue or overvalue actual trading levels. AK&M has tried to solve this problem by receiving stock quotes from 400 market participants, consisting of over 4,000 stock quotations per day. They then eliminate extreme prices, 10 per cent of the highest and lowest prices and take an average price to calculate the index. Skate Press receives price quotes from 47 market participants on a regular basis to calculate the Moscow Times Index.

In addition to indices prepared by third parties, there are also indices prepared by large broker/dealers in Russia. Credit Suisse First Boston has the ROS index, which is widely followed by western investors. This index is capitalisation weighted modelled on the FTSE 1000. As of January 1995, it included 30 companies and was heavily weighted towards the oil sector (see Exhibit 8.8).

SHARE REGISTRATION

Share registration remains a chronic problem. It can take weeks, even months. Registrars were almost always created by the company management and companies were not always pleased to see

Exhibit 8.6

Stocks in the AK&M bank index

Company	*Sector*	*Index*
AvtoVAZbank	Banking	Bank index/Cumulative index
Inkombank	Banking	Bank index/Cumulative index
Mosbusinessbank	Banking	Bank index/Cumulative index
Mitishinsky Bank	Banking	Bank index/Cumulative index
Neftkhimbank	Banking	Bank index/Cumulative index
Promstroybank	Banking	Bank index/Cumulative index
Sberbank	Banking	Bank index/Cumulative index
Sibirsky Torgovy Bank (Siberian Trade Bank)	Banking	Bank index/Cumulative index
SKB Bank	Banking	Bank index/Cumulative index
Tveruninersalbank	Banking	Bank index/Cumulative index
AVVA	Car manufacturing	Industrial index/Cumulative index
AvtoVAZ	Car manufacturing	Industrial index/Cumulative index
GAZ	Car manufacturing	Industrial index/Cumulative index
KAMZ	Car manufacturing	Industrial index/Cumulative index
LOMO	Car manufacturing	Industrial index/Cumulative index
Moscow Helicopter Factory	Car manufacturing	Industrial index/Cumulative index
Doka Khleb	Car manufacturing	Industrial index/Cumulative index
ZIL	Car manufacturing	Industrial index/Cumulative index
Kirishneftorgsinthesis	Chemicals	Industrial index/Cumulative index
Tomsk Neftkhim Kombinat	Chemicals	Industrial index/Cumulative index
Red October	Confectionery	Industrial index/Cumulative index
Novoroscement	Construction	Industrial index/Cumulative index
Brask Aluminium Factory	Metals	Industrial index/Cumulative index
Norilsk Nickel	Metals	Industrial index/Cumulative index
Sayansk Aluminium Factory	Metals	Industrial index/Cumulative index
Sredneural Medeplav Factory	Metals	Industrial index/Cumulative index
Nijnitagil Metal Kombinat	Metals	Industrial index/Cumulative index
Novolipetsky Metal Kombinat	Metals	Industrial index/Cumulative index
Gasprom	Oil and Gas	Industrial index/Cumulative index
Komineft	Oil and Gas	Industrial index/Cumulative index
LUKoil	Oil and Gas	Industrial index/Cumulative index
Purneftegaz	Oil and Gas	Industrial index/Cumulative index
Yuganskneftegaz	Oil and Gas	Industrial index/Cumulative index
Bratsk LPK	Pulp and Paper	Industrial index/Cumulative index
Siktivkarsky LPK	Pulp and Paper	Industrial index/Cumulative index
Unified Energy System of Russia	Utilities	Industrial index/Cumulative index
Olbi Diplomat	Retail	Cumulative index
GUM	Retail	Cumulative index
Far East Shipping Co.	Shipping	Cumulative index
North Western Shipping Co.	Shipping	Cumulative index
Baltisky Shipping Co.	Shipping	Cumulative index
Murmanskoye Shipping Co.	Shipping	Cumulative index
St Petersburg Telecom	Telecommunications	Cumulative index
Rostelecom	Telecommunications	Cumulative index
Moscow Telephone Company	Telecommunications	Cumulative index

Exhibit 8.6 *continued*

Novosibirsk Telephone Company	Telecommunications	Cumulative index
Lenenergo	Utilities	Industrial index/Cumulative index
Irkurskenergo	Utilities	Industrial index/Cumulative index
Mosenergo	Utilities	Industrial index/Cumulative index

Source: AK&M.

Exhibit 8.7

The Moscow Times Index

Stocks included in the MT Index

Company	*28/11*	*29/11*	*Average Price (1000s)* *30/11*	*1/12*	*2/12*	*Change over the week*
AvtoVAZ	30.80	30.80	30.80	30.80	23.30	−7.50
Bratsk Aluminium	59.65	59.65	63.05	56.80	63.60	+6.55
Far Eastern Shipping	142.90	177.70	177.70	177.70	177.70	+34.80
GAZ Auto Plant	10.00	10.00	10.00	14.60	14.60	+4.60
Gazprom	0.88	0.88	0.88	0.88	0.88	0
GUM	21.35	23.40	23.40	23.40	23.40	+2.05
Inkombank	307.00	307.00	307.00	307.00	307.00	0
KamAZ	9.70	9.70	9.70	9.70	9.70	0
Komineft	24.00	24.00	24.65	24.65	24.65	+0.65
Krasnoyarsk Aluminium	37.85	37.85	40.40	42.20	44.80	+12.35
LUKoil Holding	137.50	130.85	124.45	124.45	117.35	−20.15
LUKoil Kogalym	133.85	127.60	127.60	127.60	127.60	−6.25
LUKoil Langepas	31.00	31.00	31.00	31.00	31.00	0
Neftekhimbank	3.45	3.45	3.45	3.45	3.45	0
Nizhnevartovskneft	52.00	52.00	52.00	52.00	52.10	+0.10
Norilsk Nickel	35.45	35.45	35.45	35.45	35.45	−1.75
Noyabrskneftegaz	23.20	23.20	23.20	18.65	14.60	−8.60
OLBI-Diplomat	11.00	11.00	6.75	6.75	6.75	−3.25
Promstroybank St P	53.00	53.00	53.00	53.00	53.00	0
Purneftegaz	16.80	16.80	16.80	16.80	16.80	0
Red October	14.50	14.50	14.50	15.50	15.50	+1.0
Rostelecom	14.30	14.30	14.30	14.30	14.30	0
Sayansk Aluminium	75.80	75.80	79.20	76.30	76.30	+3.15
Sberbank	85.00	85.00	88.00	88.00	88.00	−3.0
St Petersburg Telephone	46.50	46.50	46.50	46.50	46.50	0
Surgutneftegaz	0.56	0.56	0.56	0.56	0.56	0
Tomskneft	25.60	24.70	24.70	24.70	24.70	−0.90
Unified Energy System	48.00	50.05	50.05	50.05	50.05	+2.05
Yuganskneftegaz	72.60	67.85	67.85	67.85	67.85	−5.25
ZIL	18.00	18.00	18.00	18.00	18.00	0

Exhibit 8.7 *continued*

Other OTC stocks not included in the MT Index:

Company	*28/11*	*29/11*	*Average Price (1000s)* *30/11*	*1/12*	*2/12*	*Change over the week*
Megionneftegaz	10.55	10.55	10.15	10.15	10.15	−0.40
Condpetroleum	24.90	24.90	19.40	19.40	19.40	−5.50
Mosenergo	0.42	0.42	0.42	0.42	0.42	0
Vareganneftegaz	16.20	16.20	16.20	16.20	16.20	0
Irkutskenergo	14.05	14.05	14.05	14.05	14.05	0
MMM	5.00	5.00	5.00	–	–	0
Kirishinefteorgsintez	–	–	–	13.00	13.00	–
Orenburgneft	4.70	4.70	4.70	4.70	4.70	0
Chernogorneft	176.80	185.80	184.30	184.30	184.30	+7.50
Samotlorneft	19.50	19.50	19.50	19.50	19.50	0
Apatit, Murmansk	15.00	15.00	15.00	15.00	15.00	0
LUKoil-Urayneftegaz	19.20	19.20	19.20	19.20	19.20	0
Novolipetsk Metal	25.00	25.00	25.00	25.00	25.00	0
Tebukneft	10.15	10.15	10.15	10.15	10.15	0
AVVA	8.00	8.00	8.00	8.00	8.00	0
Angarsknefteorgsyntez	57.60	57.60	57.60	57.60	57.60	0
Perm Motor	5.80	5.80	5.80	5.80	5.80	0
Moscow Telephone	326.00	326.00	326.00	326.00	326.00	+24.40
Sverdlovskenergo	22.10	22.10	22.10	22.10	22.10	0
Permnefteorgsyntez	4.00	4.00	4.00	4.00	4.00	0
Aviastar	2.00	2.00	2.00	2.00	2.00	0
Priobneft	45.70	45.70	45.70	45.70	45.70	0
Hotel Kosmos	0.30	0.30	0.30	–	–	0
Primorskoe Shipping	–	–	–	13.90	13.90	0

The Moscow Times Index is a daily average of the 30 Russian stocks with the largest market capitalisation that are traded over the counter and meet a select criteria. The criteria have been devised in consultation with The Moscow Times Index Advisory Board, on which the members are: Alfa Kapital, Ernst & Young, Grant Financial Center, Milbank Tweed, RINACO Plus, Skate Press Consulting Agency, Troika Dialog.
The criteria seek to ensure that the stocks are reasonably liquid and that at least 25 per cent of all shares are available for investment. The daily price of the stock is derived from the average of quotations from at least three separate market-makers.
1 Sept, 1994 = 100.
The index is compiled by the Skate Press Consulting Agency and audited by Coopers & Lybrand.

Source: Moscow Times.

their stock being bought and their control threatened. Often the only evidence of ownership was in a personal computer, perhaps in a remote location, and proof of ownership depended on a print-out with the customer's name on it. Even the giant Gazprom does not have a functioning register.

The market grew fast and there was little time for formal training of professionals and no programmes providing for such training. The market itself trained the participants in their various roles. The legal environment was chaotic: 'There are Soviet laws, new laws and presidential decrees', says one broker, 'and most of them are in conflict. There is not one area of law governing securities that is clear. It is all interpretation.' Today, there is greater clarity 'but not much', he said. One thing that has improved is the availability of information: 'Remember, this was an information-starved country, people didn't talk to each other about anything.' Now various sources, such as Troika Dialog, publish daily, weekly and monthly market summaries and information.

Exhibit 8.8

Stocks included in the ROS index

Company	*Sector*
Krasnoyarsk Aluminium Factory	Aluminium
Sayansky Aluminium Factory	Aluminium
Brastk Aluminium Factory	Aluminium
LUKoil	Oil
Yuganskneftegaz	Oil
Komineft	Oil
Surgutneftegaz	Oil
Tomskneft	Oil
Purneftegaz	Oil
Noyabrskneftegaz	Oil
Kogalymneftegaz	Oil
Kondpetroleium	Oil
Chernogorneft	Oil
GUM	Retail
Rostelecom	Telecommunications
St Petersburg Telephone Company	Telecommunications
Novosibirsk Telephone Company	Telecommunications
Unified Energy System of Russia	Utilities
Irkurskenergo	Utilities
Mosenergo	Utilities
Far Eastern Shipping Co.	Shipping

Source: CS First Boston.

The participants, both government and private, are now clearly trying to develop the capital market in a more rational way: new legislation is emerging and there is more to follow. By early 1995, the madness of the previous year had been transformed into what one broker described as 'a deep bear market'.

RESULTS OF VOUCHER PRIVATISATION

The voucher stage of privatisation ended on 1 July 1994 and its overseer, the state Property Committee, lauded its success. Others, such as the Mayor of Moscow and critics in the state Duma, accused the committee's chairman, Anatoly Chubais, of 'destroying the Russian economy'. A report by the Reform International Foundation was suitably impressed by the number of joint stock companies created, but pointed out that there is a lack of a broad spectrum of private owners, production efficiency has not been increased and a social security network has not taken shape because of the small revenues from privatisation. In addition, the report said, there has been a failure to break down monopolies, create competitive markets and attract significant foreign investment, all of which were official first-stage goals. It commented that there had been 'misconduct, violations of rules, and corruption among officials'. Indeed, the deputy head of the committee, Vladimir Mashevsky, was detained by police for accepting a Rb9 million bribe for his part in privatising a Tyumen defence company. Interior Ministry officials were reported to be seeking seven million vouchers and Rb1 billion that had disappeared from Neftalmazinvest, an investment fund controlled by the committee itself.

Nonetheless, the dedication of Mr Chubais to privatisation was never in question and the

The share of the state sector in the economy is shrinking

share of the state sector in the economy had shrunk to about 10 per cent by the start of the second stage, which involves the sale of company shares for money. Anyone with sufficient funds can now buy shares in the companies that underwent privatisation in the first stage or any other state-owned businesses that still exist. The shares of most former state-owned enterprises, initially sold for vouchers, now trade freely on the secondary market.

Many of these shares were highly liquid from the start; those of United Energy Systems of Russia, KamAZ, Yuganskeftegaz and the GUM department store were accepted as collateral security by all banks. Later, the larger Russian oil companies, non-ferrous metals plants, power engineering and telecommunications companies floated their stocks and regional firms sold shares on regional stock exchanges. Trades in large numbers of shares in some companies began selling for hundreds or even thousands of times their face value. Shares in several manufacturing companies began to enjoy the sort of high liquidity previously known to commercial bank and trading company shares. Most trading is over-the-counter and industrial shares account for a significant part of it (See Exhibit 8.9 – pp 130-131). About 90 per cent of the shares traded through the Professional Association of Securities Dealers (PASD) are shares in manufacturing firms. Trading volume of more than Rb1 trillion a month was logged in 1994.

While all company shares appreciated heavily on a monthly basis, some rose in sensational terms. Russia's largest oil company, LUKoil, saw its nominal Rb125 shares selling for US$35; Kogalymneftegas, a LUKoil subsidiary, saw its Rb500 shares go to US$59; another gas firm, Yuganskeftegas, saw Rb200 shares going for US$60. When the latter company was privatised at a voucher auction, each voucher invested in the firm was exchanged for 18 shares, meaning that each voucher invested could be worth US$1,000. When Rostelcom's shares were divided into smaller shares, one employee with 40 shares gained US$3,200. The price then reached US$6, giving him a potential yield of US$19,200 if he wanted to sell. It is important to note that many Russian investors did not share that sort of good fortune. For a time much attention was focused on the MMM pyramid scam (and similar bearer issues) but the collapse of the pyramid and the jailing of MMM's owners on tax charges led to new legal measures to avoid such schemes.

The Russian government now promotes the development of the market in privatised shares, but not the one in bearer stocks, such as the MMM variety. A recent ruling by the Finance Ministry on the mandatory re-evaluation of fixed assets has eased procedures for secondary share issues. Foreign investors became an important factor during 1994. The Moscow-based investment firm, Grant, estimated that foreign investments in Russian securities were growing at around US$100 million a month in late 1994 and forecast a total of US$4 billion by the end of the year. Small private investments also boomed during the year. In 1993 small private investors purchased 13 per cent of the shares in privatised companies, but in the first half of 1994 the figure rose to 20 per cent. At the end of voucher privatisation, the state Property Committee estimated that about 15 per cent of industrial shares were in the hands of company managers, 40 per cent were held by company employees, 15 per cent had been bought by investment funds, 5 to 7 per cent were owned by small private investors, and between 23 and 25 per cent of industrial shares remained in the hands of the state. But while shares are still changing hands, the ownership of Russia's largest companies must remain uncertain.

Many observers believe that the balance sheet value of state assets undergoing privatisation was underestimated or deliberately understated and that the nominal value of the investment voucher (Rb10,000) was excessively low. This resulted in a sort of fire sale in which shares went for next to nothing. Critics say that the ensuing rapid rise in share prices was carefully planned to profit a few well-informed sources who had bought up investment vouchers from the needy population at cheap prices, and with dealers setting up in metro stations and travelling out to remote rural areas to strike deals with peasants. Whatever the truth, the voucher privatisation has left behind an estimated 40 million shareholders in Russia, and about 70 per cent of Russia's industry has been registered as joint stock companies. It is a considerable achievement.

THE MMM STORY

In the end, it was not the official regulators but the tax authorities that put a stop to the MMM scam and jailed those responsible. MMM is made up of 29 companies, headed by the Greek-born Sergei Mavrodi. Its voucher fund, which was Russia's largest in terms of shareholders and the second largest in terms of vouchers, was licensed by the state Property Committee (GKI), while the problem investment fund itself came under the Ministry of Finance. Four separate regulatory bodies were sure that MMM was running a pyramid scheme and using misleading advertising, but seemingly could not do anything about it. Eventually, the tax police stepped in and put Mavrodi and his brother behind bars on tax avoidance charges; but the two promptly launched another scheme based on MMM 'tickets', a term used to bypass legislation on shares.

The government's first reaction was to do nothing very much and indeed there seemed to be nothing in the letter of the law to prohibit pyramid schemes. Although the authorities later recognised the explosive nature of the problem, it lacked the mechanism and the leadership to respond swiftly. Responsibility for the financial market is split between the Finance Ministry, the Central Bank, the GKI and the Anti-Monopolies Commission (AMC). The AMC has the authority to supervise organised commodity and financial markets, but cannot make its own rules – that requires either a presidential decree or a law passed by parliament. President Yeltsin, anxious to short-circuit pressing economic problems, has been issuing a lot of decrees. One, issued in July 1994, forbade financial companies from advertising projections of future performance; but the decree does not catch unregulated companies, or the subsidiaries of regulated companies either, and until 1 January 1995 not all investment companies needed a licence. The AMC's only course of action was to send letters to MMM-type companies asking about their activities and the nature of their investment.

Even in August 1994, MMM, Tele-Market and several other suspicious funds were still advertising on TV and other media. Many, including MMM, had removed their financial guarantees in accordance with the decree, but others had not. The Dutch-registered GMM, for example, was advertising hard currency returns of at least 28 per cent. The government's response was a draft law in early September which bans advertising by unlicensed companies, prohibits subliminal advertising and limits companies to two commercials an hour on TV or radio. MMM has since been banned from advertising on state-run media.

The AMC contacted Britain's Securities and Investments Board (SIB) to ask how it deals with similar scandals in the UK, and whether the SIB's structure and powers would work in Russia. Unlike Russia's Finance Ministry, the SIB has the power to freeze the worldwide assets of a firm if its activities are deemed detrimental to investors' interests. Investment legislation is high on the agenda, with parliamentary working committees looking into the whole area of securities regulation.

In a press statement issued after the MMM débâcle, the GKI noted that, in addition to teaching Russian investors about the risks of investing: 'MMM also teaches another lesson, that the irresponsibility of the Russian bureaucracy is the greatest danger for the Russian capital markets. MMM teaches that if we depend on bureaucrats for regulation, they will destroy faith in the marketplace. They have no interest in stopping frauds like MMM. The irony is that they ignore frauds like MMM and at the same time interfere everyday with honest and legitimate businesses. Bureaucrats are not interested in protecting investors, they are only interested in increasing their own power.'

REGISTRATION, CLEARING AND SETTLEMENT

It could take up to six months to register a share transfer in Russia, although most deals now take less time than that, since there are few proper registers and few companies offering custodial services. Clearing and settlement are slow. One of the biggest problems for the market reformers has been the share registrars, whose independence and integrity are crucial because registration, not the share certificate, is the only legal proof of ownership. Only in the autumn of 1994 did the first rules for registrars appear (and they were deemed inadequate) the most important of which was that companies with more than 1,000 shareholders must use a separately incorporated registrar, which may not trade or issue the shares.

The Capital Markets Surveillance Unit, a project funded by USAID and administered by Price Waterhouse, examined registers used by companies with more than 1,000 shareholders and found that 15 per cent were held by the companies, 12 per cent were at brokers, and 18 per cent at banks and investment firms, while fully 50 per cent were so-called 'pocket registrars', set up to circumvent the rules by firms with 'red directors' (Soviet-era bosses determined not to lose control of their companies). Most enterprises maintained their own registry unsystematically and only inscribed their employees, while the other shareholders could not get any dividends or information on the company. The pocket registrars sometimes have good reason to keep their registers secret, especially from Russian criminals who use registers to identify shareholders from whom to extort shares: but usually they are obstructive for other reasons. Most lack the software or the infrastructure to run their operations properly, and many are controlled by the company's administration, which instructs them not to tell brokers anything.

There is now widespread interest in improving and centralising share registration in a way that would not interfere with the market, but would promote its integrity and help enforce the laws already passed. Indeed, some Moscow brokers are setting up independent registrars. They will receive some funding from USAID, which is also financing trials with independent share regulators in Vladimir, St Petersburg and Kursk, as well as testing two registration software packages. In St Petersburg many banks have set up share registries. The Central Bank wants banks to act as sole depositories, registrars and custodians.

However, because the law remains vague, there are still problems. Some companies have strange issuing procedures. The ZIL automaker issued both 'shares' and 'share certificates', the first representing individual shares, the second multiples of them. There is much confusion over

Exhibit 8.9

Over-the-counter share prices of the largest Russian Corporations

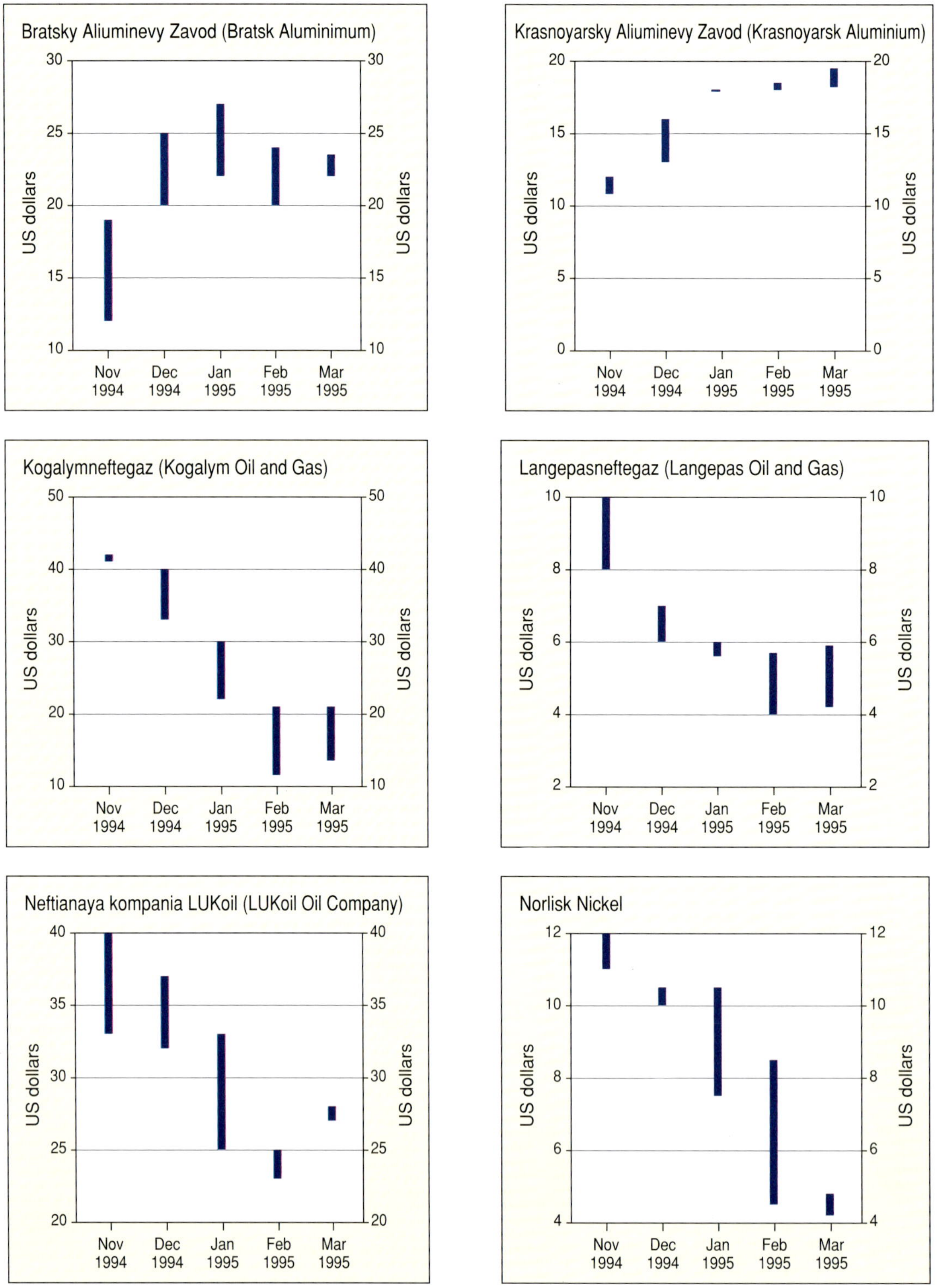

Exhibit 8.9

Over-the-counter share prices of the largest Russian Corporations

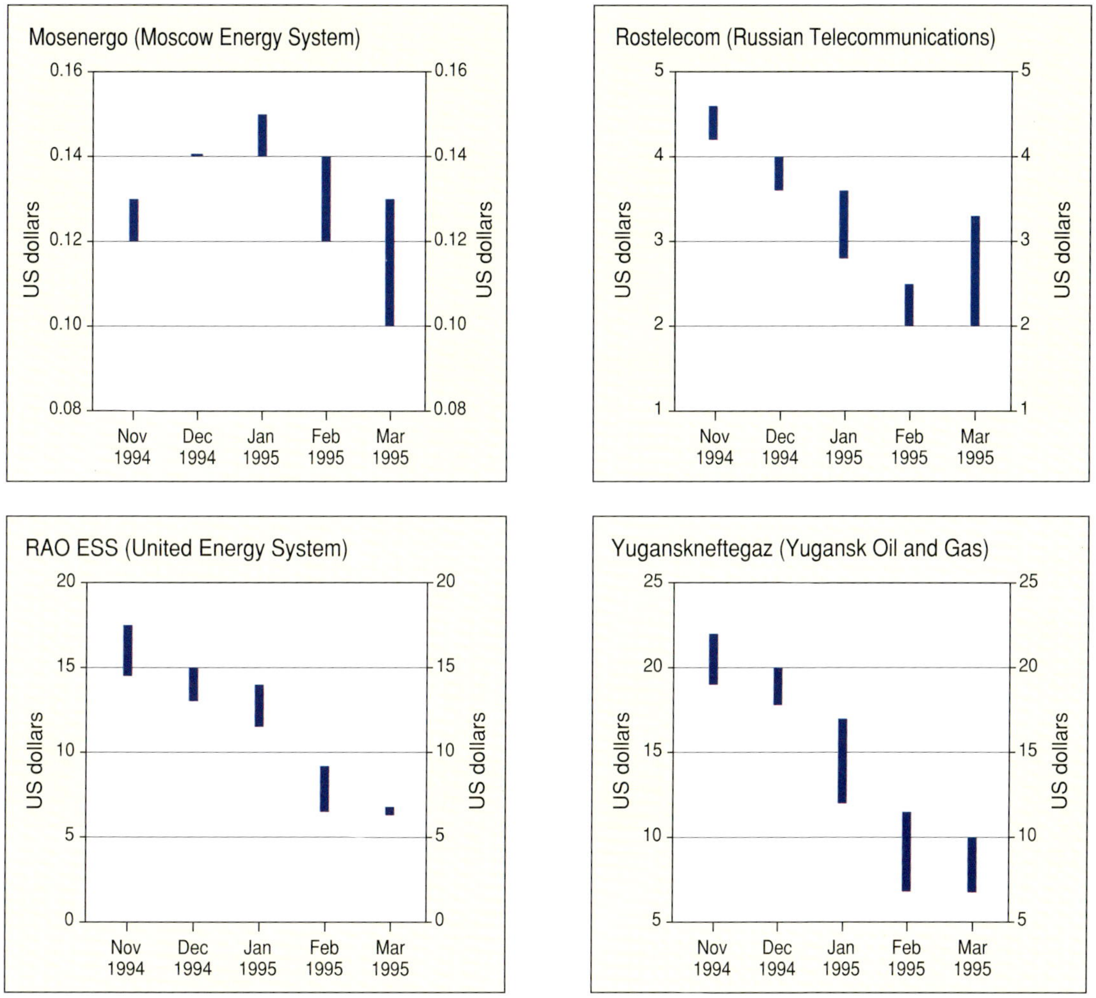

Shares in manufacturing companies began to enjoy high liquidity in 1994

the proper levels of registry fees. While these should reflect the expenses incurred by the registrar, that still leaves some room for abuse. Some registrars charge only the share buyer, others also charge the seller. It is common to charge 1.23 per cent of the purchase price, which brokers think is far too much.

Brokers and investors also want the shareholder's right to information to be legally defined. Shareholders do not have full right of access to information on the registry. Registrars want a legal definition of the proof of share ownership required for registration, given that shares can be bought at closed subscriptions, share shops, even grocery stores. There is also the danger of the same shares being sold more than once between registrations. This problem is worse in the regions because of poor communications and the time it can take to register a purchase when the broker or investor might have to travel 1,000 miles to record the transaction. This has led to many brokers trading bearer securities because they carry no registration problems.

Several organisations are tackling the clearing and settlement problems. One of these is the Rinaco Depositor Company, part of the Rinaco Russian Investment Group, which began as the firm's registrar then branched out into custodial and depository services for voucher investment funds. In Moscow, the project with the best support from brokers is the Depository Clearing Company (DCC), backed by USAID, whose advisory committee includes such big players as Troika Dialog, CS First Boston, Grant, Chase Manhattan, Brunswick, NikOil and Olma. Deloitte and Touche is senior adviser. But the entire Russian back office industry faces an uphill struggle. At one end of the scale are the small registrars of shares which few are interested in trading; at the other end are the bigger, possessive registrars which resist the idea of centralised organisations.

The issue is complicated by the lack of clarity in the legal status of nominee holdings. Many Russian brokers do not have a back office and register shares in their own names. The acceptance of nominee holdings by registrars would enable the transfer of ownership to be made easier. Nominee shareholdings are essential in Russia. Zil issued 200,000 shares and it is inconceivable that each could be registered separately. Legal clarification could also settle the issue of book entry (who maintains it, the issuer or the registrar?) and force issuers to recognise nominee shareholders. As long as the rights and duties of nominee holders are not clearly defined, there is uncertainty about who can act as depository and custodian. Meanwhile, business is booming for the few foreign custodians. CS First Boston's custody service for its own clients grew to cover US$1 billion-worth of paper in less than a year. There were reports circulating in 1994 that both Chase Manhattan and Citibank would soon be offering custodial services.

In clearing and settlement, traditional turf wars take their toll on the poor infrastructure. It can take a week or two to transfer money between institutions in the same street, or a month between cities, so many share purchases are made in person. Brokers and dealers should maintain client accounts but some do not, because of a potential problem with the authorities. Maintaining client accounts is not clearly defined in law, because monetary accounts come under the Central Bank's authority, and brokers claim it is unthinkable to open one account at a bank and another at a brokerage because it would make the whole system too complicated. One remedy is for the broker to buy a bank, or the dealer could set up an account at a bank with agreements for transferring cash. But in Russia there is nothing to stop the bank from front running. In August 1994, DCC got around the problem by setting up its own bank, Depository Clearing Bank, which hopes to act as paying agent for several issues, collect dividends and interest payments and settle trades.

The Moscow Interbank Currency Exchange (Micex), has extensive experience in securities clearing and settlement through its treasury bill operations, where it acts as sole registrar, custodian and depository. Micex is looking for new business because currency trading is gravitating to the OTC market. It has the resources to develop a securities clearing system, as well as a powerful backer in the Central Bank, which is a member of the exchange. Micex's depository is electronic and, with its optical fibre communications, comparatively expensive. It also plans to go into the clearing and settlement of taiga bonds, which could provide a launch pad for future stock market operations.

THE PROSPECTS FOR THE LAW ON SECURITIES

In the autumn of 1994 there was some progress in the legislative regulation of the securities market. The stormy financial speculations of recent months certainly proved an additional impulse to the development of the law. In September and October there were noticeable changes, with the first section of the Civil Code adopted by the state Duma on the third reading. The government hurriedly submitted to parliament a draft law on joint stock companies and a draft law on the securities market was prepared. Finally, the presidential decree 'On Measures for the State Regulation of the Securities Market in the Russian Federation', appeared on 4 November.

In the opinion of the EPIcentre think-tank: 'The given package of draft laws resolves almost all the problems connected with the legal regulation of the securities market.' The Civil Code 'is the base of the pyramid', in the field of legal regulation and even contains a special chapter devoted to securities, the organisation said in a report published in December. The Civil Code defines a security as 'a document certifying property rights, the realisation or transition of which are possible only on its presentation. For this purpose, securities should be of a standard form and have obligatory requisites'. In addition, the Civil Code gives a supplementary definition: 'In cases stipulated by law or defined by law, it is sufficient to prove that the securities are registered in a special (physical or electronic) register in order to realise and transfer the rights certified by the securities.' This is important as non-documentary securities have already emerged in the market. Moreover, the Ministry of Finance is preparing for a huge treasury bond issue in 1995. The important thing here is the demand that: 'Only an official registrar can maintain such a register and he must be responsible for the conservation of entries, maintaining their confidentiality and the correct submission of the corresponding data.'

The Civil Code classifies securities by kind and only nine kinds are recognised: government bonds, bonds, bills, cheques, deposit and savings certificates, bearer bankbooks, endorsement bills, shares, and privatisation securities (although vouchers have ceased to exist and the issuing of other such securities seems unlikely). In addition, three categories of securities are set down: bearer securities (property rights belong to the bearer), registered securities (rights belong to the person indicated on the security) and warranted securities (rights belong to the person indicated in the security or to a person indicated by the owner through his order).

The distinctive features of the transfer of rights to securities are: (1) rights resulting from ownership of the bearer security may be transferred by simply handing over the security to another person; (2) transfer of rights to a registered security is performed through concession, which does not involve the previous owner in any liabilities for non-fulfilment of an obligation resulting from ownership of the security; and (3) transfer of rights to a warranted security is realised by means of a transferring registration or endorsement. In this case, both the initial owner and all other owners bear joint responsibility for the corresponding obligation. EPIcentre regards the Civil Code as 'a pure framework' for securities legislation which 'leaves a broad field for other legal enactments'. It also indicates that the specific definitions, order and procedure of the emission and circulation of securities 'shall be determined by the laws on joint stock companies and securities'.

The draft law on joint stock companies would permit the emission of two categories of shares: ordinary and preferred. An ordinary share gives its owner the right to one vote at the general meeting of shareholders, to receive dividends from company profits after reserves have been restored, and dividends on preferred shares have been paid out, as well as to a part of the property on the liquidation of the joint stock company. A preferred share gives its owner the right to enjoy preference over an ordinary shareholder in case of distribution of profit and property of the company on liquidation. The right to vote on preferred shares can only be granted by the company if this is stipulated in the company's charter. Owners of preferred shares may vote at the general meeting of shareholders if the company has not paid promised dividends for a term of two years.

One important innovation of the draft law is a prohibition against the emission by joint stock companies of bearer shares (a direct consequence of the MMM scandal and others). The bearer shares of about 10 issuers are already circulating and they will have to be converted to registered shares. Also the requirements on the maintenance of the shareholder registers are becoming more strict and such a register must contain the following information: (1) full name of all shareholders (including the names of enterprises); (2) data of shareholders (locations and account numbers of legal entities, passport data, and residential addresses of private individuals); (3) quantity, category, face value of the shares owned by each shareholder); (4) dates of acquisition of shares; and (5) grounds for acquisition of property rights to the shares (including data from the documents confirming the facts of transactions with the shares).

A joint stock company may entrust maintenance of the register (if there are over 100 shareholders this becomes an obligation) to a bank, depository, or other specialised institution which has the corresponding licence. This could be burdensome for small companies, as the costs of such services are rather high. Requirements covering the confirmation of shareholders rights are more stringent. In particular, documentary emission of shares should be accompanied by the obligatory distribution of the share certificates, which should contain all the data indicated in the law (one item missing would render the certificate invalid).

A joint stock company has also the right to issue bonds. Unlike shares, bonds can be bearer bonds (for registered bonds maintenance of a register, like the shares register, is obligatory). Interest on bonds should be paid at least once a year. If the company fails to pay interest or a bond credit it can be declared bankrupt at the demand of any shareholder. The issue of convertible bonds is permitted (owners enjoying priority in acquiring shares or the right to change bonds into shares). When bonds are issued, owners must receive a certificate which, as in the case of shares, must contain all relevant data and would be rendered invalid by omissions.

Distribution of shares should end within six months of the registration date of the prospectus of the issue, the draft law lays down. In public distributions, the total nominal value of issued shares may not exceed by more than five times the volume of the company's charter capital. An open joint stock company may not perform public distribution of the issued shares if its charter capital does not exceed ten times the minimal charter capital permitted for such companies. As of October 1994, public distribution of shares is allowed only for stock companies with charter capital of Rb200 million or more.

In general, the new law on joint stock companies 'is a normal law for normal companies', EPIcentre comments. It gathers together in one act all the norms scattered between different laws, presidential decrees and government resolutions. 'The only problem is that stock companies in Russia are not normal. A large number of closed joint stock companies with thousands of shareholders can be regarded as a consequence of the premature (1987–92) privatisation laws. The draft law now introduces a norm: any more than 50 people and a closed joint stock company must re-register as an open joint stock company, and this can produce conflicts. The stock companies emerging from the transformation of state enterprises also bear a large number of specific features connected with the preservation of controlling blocks of shares held by work collectives or the administration. All this differs from the classical notions of joint stock companies in the US or Western Europe. Thus the problem of implementation of the law's requirements in real life is a matter for discussion.' Perhaps all that is left 'is to wait for amendments from economic reality', EPIcentre said.

The draft law on the securities market was prepared by a working group from the state Duma and the Finance Ministry. In essence it defines the activities of brokers and dealers, deals with management of securities, clearing, collection, verification, documentation and depository activities. It also includes registration, which is to be performed on an agency contract basis. The emitter himself can be a register holder. The holder is obliged to open personal accounts in the register of owners; introduce all necessary changes and additions; perform operations on owners' accounts only at their instructions; inform owners of the rights conferred by securities and the means of realising such rights; give the owners information provided by the emitter; and strictly observe the procedure for transfer of the register on the abrogation of the contract with the emitter.

EPIcentre comments that all participants in the securities market can combine all six types of activity (broker, dealer, securities management, clearing, depository activities and registration), where formerly a broker could not be a dealer. 'We are not sure that such liberalisation is reasonable,' it said, 'as a prohibition against combining brokers' and dealers' activity exists in the laws of many countries and is targeted at the prevention of fraud. Certainly, it is easy to evade this law, but why should we make life easier for swindlers?' Organisation of trade on the securities market (the rendering of services that facilitate the conclusion of legal deals with securities by participants in the market) is best performed by a stock exchange, which does not combine organisation of trade with other types of activity, apart from depository activity, maintenance of the register, and the determination of mutual obligations, EPIcentre believes.

The emission procedure is described in detail. The emission prospectus is registered if the securities are distributed: (a)among a potentially unlimited circle of investors; (b) among a group of persons, not less than 100, known in advance; or (c) when a general volume of emission exceeds 1,000 minimal wages. Registration or refusal of the emission is given within 30 days of submitting the documentation. General requirements for the emission are described in detail and are in accordance with present practice. The emitter submits an account on the emission of securities to the registering body within 30 days of distribution. The registering body should register the results of the emission within two weeks, after which it takes full responsibility for the completeness of the account.

State regulation of the securities market is performed by the Federal Commission for Securities and Stock Market issues, which is responsible to the president (he appoints all 12 members). The commission distributes licences among market participants, suspends or annuls licences, establishes the obligatory norms of efficiency for the institutions (excluding banks), and verifies the performance of participants. 'The present law on the securities market is in general very broad and detailed from the point of view of the present registering body (the Ministry of Finance)', EPIcentre said. That is, it contains a large number of norms that do not require further explication or interpretation. But 'It is excessively liberal, there are practically no tough norms that would change the present practice (although the new draft law does contain such norms). The main innovation is the Federal Commission for Securities, which is granted broad functions in regulating the securities market and its activities virtually removed from public control. It is responsible only to the president. This results in a reduction of legislative regulation of Russia's securities market and increases the importance of the bureaucrat, i.e. of subjective state regulation. This is a rather sharp turn from liberalism to bureaucratisation of the securities market', EPIcentre said.

The presidential decree does not add anything to the debate, repeating almost word for word some of the provisions of the existing law on the securities market. Its main aim seemed to be to give a legal basis to the Federal Commission for Securities and the stock market. The president tends to rush his decrees to issue them a bit earlier than the law, so as not to lose the initiative in conducting reforms. Vice Premier Anatoly Chubais, who ran the voucher privatisation as the head of the state Property Committee, will chair the commission.

In the 1992–94 period, Russia's securities legislation 'was very loose', EPIcentre says, and the adoption. of the new legislation 'will be a big step forward'. The drafts are 'more or less consistent in liquidating the conditions for fraud on the financial market. In this sense the law on joint stock companies seems to us very important and comprehensive. It does not directly prohibit the establishment of pyramid schemes; however, it restricts this activity in such a way that a pyramid can exist only for a short time and will not have macroeconomic consequences as at the end of the summer and autumn of 1994.' The developing system of regulation of the securities market 'shows a clear tendency toward stabilisation. It fixes the existing practices and is based on the present forms of normative regulation. A systematisation of normative provisions is taking place'.

But the think-tank sees one main drawback to the draft laws. They are all rooted in a definite scheme of normative regulation, which is rather distant from the facts of life for joint stock companies. 'The legislator proceeds from the fact that shareholders acquire shares because they are interested in dividends, that corporations are interested in maintaining stable rates of their shares, and that the price of a share is determined by a capitalised dividend, etc. Actually, the typical small-scale Russian shareholder owns shares that he got free of charge, and if the majority of stock companies and investment funds are unable to pay, they could at least protect the shareholder from inflation (meaning shares have a negative value). Russia's market becomes interested in dividends only when the dates of their payout draw near, and for most of the financial year participants are interested only in speculative fluctuations in the price of shares, and there is a huge gap between share prices and the level of dividends. The legislator does not wish to see this gap and proceeds from the fact that life should be within the framework of the normative scheme.' The paradox is that the stabilisation of the legislation on joint stock companies and the securities market is taking place at the very moment when these companies and the market itself are highly unstable.

The laws remained drafts at the end of 1994 and, no doubt, considerable changes are possible. The presidential decree remains in force until the law on the securities market is finally adopted. Future evolution of the legislation will be linked with pressures emanating from different groups: the banks, the Ministry of Finance, the Central Bank and professional participants in the securities market. EPIcentre expects 'even broader liberalisation of the laws as compared to the drafts'.

IX

TAXATION AND ACCOUNTANCY

Price Waterhouse, Moscow

OVERVIEW OF THE FISCAL ENVIRONMENT

SCOPE OF APPLICATION

The present Russian tax system is in its infancy and as a result has been developing rapidly and is subject to constant change and interpretation. This is especially true with the tax system that applies to banks. In December 1991 the Russian authorities introduced a new banking income tax law which was effective from 1 January 1992. At the end of 1993, a Presidential Decree (Decree 2270) abolished the banking income tax law and required banks to be taxed under the Profit Tax Law, similar to regular enterprises, effective 1 January 1994. However, instructions, regulations, and other taxation documents clarifying tax procedures have been issued which only apply to banks. The result is that taxation as it applies to banks is a subsection of the overall Profit Tax Law.

The primary legal documents relating to the profits tax calculation for commercial banks include:

- Law 2116-1, 'On Profit Tax from Enterprises and Organizations', dated 27 December 1991. This law establishes the procedure of calculation of taxable base and provides guidelines for the enterprise's income and expenses.
- Decree 490, 'On Calculation of Taxable Profit to be paid by Banks and other Credit Institutions', dated 16 May 1994. This decree describes the instruction for taxation of the bank's activities.
- Resolution 552, 'Regulations on Composition of Costs included into the Cost of Production and on the Order of Calculation of the Financial Results which are Subject to Profit Tax', dated 5 August 1992. Although these regulations are not specific to financial institutions, the law states that the provisions of this resolution are effective for banks unless they are directly contradicted by Decree 490.

At present, the legislative basis for taxation of financial institutions is minimal but is growing steadily. In addition to the above documents, the Central Bank of Russia, the Ministry of Finance and the State Tax Inspectorate offer clarifications and amendments through instructions, letters and other informal publications. Notwithstanding these documents, the treatment of many transactions remains unclear, especially new products and services.

One of the many problems that exist in the Russian profit tax framework is that many of the documents published are contradictory towards one another. This is highlighted by the fact that there is no legal hierarchy of tax legislation. It is difficult for the taxpayer to function in an environment where the President issues Decrees, the Duma issues laws and regulations, the Central Bank and Ministry of Finance issue instructions and the State Tax Service issues clarifications. There are many instances when two or more of the above documents contradict one other on the same issue. The reality of the situation is that taxes are applied differently from region to region.

The rate of change and clarification is dramatic. It is not impossible for the authorities to change their position regarding the tax treatment of a specific activity or transaction three to four times in one week. Therefore, it is essential that taxpayers are fully up to date and check with their advisers prior to acting.

SYSTEM OF BANKING TAXATION

The Russian system of taxation is a classical system of taxation, where income is taxed in the hands of the company and again on distribution to shareholders. Under Russian law, all Russian legal entities, whether they have foreign investment or not, are subject to the profit tax law. Foreign entities that have a taxable permanent establishment in Russia are also taxed under this law. Russia is a very high-tax jurisdiction and careful planning is necessary to limit the impact of very high effective taxation.

The law has not been developed to deal with complex issues that have been addressed in more mature systems. As such, many concepts familiar to foreign financial institutions and tax specialists are unknown in Russia and therefore there is potential for successful tax planning.

Russian taxes provide revenue for three tiers of the budget: federal, regional and local. The primary taxes paid to the budget are:

- Profit tax
- Value added tax (VAT)
- Housing (social) tax
- Road use tax
- Customs duties
- Securities tax
- Exchange tax
- Payroll taxes
- Excess wages tax
- Withholding tax

Depending on the bank's activities, any of these taxes can be significant.

PROFIT TAX

The profit tax rate for banks is a minimum of 35 per cent and a maximum of 43 per cent in 1995. This rate comprises two elements: 13 per cent for the Republican (Federal) budget and, depending on the region, between 22 and 30 per cent for the regional budgets.

For purposes of calculation of taxable profit the following types of income (net of VAT) are to be included but not limited to:

- interest income;
- commissions and other fees charged for services;
- payment for retail banking services;
- income for trust and custody services;
- gains/losses of realised currency transactions; and
- other income not specifically exempted.

More importantly, the primary types of income that are exempt from tax are:

- income from state securities, this includes interest, gains/losses on sale, and commissions for placement; this exemption applies for the primary and secondary markets for T-bills (GKOs) and for only the primary market on 'MinFin' bonds; and
- unrealised revaluation gains.

The following types of income are paid net of withholding and therefore are not subject to profit tax:

- dividends and interest paid on shares, bonds and other securities issued in the Russian Federation are subject to a withholding rate of 18 per cent.

For purposes of the profits tax calculation the following expenses are disallowed:

- loan loss provisions/write-offs on hard currency loans;
- the general loan loss provision for rouble loans;
- excess over statutory limits for loan loss provision/write-offs on rouble loans (the provisions required for international purposes are generally higher than statutory requirements);
- interest expense greater than 3 per cent over the Central Bank rate on interbank loans;
- training expense, unless provided by a licensed Russian educational institution;
- advertising, travel and entertainment expense over very small norms;
- non-mandatory insurance payments; and
- penalties.

In addition to the above, certain tax concessions exist. Tax concessions can only reduce the taxable base by a maximum of 50 per cent percent. They are as follows:

- net operating losses (carry-forward is five years);
- payments to reserve fund (up to 25 per cent of charter capital);
- payments to qualified charities;
- expenditures for technical qualifying equipment; and
- charitable payments.

SIGNIFICANT PROFIT TAX POLICIES

Cash basis

For tax and accounting purposes banks are primarily on the cash basis.

Loan loss provisions

In December 1994, the Central Bank required banks to calculate a loan loss provision based on mandatory classifications. The provisions ranged from a general reserve 2 per cent on all performing loans to 100 per cent for significantly over-due loans. The Central Bank guidance required the banks to reduce their taxable base by the calculated provision to the extent of profits before the reduction. The remaining portion was to be included on the balance sheet and amortised over five years to the taxable profit and loss. This policy was considered unacceptable to the Tax Inspectorate due to the significant effect it would have on tax collections. It was estimated that 20 to 25 per cent of all banks would have no tax liability if the provision was considered a reduction to the taxable base.

Therefore, during the first four months of 1995, the Tax Inspectorate informed the banks that the provision for loan losses would not be deductible for tax purposes. It is unclear what the final position will be, but the current thought is that the general provision will not reduce the taxable base and the specific provisions will reduce the taxable base. This matter is likely to change significantly during 1996.

Provisions for hard currency (non-rouble) loans remain not deductible for tax purposes.

Foreign exchange gains/losses

Banks are required to revalue their assets and liabilities denominated in foreign currency twice a week, when the Central Bank issues revised exchange rates. The resulting gain/loss is reflected in the profit and loss accounts of the bank. Until early December 1994 these exchange gains/losses were included in the tax base. Based on an instruction at the beginning of December 1994, these gains and losses on revaluation are now not subject to tax.

The revaluation is reduced by the amount attributable to shareholders' equity.

Depreciation

The current Russian calculation of depreciation for tax purposes applies the former USSR depreciation periods for each specific type of asset. These periods tend to be excessively long and, due to rouble devaluation, become worthless over time. For example, the depreciable life of a building and a computer is 100 and 10 years, respectively. Depreciation is calculated on a straight-line basis.

Interest expense

The deductibility of interest expense paid on deposits is specifically provided in the instructions without limit. However, interest expense paid on loans is limited to 3 per cent greater than the Central Bank rate. In 1994, the Central Bank rate fluctuated between 130 and 210 per cent. In addition, interest expense on loans used to finance the purchase of fixed or intangible assets is not deductible. The treatment of interest expense on hard currency loans is unclear at the present time.

Management charges

Intercompany charges will be fully deductible for tax purposes provided they are for services the company cannot provide for itself. Currently, the concept of transfer pricing is not in the tax legislation but this concept is developing.

Consolidation

The Russian tax law does not provide for consolidation among group companies, regardless of ownership percentages. Additionally, there is no form of an offset on dividends paid to a controlled group company. The result is that parent–subsidiary structures are very costly and are not widespread in Russia. Groups tend to be structured as brother–sister companies in order to avoid the multiple layers of taxation.

In practise, branches in separate regions are taxed separately from the head office. Although the tax law provides for consolidation within one company (head office and its branches), no mechanism exists to calculate and disburse the regional portion of the profit tax paid. Therefore, each regional Tax Inspectorate taxes separately any branch that is in its region. If a branch or head office is in a loss position it will not be consolidated with the rest of the company and the loss portion will go unutilised within the company for profit tax purposes.

PENALTIES AND INTEREST

The taxation system is in an early stage of development and is subject to varying interpretations and constant changes, which may be retroactive. In certain circumstances the Tax Authorities can be very aggressive in assessing interest and penalties, especially with banks. Although the actual tax due on a transaction may be minimal, penalties plus high rates of interest can be significant. The penalties range from 10 per cent for failure to file to 500 per cent of the transaction for fraud. The most common penalties for errors and omissions are 100–200 per cent of the *transaction value* (not the tax due). In addition to penalties, interest is charged in the amount of 0.7 per cent per day (255.5 per cent per annum).

VALUE ADDED AND SPECIAL TAX

All comments below on VAT apply to both VAT and the so-called 'special tax' which is also a VAT, although it must be accounted for separately.

The following services are not liable to VAT:
- 'the granting and transfer of loans, operations on deposits, settlement accounts, current and other types of accounts'; and
- 'operations connected with the circulation of money, banknotes or anything else which is a legal means of payment and operations connected with the circulation of securities (shares, guarantees, certificates and bills of exchange);

For example
- interest on loans;
- transaction charges on bank accounts;
- the buying and selling of shares as principal;
- discounting bills of exchange; and
- the issue of bonds.

The following are subject to VAT:
- *any kind of brokering services*, i.e. where the bank acts in the name of and under the guarantee of the client;
- fees for acting as trustee;
- the issue of guarantees or any other kind of obligation which the bank takes on for a third person;
- factoring;
- leasing;
- safe custody services;
- consultancy and information services;
- giving investment advice; and
- management services charged to subsidiaries or branches.

The bank will only be able to recover VAT paid to the extent of the ratio of non-exempted services over total services. In the normal course of business, many banks have a very low ratio of non-exempted services and therefore VAT represents a significant cost to a bank.

VAT CHARGES

As of 1 April 1995 services performed on the territory of the Russian Federation by a Russian legal entity will be liable to VAT at the rate of 21.5 per cent (this includes the special tax of 1.5 per cent) unless the services can be treated either as 'exported services' or are covered by another specific exemption from VAT.

VAT EXEMPTION FOR EXPORTED SERVICES

In line with other VAT jurisdictions, Russian VAT legislation provides that services qualifying as 'exported services' will not be liable to VAT in Russia. However, a recent ruling issued on exported services is far from consistent with other VAT jurisdictions and gives an extremely restricted definition of what constitutes an exported service.

This ruling effectively provides that, subject to a small number of exceptions, all services 'realised' (i.e. generally paid for) after 1 December 1994 by a Russian registered entity are chargeable to Russian VAT unless they are *physically performed* outside the CIS. A tax inspector will require proof that services have been physically performed outside the CIS (e.g. copies of the air tickets for the employees concerned).

For example, unless physically performed outside the CIS, the services supplied by a bank to a foreign parent will not qualify as exported services even though they are supplied to a foreign entity.

VAT IMPLICATIONS FOR CHARGES TO FOREIGN ENTITIES

If the services to be supplied to a foreign entity fall within the category of Vatable services, the Russian bank will be obliged to charge VAT at 21.5 per cent on the provision of services to the

Statue of Peter the Great, St Petersburg

foreign entity. On the assumption that the foreign entity has no registration for tax in Russia, this VAT will represent a cost to the foreign entity as it will not be entitled to recover it. If the services in question fall within the category of exempt services, obviously no liability will arise.

VAT ON PURCHASES

Banks suffer a number of restrictions on the amount of VAT they may reclaim on their purchases. In particular, a bank is not allowed to reclaim VAT incurred on any fixed assets acquired.

REVERSE CHARGE VAT

It is very likely that the new VAT law will contain a reverse charge on the purchase of services from outside Russia. The reverse charge VAT will also be levied at 21.5 per cent.

VAT PENALTIES

The penalties for failure to include a Vatable service supplied by a Russian bank on the company's VAT return or for an overclaim of VAT on purchases could, if the matter came to the tax inspector's attention, be as follows :

(i) 100 per cent of the tax due if the company fails to include this amount on its VAT return and the Inspector is of the view that this is a concealed object of taxation.

This amount can be increased to 200 per cent of the tax due in the case of a repeated violation and up to 500 per cent of the *income concealed* (i.e. not the tax on the same) if the concealment can be proved before a court to be premeditated.

(ii) Interest at the rate of 0.7 per cent per day (255.5 per cent per annum).

Tax inspectors generally focus on VAT during the course of tax inspections, since they regard it as one of their easier and more profitable targets.

TURNOVER TAXES

Russia taxes the gross revenues (before expenses) of banks as well as other entities at rates between 2.3 and 2.8 per cent. These taxes are paid regardless of overall profitability and are especially onerous to high turnover–low margin entities such as banks. In essence, the bank must increase its margins by these taxes. The turnover taxes are as follows:

Social housing tax	1.5 %
Road-use tax	0.8 %
Tax on the name 'Russia'	0.5 %

The rates for these taxes vary from region to region. The above amounts are for the Moscow region.

PAYROLL AND EXCESS WAGES TAXES

Russian law distinguishes the Contract of Labour (employee), which is regulated by the provisions of the Labour Code, from the Contract of Labour Assignment (independent contractor), which is subject to the Civil Code regulations.

There are some differences in taxation of income received by the contractors. This does not offer significant savings. Only if an individual is a 'registered entrepreneur' is the company allowed to pay gross.

All permanent staff should be hired under the Contract of Labour. The Contract of Labour Assignment can be used mainly for performance of one-time jobs.

Exhibit 9.1

Wage taxes and deductions

Taxes and payments (%)	*Contract of Labour*	*Contract of Labour Assignment*
Personal income tax	in accordance with the statutory provided rates	
to the Pension Fund	28.0	28.0
to the Social Insurance Fund	5.4	–
to the Medical Insurance Fund	3.6	3.6
to the Employment Fund	2.0	–
Transport tax	1.0	1.0
Tax for educational needs	1.0	1.0

Presently the approximate combined payroll tax rate of 84 per cent consists of 41 per cent incurred on wages paid to employees, as shown in Exhibit 9.1, and a 43 per cent Excess Wage Tax on any payments made over six times minimum wage (currently Rb20,400). In addition to the employer portion, the employee is required to pay 1 per cent of the salary to the pension fund. As a result, it is important to evaluate other payroll structures in order to minimise these taxes.

Expatriate payroll planning

The most tax effective structure of employing expatriates working in Russia is to employ them through an offshore management company in a country that has a double tax treaty with Russia. Based on the current interpretations of the regulations, there will be no Russian payroll tax or excess wage tax liability to the Russian bank entities. The management charge should be able to be paid free of withholding because of an exemption in an applicable treaty and should be tax deductible to the Russian bank if correctly structured.

Expatriates are not currently taxable in Russia unless they are present in the Russian Federation for 183 or more days in a calendar year. Most of the planning opportunities revolve around this requirement.

WITHHOLDING TAXES

A Russian bank is required to withhold 15 per cent on interest and dividend payments (18 per cent if the payments are to another bank). In addition, the bank is required to withhold 20 per cent on royalty payments and payments made offshore which are considered Russian source income. Unfortunately, Russian 'source' is not defined in the Russian law or regulations and as a result the Russian tax authorities consider almost any amount paid from Russia to an offshore account as Russian source.

The withholding taxes can be reduced or eliminated by an applicable double tax treaty. Unfortunately, withholding clearance under a double tax treaty has sometimes been difficult to obtain.

OTHER TAXES

- Property tax is paid at a rate of up to 2 per cent on qualified assets. Banks are not subject to property tax on loans and cash balances.
- Securities tax is paid at a rate of 0.3 per cent and 0.1 per cent on the purchase and sale of securities and government securities, respectively.
- There are potentially 10 to 15 additional taxes/fees, depending on the bank's activities.

REPORTING REQUIREMENTS

The tax reporting requirements are burdensome. For profit tax purposes the bank files an estimate of its taxable base at the beginning of each quarter. The estimated taxes are then paid in one-sixth increments twice a month. At the end of the quarter, the bank files a declaration based on actual results and pays the difference or applies the overpayment to the following quarter. The final tax return is due on 1 April of the following year. All enterprises are required to report on a calendar year.

If the bank is considered to be a 'large' VAT payer, then the bank will be required to file a VAT declaration on a monthly basis with payments every 10 days. The tax filing requirements for the other taxes range in frequency from three days after the transaction to each quarter.

TAX AUDITS (BY THE TAX AUTHORITIES)

Russian banks should expect to be audited by the Tax Inspectorate at least once every two years. The primary focus is to verify proper documentation for deductions and to review for breaches in the regulations. As it is very difficult, if not impossible, to comply with every regulation and filing requirement, it is likely that the Tax Inspectorate will be able to assess interest and penalties on violations and understatement of tax. Banks must pay close attention to compliance matters if they wish to minimise the assessment to the greatest extent possible.

In addition to regular audits, a 'tax police' has been formed to bolster the Tax Inspectorate's enforcement of the law and collection of tax. The formation of this body was considered necessary in the wake of significant taxpayer non-compliance. Unfortunately, this group has also been used for political reasons, especially with high profile companies. It has very extensive power.

TAX TREATIES

In a statement issued by the Ministry of Foreign Affairs on 13 January 1992, Russia agreed to honour the tax treaties signed by the former Soviet Union until new tax treaties are drawn up between Russia and individual countries.

ACCOUNTING PRACTICES

INTRODUCTION

Accounting for banks is regulated by a number of sources. The primary regulation is issued by the Central Bank of Russia. Other sources of regulation include Presidential decrees, Laws of the Russian Federation (previously Laws of the Supreme Soviet) and acts of the Ministry of Finance. Laws issued in the time of the Soviet Union are still in force unless superseded by more recent legislation.

As to accounting regulation, the Central Bank has established a standard chart of accounts and instructions on how transactions are recorded within the accounts. The accounting is substantially cash-based as the primary focus for the financial statements has been the profit tax calculation. Regulations issued in the last half of 1994 indicate that the focus is shifting away to one of greater prudence, in the face of strong resistance from the tax authorities.

CONVERGENCE OF RUSSIAN ACCOUNTING RULES TO INTERNATIONAL PRACTICE

During 1994 the Central Bank also required the preparation of supplementary financial statements each quarter. These statements, termed 'broadly adapted financial statements' (BAFS) or 'Instruction no. 17 accounts', were designed in co-operation with the World Bank. The BAFS are a much closer approximation to International Accounting Standards. The primary difference between the BAFS and the statutory accounts described above is that the underlying concept of prudence is present in BAFS. The BAFS also include accruals and make additional disclosure. However, there is no requirement for BAFS to be audited or published.

The primary differences between the BAFS and IAS financial statements are that BAFS do not require the following:

- consolidation of subsidiaries;
- accounting for hyperinflation;
- recognition of deferred taxation;
- judgemental approach for provision for loan losses (a mechanistic approach which usually results in low provisions is prescribed); and
- consideration of issues such as going concern and contingent liabilities.

Most of the major Russian banks now produce annual financial statements prepared under International Accounting Standards and audited by an international audit firm. Foreign investors and counterparties should ask for these and should not attempt to analyse the Russian statutory accounts, which can be misleading.

FINANCIAL STATEMENTS

There are currently more than 50 types of different reporting documents that must be submitted to the Central Bank on a periodic basis. As related to financial statement reporting, the primary document required on a monthly basis is a balance sheet. On a quarterly basis, a profit and loss statement must also be submitted. On an annual basis, the required financial statements must also include a statement of profit allocation and a statement of reserve movements.

The annual balance sheet and profit and loss statement must be audited by an independent auditor licensed by the Central Bank.

The balance sheet is divided into various sections based on the type of activity and the type of customer. For instance, separate sections exist for foreign currency activity (nostros, loans, deposits), security operations, transactions with individuals, settlements with banks, etc. The types of accounts are generally the same as those found in western banking financial statements; it is the grouping of these accounts which differs.

The balance sheet of a bank includes an accumulation of all the bank's branches. Interbranch activity and balances are not eliminated. Additionally, consolidation of subsidiaries is also not performed. There is little disclosure of supplementary information.

Capital adequacy is measured as a ratio which is superficially similar to the risk-weighted asset ratio established by the Basle Accord. However, technical features of the calculation mean that the Russian measure is very much less stringent than the Basle one, and most Russian banks are severely under-capitalised.

SIGNIFICANT ACCOUNTING POLICIES

Accounting rules are prescribed by the various legislative bodies, primarily the Central Bank. An underlying conceptual framework on which to develop the accounting methods does not exist. Accounting tends to follow the legal form of the transactions rather than trying to capture the economic substance.

The balance sheet is prepared in roubles, with foreign currency accounts revalued twice weekly based on the Central Bank rate. All foreign currency accounts are revalued, except for share capital and fixed assets. The resulting gain or loss is recorded into account 19, which is classified in the capital and reserve section of the balance sheet.

Most banks record income and expenses on the cash basis, although both cash and accrual methods are permitted for revenue and expense recognition.

Beginning in December 1994, provisions for loan losses are recorded for rouble loans. The provision is calculated on a loan-by-loan basis with reference to the payment status of the loan and the underlying collateral. Loans are categorised into five groups, with provision percentages ranging from 2 to 100 per cent. The loan loss provision is charged to the profit and loss statement unless it exceeds available profits, in which case it is charged to a balance sheet reserve. This whole area is under attack by the tax authorities and is likely to change.

A provision of 50 per cent is also required for any investment securities not quoted on an exchange. Quoted securities are recorded at lower of cost or market. Provisions against securities are included in the profit and loss statement.

Other assets and liabilities are recorded at historical cost, except that fixed assets are subject to periodic revaluations to factor in inflation. Revaluation indices are provided by the Russian government. The credit is made directly to reserves.

Depreciation on fixed assets is charged on a straight-line basis using rates specified by the Ministry of Finance.

Taxation is recorded for amounts due in the current year. Deferred taxation is not recorded.

Certain expenses which are not deductible for tax purposes are not recorded in the profit and loss statement but rather recorded directly as a charge against reserves. These can total substantial amounts.

The material contained in this chapter is current through 1 April 1995, and, unless otherwise indicated, is based on information at that time. In addition the lists provided are not intended to be all-inclusive.

X

BANKING REGULATIONS

Dr. Hermann Schmitt[1]

Pünder, Volhard, Weber & Axster, Frankfurt/Moscow

THE REGULATORY ENVIRONMENT

The Russian banking system has experienced a period of rapid change over the past seven years. Since January 1 1988, the principle of full economic accountability has been applied to the state banks which existed on that date (Gosbank, Vnesheconombank, Sberkassa, Stroibank). This principle means that banks are for the first time responsible for the manner in which they use their resources and are allowed to conclude loan agreements with state enterprises directly. Less than three years later, on 2 December 1990, the Supreme Soviet of Russia – the USSR still existed at that time – adopted the Act on Banks and Banking in the Russian Federation (the Banking Act) and the Act on the Central Bank of the Russian Federation (the Central Bank Act). They provide for the existence of a Central Bank as a regulating body and an unlimited number of commercial banks, both private and state-owned. It is obvious from the terminology and the techniques applied that banking laws of capitalist countries served as blueprints for these laws. Notwithstanding a number of amendments, both the Banking Act and the Central Bank Act are still in force.

Banking has seen a period of rapid growth, both in terms of the number of banks and in terms of their turnover and profits. While there existed only a negligible number of private banks at the end of 1991, there were 1,900 private banks at the end of 1993 and their number had grown to 2,400 by the end of 1994 (with about one-third of them having a foreign exchange licence). The list of the world's thousand largest banks published in *The Banker* in 1994 showed five Russian banks, ranking between 425th and 996th position. According to a press release of the International Moscow Bank (which ranks 13th in the semi-official list of the top 100 Russian banks) their return on assets ranging between 11.82 per cent and 1.58 per cent would place these five Russian banks among the 255 top earners.

This stormy development of the banking industry, coupled with sometimes inexperienced management and insufficient application or enforcement of existing legislation, also resulted in the collapse of a number of banks, which were widely reported by the press. Some 570 banks apparently incurred significant losses in 1994 as a result of non-repayment of loans. Several banks have lost their licences because of non-compliance with regulatory standards (65 in 1994, 41 during the first two months of 1995). It is likely that the process of weeding out the market has not yet come to an end (about 100 banks are under investigation by the Central Bank).

However, this should not divert attention from the fact that the banking sector is one of the areas where reforms have already been successful. Notwithstanding the well-known adverse

---

[1] The assistance of Mr. Alexei E. Vladimirsky, in the preparation of this article was highly appreciated.

macroeconomic factors, such as hyperinflation, payment crisis and general economic decline, many banks have done surprisingly well, and that is not only by Russian standards. Foreign bankers are of the opinion that supervision by the Central Bank has recently become much tighter. The training of personnel has visibly improved. According to the Deputy Minister of Finance, Mr. Kosmin, 28 Russian banks are already operating at western standards. The importance of banking in Russia will presumably increase now that the privatisation process has entered its second phase, known as cash privatisation, which started on 1 July 1994.

THE CENTRAL BANK OF RUSSIA

The Central Bank of Russia (the Central Bank) is the successor to the former Russian State Bank (Gosbank). While Gosbank directly granted loans to the various state ministries and industries, the Central Bank is now only a regulatory institution. It grants licences to commercial banks and other banking institutions, supervises their activities, and is the guardian of the Russian currency, the rouble. The Central Bank is legally independent of the Russian government. It consists of a General Department, which is headed by a Board of Directors, and a number of chief territorial administrations in the Russian republics (some of which are called national banks) and local branches. The Chairman of the Central Bank is not nominated by the government, but elected by the state Duma upon the proposal of the President. However, according to a Decree issued by President Yeltsin on 10 June 1994 'on Improving the Banking System in the Russian Federation' (no. 1184), the Chairman of the Bank of Russia takes part in cabinet meetings, whilst the Ministers of Finance and of Economy participate in meetings of the Board of Directors of the Central Bank. The state Duma recently refused to elect Mr. Yeltsin's candidate for the position as the chairman of the Central Bank, Ms Paramonova. She therefore performs the function of acting chairman of the Central Bank.

SELF-REGULATORY BODIES

The Association of Russian Banks is not a government agency but a private organisation set up by the banks themselves. However, it has a legal basis in Article 3 of the Banking Act, where it is stipulated that it can co-ordinate the activities of private banks. It comprises today 934 banks with some 3,900 branches. Its activities are limited to representing its members' interests *vis-á-vis* the public and the media, promulgating non-binding guidelines and so forth. It also provides its members with services such as training, consulting, independent clearing centres and technical support. However, it is possible that some regulatory tasks will be assigned to the Association of Russian Banks at some time in the future.

OTHER AGENCIES

Various republican and regional administrative bodies have repeatedly tried in the past to gain some control over banking activities by passing legislation to this effect and/or issuing orders to banks. However, these activities have had no constitutional basis. In order to clarify the situation, Mr Yeltsin stated in the above-mentioned Decree No. 1184 of 10 June 1994 that such legislation or other regulations are without legal effect.

REGULATORY ISSUES

BANKING SYSTEM

A 'bank' under Russian law is a commercial institution having the right to accept cash deposits from legal entities or natural persons and to engage in banking operations in general, while other credit institutions may only engage in certain specific banking activities. In addition, the 'Russian banking system' comprises the former USSR state banks Foreign Trade Bank (Vneshtorgbank) and Savings Bank (Sberbank) as well as development banks which may be established for the purpose of implementing special programmes in a specific republic or region (article 2 of the Banking Act). Banks may, in addition to the classic banking operations of accepting deposits and granting loans, engage in a variety of other banking activities some of them listed in the Banking Act, provided that these are covered by licences held by the individual banking institution concerned. Banks may engage in broker services, trading of shares and other securities as well as underwriting. Banks are not allowed to manufacture or trade in goods or to engage in the insurance business.

LICENSING

General requirements

Any banking activities (as defined in Article 5 of the Banking Act) may only be engaged in after a licence has been obtained from the Central Bank. Applicants for a banking licence have to submit:

- evidence showing that they are duly incorporated within the Russian Republic;
- a business plan, including a summary of the circumstances which justify the foundation of the bank;
- detailed information concerning the professional qualifications and personal reliability of the bank managers.

The minimum number of founders for a bank required under the Banking Act is three, although a joint stock company or (since the enactment of the first part of the Civil Code of the Russian Federation on 8 December 1994) a company with limited liability can be set up by only one founder. The reason for the requirement for banks to have at least three founders is to give additional credibility to the bank. The present version of the Banking Act does not provide any details as to the legal form which banks must take. According to a Central Bank Directive, almost any legal form is permissible, including partnerships or co-operatives, provided that the number of founders is at least three.

Refusal of a licence

It is important to note that the Central Bank may refuse to grant a banking licence only if the legal documents presented are not in compliance with the applicable legislation or if the financial circumstances of the founders are unsatisfactory. In all other cases, the licence has to be granted within three months (which is to be extended to six months under a draft revised Banking Act presently going through the legislative process).

Clarity of name

The term 'bank' is reserved for institutions which hold a banking licence under the Banking Act. Only holders of such a licence may call themselves a bank.

Foreign banks

The number of foreign banks holding banking licences in Russia reached thirteen at the end of March 1995. Among these are ABN AMRO, Bank Austria, BNP/Dresdner, Chase Manhattan, Citibank, Crédit Lyonnais, First Boston, ING and West LB. The business of foreign banks is regulated by the Banking Act, 'the Central Bank Directive on Terms and Conditions for Opening Banks with Foreign Investment in the Russian Federation' (Directive No. 14), Presidential Decrees No. 1184 of 10 June 1994 and No. 1925 of 17 November 1993 on Activities of Foreign Banks and Joint Venture Banks with Non-Resident's Investment in the Russian Federation. According to this

Relief on the side of the Space Monument, Moscow

legislation, a foreign founder or co-founder of a Russian bank, or of a Russian branch of a foreign bank must, in addition to satisfying the requirements to be met by domestic applicants, provide information on its present and past financial circumstances and, in the case of natural persons, - submit recommendation letters by a leading bank and other reputable institutions of their home country.

Reciprocity

A precondition for obtaining a banking licence is that the home country of the foreign applicant adheres to the principle of reciprocity in this respect. Russian banks must have the right to receive a similar licence in that country under comparable conditions.

Restrictions on foreign banks

Foreign natural persons or legal entities are only allowed to hold shares in banking institutions to the extent that the participation of foreign capital within the banking system of the Russian Federation does not exceed 12 per cent of the total capital of banks registered.

According to official Russian figures for 1995, foreign investment in banking capital is somewhere between 8 per cent and 12 per cent, which is exactly within the limits set by Russian law and which can be regarded as reasonable compared with the 10 per cent in western Europe and 20 per cent in the US. The Central Bank has publicly spoken in favour of a more liberal treatment of foreign banks in Russia. Furthermore, according to Presidential Decree No. 1925 of 17 November 1993, until 1 January 1996, newly established foreign banks may only do business with non-residents. This moratorium on foreign banks has been advocated by Russian banks out of fear that they may be overridden by foreign competition before they can stand on their own feet. The moratorium has meanwhile been lifted by Presidential Decree No. 1184 of 10 June 1994, but only for banks that have been already established and subject to the condition that the home country of the foreign bank has concluded an agreement with the Russian Federation on the encouragement and protection of capital investments. Until 1 January 1999, banks with foreign participation may only open accounts for Russian residents if the customer makes an initial deposit equivalent to a minimum of 50,000 Ecu (this means that foreign banks are precluded from serving ordinary consumers). In addition, foreign banks maintaining accounts for Russian residents may not trade in shares in corporations based in Russia.

BANKING REGULATIONS

Lending/exposure limits

The Central Bank has established maximum equity/debt ratios, limits on lending to an individual borrower (risk diversification) and limits on hard currency and exchange rate risks. The specific and concrete ratios are fixed by means of repeated amendments to Directive No. 1 of the Central Bank dated 30 April 1991 'on the Procedure for Regulating the Activities of Commercial Banks'. The value of the assets of a bank is assessed by applying risk coefficients to six different groups of risks (examples: group 1: cash; group 2: government securities; group 3: local authorities securities; group 4: long-term loans; group 5: other securities; group 6: outstanding bank debts, intangibles).

Capital requirements

The Central Bank sets minimum equity (charter capital) requirements for banks. Since 1 April 1995, an equity requirement of Rb6 billion or Ecu1 million applies to banks having a general licence and Rb1.5 billion or Ecu250,000 for banks having a limited licence not including the right to deal in foreign currency; the minimum capital requirement shall be increased to Ecu5 million by 1 January 1999.

Reporting requirements

The Central Bank exercises its supervisory functions on the basis of balance sheets submitted to it regularly accompanied by financial statements showing the actual financial position of the bank. In addition, banks have to promptly inform the Central Bank when correspondent accounts are opened for the purpose of providing large loans (exceeding 20 per cent of the bank's capital). The Central Bank may at any time and at its discretion carry out full or selective checks to satisfy itself as to the accuracy of the financial accounts and other information submitted by any bank. For this purpose, the Central Bank may inspect all books and records of the bank concerned. In addition, regular audits must be carried out by an auditing company holding a special licence.

Deposit protection

The Central Bank is entitled to determine the procedure for the formation of deposit protection funds designed to protect bank customers from losses if a bank collapses. These funds are financed by the member banks. To date, no such deposit protection funds exist, but they will be set up in the near future. Both Presidential Decree No. 1184 of 10 June 1994 and the draft revised Banking Act provide for mandatory deposit protection.

Liquidity

Banks are obliged to 'ensure a necessary level of liquidity' in conformity with the requirements set by the Central Bank (Article 24 of the Banking Act, Directive of the Central Bank of 30 April 1991).

Mandatory reserves

The amount of the mandatory reserves to be deposited by any bank with the Central Bank is fixed as a percentage of the 'total sum of money attracted' by the bank concerned. Credits from other banks, funds made available by the Central Bank for specific government programmes of the Russian Federation, deposits on current foreign currency accounts, and several other forms of deposits are not taken into account in this respect. The specific quotas of mandatory reserves are established by the Board of Directors of the Central Bank ('Regulation for the Formation of a Fund of Obligatory Reserves' dated 15 February 1994, chapter 3).

Capital investment

Banks are subject to restrictions as regards the investment of funds deposited with them 'for the purchase of shares in legal entities'. In addition, according to the Central Bank Directive No. 145 of 17 February 1995, banks may not use shares in companies which they own as part of the bank's equity. The Banking Act does not provide for a limit on capital investment by a bank in an individual enterprise. However, according to chapter 9.5 of the state programme for the privatisation of state and municipal enterprises (presidential decree no. 2284 of 24 December 1993), a bank shall not acquire more than 10 per cent of the shares in a stock company being privatised.

Confidentiality

Banking institutions have to 'guarantee' confidentiality as regards any operations, accounts or deposits by clients and banking correspondents. In addition, bank employees are personally subject to a statutory obligation to maintain such confidentiality. Nevertheless, ordinary courts of law, arbitration courts, investigation authorities and the tax office 'may' be provided with information concerning banking operations and accounts. Furthermore, hard currency accounts have to be automatically registered by the bank with the tax inspection authority. Any hard currency operation involving a capital transfer to a foreign country (meaning a transfer of money for more than 180 days) is subject to prior authorisation by the Central Bank. In this respect, commercial banks are acting as currency control agents, accountable to the Central Bank (Article 1, paragraph 11 Foreign Currency Act).

BANKS AND THE LAW

Savings

Any bank holding the required licence has the right to accept saving deposits from individuals. Individuals may have several accounts at different banks. Thus, there are no special savings banks exclusively entitled to accept saving deposits. However, Sberbank ('Savings Bank'), which is the successor to the former Sberkassa of the USSR and still has more than 35,000 branches nationwide (compared with only 5,000 branches of all other Russian banks, not counting the state-owned Agroprombank) holds most of the private savings accounts of the Russian population (and continues to be the largest Russian bank). Apart from its dominance in terms of number of branches, Sberbank enjoys the privilege of having all deposits on any accounts maintained with it by private individuals guaranteed by the state.

Cross-border transactions

Banks holding a special licence may open direct correspondent accounts at foreign banks, including western banks. Some Russian banks are accepted by national investment guarantee organisations as guarantors for short-term deals (for example Foreign Trade Bank, International

Moscow Bank, Tokobank, Mosbusiness Bank). Many banks have access to SWIFT and Reuter telecommunication facilities. Consequently, the monopoly of the Foreign Trade Bank no longer exists (though it is still the second-largest Russian bank).

Mortgage banks

The Russian government established a mortgage bank in 1993 in order to support the private financing of housing. However, this bank is still engaged in the process of preparing for its future business activities. The main reason for this is that there is still no adequate legislation governing the provision of collateral in general or, more specifically, the mortgaging or pledging of land and/or buildings.

Investment banking

The investment banking practised in Russia is still very rudimentary, but will presumably develop very quickly. The voucher privatisation scheme was completed on 1 July 1994, and the majority of shares in many former state-owned companies are already in the hands of their employees, managers and/or other private individuals. Banks are accepting instructions from domestic and foreign investors to acquire such shares through a network of agents all over the country. Banks also may participate in the second privatisation phase (cash privatisation) by purchasing shares for their clients. Reportedly, up to US$500 million of foreign capital per month were invested in the acquisition of shares in Russian companies in 1994.

Trading in treasury bills

Trading in treasury bills, the most popular of which are called GKOs (*Gosudarstvennaya Kratkosrocshnaya Obligatsiya*) and have maturity dates of three or six months, is one of the most active markets. An important exchange for treasury bills in Russia is the Moskovskaya Meshbankovskaya Valutnaya birsha (Moscow Interbank Currency Exchange), where more than fifty banks are at present admitted to trade. A large part of the debt of the Russian state is financed by means of such bills.

Traditional lending

Traditional lending plays a very limited role. In view of hyperinflation, private banks are generally not prepared to lend funds for a term of more than three months.

Restrictions on bank ownership and management

The equity capital of banks may not be held by state organisations, political organisations or public foundations (such as charitable organisations). Civil servants may not hold positions in banks.

REGULATORY OUTLOOK

REVISIONS OF BANKING ACT

The main objectives of the proposed amendments to the Banking Act and to the Central Bank Act are to make existing regulations more precise, to clarify definitions, and to incorporate provisions into the Acts which are already contained in Presidential Decrees or Central Bank Directives. In addition, the supervisory and regulatory powers of the Central Bank are to be increased. It is not expected, however, that the new Banking Act will provide for material changes in the basic principles of banking legislation. According to the draft laws, banks may only be organised as stock companies or limited liability companies, there will be more specific provisions on the various forms of bank capitalisation, a bank register will be published by the Central Bank, the Duma will be explicitly empowered to set a maximum limit for financing through banks with foreign participation, domestic banks will be allowed to open branches without the explicit permission of the Central Bank, capital-adequacy regulations will be more detailed, confidentiality regulations will be improved, correspondent accounts may be opened without Central Bank permission, and separate deposit protection funds may be established by groups of banks, etc.

SECURITIES MARKET

Given that banks are important players in the securities market, they will also play a significant role as regards the restructuring of that market. In accordance with Presidential Decree No. 2063 of 4 November 1994 on 'Measures for State Regulation of the Securities Market in the Russian Federation', a Federal Securities and Stock Market Commission has been established under the chairmanship of AB Chubais (who is also First Deputy Prime Minister of the Russian Federation and former Privatisation Minister). The Commission consists of representatives of various ministries, committees and organisations, including the State Property Fund (the government's privatization agency), the Ministry of Finance and the Central Bank. The purpose of the commission is to regulate the activities of professional participants in the securities market, to co-ordinate the drafting of normative acts' (legal regulations) on questions of the securities market, and as an SEC-type organisation to confirm standards for the issuance of securities and prospectuses. Under a recent Decree issued by Mr Yeltsin, the Commission was granted the status of a ministry of the Russian government.

A draft 'Federal Securities Market Act' has been submitted to the state Duma. In order to protect investors, this draft Act contains comprehensive rules of conduct for parties participating in this market. It is further stipulated in the draft that the Federal Commission continues to be the government authority in charge of regulating the securities market and the activities of parties dealing in securities. The Commission is to have extensive powers. It shall supervise the future development of the securities market and set standards for the registration and issue of securities and prospectuses, create unified rules of conduct for securities trading and recording and public trading, settlement and depository schemes and provisions for the registration of exchanges and licensing of their operations.

XI

RUSSIAN BANKING: THE WAY FORWARD

Although the number of Russian banks has grown rapidly and vast profits have been made while the rest of the national economy lagged behind, it is difficult to see further solid growth of the sector occurring without an economic recovery. Much of the most profitable activity has been opportunistic arbitraging operations in currencies or the cheap accumulation of privatisation vouchers which, when exchanged for shares in grossly under-priced companies, produced massive gains. It is characteristic of Russian commercial banks to pay low interest on deposits, charge high interest on loans (which are always short term) and charge high commissions.

The 30 to 40 banks that have emerged as strong viable institutions are surrounded by hundreds of others that are little better than bucket shops or money changers. Any decisive downturn in the Russian economy would certainly endanger the existence of many banks; in fact most banking observers forecast widespread bankruptcies among smaller concerns in the 1995–97 period. Many will not be able to meet the official rules on authorised capital and assets and will have their licences revoked. This has already happened to about 100 banks. Other small provincial banks will be swallowed up by the Moscow giants. A plethora of mergers and liquidations will see banking empires rise. Even some of the larger institutions may not be safe from the vagaries of economic fortune and the predatory instincts of their fellows.

An economic downturn would put many industrial concerns out of business; in fact such an economic deterioration and a consequent wave of bankruptcies has been widely forecast. This would result in massive arrears for the banks. The Central Bank has begun to limit directed credits issued to commercial banks and has made terms for such credits more demanding. Hard currency accounts, the main source of wealth for many institutions, could get harder to build up when a more efficient and more regulated currency market cuts down on the chances for speculation. It is not necessary to take the forecasts of financial crisis literally to see the dangers.

Russia has rushed into capitalism at an alarming rate, trying to do in five years what others took generations to achieve. It has proved impossible to eliminate all aspects of the old Soviet system and mentality in such a short period of time. In discarding centralised planning the reformers seemed to throw out the very idea of planning itself. The progress toward the grand idea of a free market has, in fact, been largely unplanned and haphazard, dependent on the fits and whims of President Boris Yeltsin or the energy generated by some of his government colleagues and the reactions of the unpredictable state Duma. The IMF, which has never had to deal with an ailing economy of such size before, cannot be sure that the formulas that have not always worked in smaller countries will function in Russia. No one anywhere has any experience of transforming a giant of totalitarianism into a democracy with a free market economy.

There has been no shortage of foreign advisers, some of them distinguished Ivy League think-tankers. But as the economist Grigory Yavlinsky puts it: 'Most practical economists in Russia know little of mainstream economics; however, mainstream economists also know very little about the Russian economy. One is really no substitute for the other. The controversy between "practicians" and "macroeconomists" in Russia was really an argument over whether it was the upper or lower blade of scissors which cuts paper. In fact we need both.' For Yavlinsky, a blend of both in 'a new type of economic thinking' is necessary to solve Russia's manifold problems.

In Russia, there is a growing consensus that the assumptions about the free market in mainstream economic analysis do not include or take for granted several aspects of the Russian reality: institutional property relations, the existence of financial intermediaries playing according to fairly standard rules, indeed the basic concept of a market where buyers and sellers meet and bargain and are subject to liquidity constraints. Such matters, it is contended, are very important for economies in transition and should be 'included among the variables, rather than the data'. In short, Russia does not fit the western model, and *laissez-faire* has so far led to liberalisation of the totalitarian economy. 'We want a liberalisation which will take us away from the totalitarian economy', Yavlinsky says.

PROBLEMS AWAITING SOLUTION

Since the beginning of 1992 a plethora of government reforms, many of them generally held to be hasty, ill-thought-out stopgaps to keep things running until something better came along, has been approved. Some of these laws and decrees have been amended as recently as 1994, but still give the appearance of papering over the cracks in the system. Many of the reforms affect the banks, even laws that do not seem to directly concern them. Among these is the virtual absence of clear property rights.

Russia is in urgent need of legislation to clarify land ownership, land valuation and mechanisms for trading urban land. Russian land law now permits private ownership of land, but restricted rights of sale. Owners have a right to mortgage, but the sale restrictions and the dearth of mortgage services in banks make that right somewhat fanciful. Land is not accepted as collateral, except in the cases of family plots assigned to dwellers on the outskirts of major cities where full private ownership rights apply, including the right to sell. Russia is highly urbanised and the World Bank reports that housing assets account for a large share of national wealth – about 25 per cent of the total assets in the economy in 1990. The privatisation of housing, which started in 1990 and has proceeded rather slowly, is seen as the royal road to the emergence of a genuine housing market and the accompanying development of housing finance, of which the young Moscow Mortgage Bank is the most visible manifestation.

Over a third of the state housing in Moscow has been privatised, rather less elsewhere. The impact of private housing on the development of the financial sector lies in the fact that a house is acceptable collateral for a loan. What is lacking are instruments to finance new housing and the use of housing equity as collateral in borrowing to start a new business. Before the long-term financing of housing can increase in Russia some problems must be solved. The price of housing is still distorted by rent controls, which cuts down the investment value of new ventures. Land registration is inadequate, valuation uncertain and few real estate professionals exist. Eviction and foreclosure are not politically acceptable. Finally, under current economic circumstances, it is impossible to manage interest rate risks in Russia. One likely outcome is the development of dual-rate adjustable mortgage instruments (DRAMS) with both interest rates and payments adjusted periodically. This would allow banks to back mortgages with short-term loans repeatedly refinanced at maturity if the home-owner's payment record warrants it. Such instruments presuppose reliable economic and financial indicators, which many bankers still feel are lacking. All in all, a large-scale Russian mortgage market is probably some years in the future.

Reckless lending to real estate is not unknown in developed nations, so the World Bank feels a clear distinction needs to be made in Russia between long-term lending for residential investment and for commercial investment. It seems likely, the bank thinks, that hotels, offices and commercial building projects will for some time rely on equity-based financing schemes with a number of investors contributing. Collective real estate investment trusts exist in some of the major cities.

The fact that land cannot be used as collateral inhibits the development of rural credit markets and so hinders the reduction of government subsidies for agriculture. Further hindrance comes from the large state agencies that finance agricultural procurement and market farm products. Such work still needs to be done via directed credit programmes because the agencies and their needs are too big for the banking system to handle. Sberbank is the only institution with a presence in most rural areas and most farmers do not know how to look for commercial loans.

Most farms work with Rosselkhozbank whose requirements for granting loans are much like those of the government agency it once was. Under communism, farm credits were regarded as government transfers and were frequently forgiven. Farmers will find it difficult to change their traditional attitude to credits. Over the short term, directed credits to agriculture will certainly continue, at least until farmers can borrow against their farms. State and collective farms, now being privatised, could hardly get the time of day, much less a loan, from a commercial bank.

The World Bank suggests that directed credits should be restricted to agriculture and small-scale processing that takes place on the farm. Firms producing agricultural inputs, such as fertilisers, and agro-industry enterprises should fund themselves directly from commercial banks. This would reduce the size of directed credit programmes by as much as 25 per cent. Naturally, the bank would like to see state agricultural credits come down over time and the private banks and capital markets take over the field. Credits, however concessional, should carry clear terms and these should be enforced, the World Bank says. Interest rates on loans to agriculture should be at the level prevailing in the rest of the economy. Meanwhile, subsidies would be cheaper and more effective if they are granted with direct links to the objectives the government wants to subsidise.

But it will be a long time before centralised procurement and marketing systems are replaced by the private retail and wholesale market. One future step is likely to be providing clear titles to private farmers, with the right to mortgage lands and permitting banks to foreclose in the event of default on loan, in order to enhance farmers' access to credit. Rosselkhozbank will be around for a long time yet as the main channel for directed credits to agriculture, but it will separate the loans it makes on behalf of the government from those it makes on its own account as a fledgling commercial bank.

Another problem for banks with bad debts is the existing bankruptcy law and its enforcement. A Law on the Insolvency of Businesses was passed in 1992 and went into effect in March 1993. Although debts between companies grew in the first half of 1994, only 85 bankruptcy cases went before the 89 Russian arbitration courts. Russians say they have an abundance of laws that are easy to ignore The original bankruptcy law was followed by a series of regulations that were supposed to make it workable. When this did not work, the government set up the Federal Department for Bankruptcy Cases (FDBC) under the state Property Committee. According to law, only the arbitration courts or the debtors themselves can declare bankruptcy and liquidate a company. Now, however, the new agency will have these powers.

In other words, the FDBC aims to achieve what the law did not. It has set up 83 regional branches and examined the accounts of 3,000 debtors among the 30,000 companies that retain some government stake. In fact the main motive behind the agency seems to be that the state got tired of seeing its assets ruined by bad managers. It has strict requirements for the liquidity ratio of a firm (working capital divided by current liabilities) and the shareholder net-worth-to-debt ratio. A company is judged to be insolvent if the former is lower than two or the latter is lower than 0.1. In fact, say the Congress of Russian Manufacturers, more than 70 per cent of the country's manufacturing firms are insolvent according to the agency's criteria, which it naturally feels are too strict. While the government will undoubtedly move to save certain large companies, it is not now inclined to bail everyone out. Most of the debtors will be transferred to private ownership or reorganised with new management or, as a last resort, liquidated.

Even with intercompany debt reaching great heights, Russian businessmen seem reluctant to go to the courts. Litigation fees are high – up to 5 per cent of the amounts claimed – and the court's decision can be uncertain. The arbitration system is deemed unsatisfactory, and its administrative measures unreliable. Hence, bankruptcy is seen as a last resort, after all else has failed, and some business and banks prefer to collect money owing to them through intermediaries who use threats or violence. In 1994, amendments to the Criminal Code covered 'intentional bankruptcy', another addition to the list of interesting crimes in Russia. Observers say the rate of bankruptcy could grow by 20 per cent in the short term. This should smooth Russia's transition to market conditions, provided that bankruptcy procedures are implemented properly and fairly. The commercial banks, which are the main lenders to the private sector, could suffer acutely when some of the more fragile privatised companies go bust, as they are expected to do. Implementation of the bankruptcy laws by the courts or the FDBC would at least leave them with something to show for unwise lending.

REFORMING THE FINANCIAL SECTOR

Today the Central Bank of Russia and the government as a whole are gradually reducing directed credit programmes, except to agriculture, the conversion of military industry, and a couple of other sectors. However, the authorities still channel about 50 per cent of the total credit in the system through to earmarked projects. It is now recognised that directed credits are pernicious as well as unprofitable for the commercial banks and hinder the development of a normal banking system. While directed credit will survive in some areas, it will be increasingly labelled as subsidy and budgeted for under that label. Other directed credits will be phased out over the next few years, and by 1998 private commercial banks will allocate most financial resources. The Central Bank will continue to set a discount rate to promote its monetary and credit policies, hopefully at lower rates than in 1994, and the government will borrow in the financial market to finance what it is hoped will be a reduced budget deficit.

The government and Central Bank will proceed with the work of setting up a legal and regulatory framework to develop banking and capital markets. If the past is a reliable guide, the framework will not emerge in one seamless piece, but consist of a patchwork quilt of reforms, decrees and sundry afterthoughts. Nonetheless, it will begin to approximate what the markets need somewhere between 1995 and 1997. The Central Bank will have another stab at developing the physical infrastructure for commercial banks to function in, including a payments system. In this regard, its efforts have been partly pre-empted by some of the commercial banks which have grouped together to set up their own clearance facility. Whether the Central Bank will see this as an invasion of its power base and try to monopolise what the World Bank calls 'a legitimate private sector function', or set proper operating standards for local clearing houses, is still a matter for speculation. But it will certainly take the lead in establishing standards for risk-management control, common formats, communications protocols and settlement timing.

If private clearing houses are recognised by the Central Bank, it will try to set up new accounting and settlement procedures. This should encourage larger banks to offer clearing and settlement services to smaller banks and, because most payment orders are intraregional, the volume of transactions passing through the Central bank will get smaller, doing away with the system's major paper processing bottleneck. The long-term aim must be automation of the payments system. Facilities for electronic payments are reliable and less expensive to operate than all that is involved in the physical delivery of paper instruments. Substantial international funding will be necessary to design and put the system into practice. The World Bank believes that 'International experience dictates that technology should not drive the project until a more sophisticated infrastructure, including available manpower, is established'. Speed and sophistication may be less important than reliability and the robustness of the system as a whole, it added. Some procedural changes are already in place. A standard numbered payment order form has been proposed and bank courier routes rather than the postal system are being used to deliver payment forms.

Reform is urgently needed on payment systems to increase productivity, to enhance security, and to bring in new technologies. New technology will have a direct effect on the laws of evidence (some electronic recording media are not accepted in the courts), contracts and other property rights. Regulations governing electronic transfer of funds are necessary but, as usual, the holes in the legislation will be patched up later rather than sooner, given the amount of needlework left to get through in other legislative areas.

A programme on deposit insurance has been designed to extend protection to depositors of all failed commercial banks. The Central Bank has been collecting deposit insurance premiums since mid-1991 and putting them into a special account. The Central Bank will be responsible for covering all deposits in failed banks above the funds it has accumulated. This system extends protection to companies owning banks who have large deposits in their own institutions and who could be directly or indirectly responsible for the bank's failure. This scheme is likely to be changed to avoid the Central Bank's having to absorb substantial losses. Current opinion favours limiting deposit insurance coverage to fairly small deposits from individuals and small businesses. Those commercial banks wishing to attain the status of International Standard Banks, in a scheme being pushed by the World Bank, might well be offered lower deposit insurance premiums.

Along with property ownership and insolvency problems goes the question of security. A Law of Pledge was passed but is not very effective because it has no provisions to deal with the priority of creditors; and there is no central registration of pledges nor rules on the execution of collateral. The government is expected to do something about this eventually. A new law on joint stock companies was being debated in the Duma at the end of 1994: it addresses the establishment of commercial enterprises, limited liability status, exit and entry procedures, money lending, instalment buying, and leasing – but not to everyone's satisfaction. Again, more patching is expected when the government becomes aware of the law's shortcomings in the real world.

There is no legislation for the insurance field: the government and the state Duma are looking at the establishment of a regulatory body and rules for the creation of private insurance companies, prudential regulations, the participation of foreign insurance companies, and the reform of the whole social security system.

The Central Bank will in future limit the issuance of new bank licences to those banking projects that meet its rules on authorised capital and the relevant risk coefficients set out in its latest bulletins on the matter. It seeks to discourage further proliferation of unsound banking practices and MMM-type scandals. But while some banks will disappear, others will try to take their place, because a banking licence in Russia has so far been tantamount to a licence to print money.

REFORMING THE PAYMENT SYSTEM

SERGEI MOROZOV[1]

Russia, recently integrated into the international economy, finds itself in a particularly difficult situation: with its inconvertible currency, Russia's economy is like a horse-drawn cart on a trunk road. No matter how many dollars Russia can now earn, the United States will never exchange them for gold. Russia can buy gold only on the gold market in London at around 385 dollars per troy ounce.

Regrettably Russia's inconvertible roubles can be used only with great difficulty to buy goods and services on the international market. To buy such goods and services, one must first exchange roubles for dollars on the foreign exchange market, at very unfavourable rates of exchange, and use the dollars to pay for those goods and services.

The overrating of the dollar pushes Russia's domestic prices higher and impedes further development of domestic production. This is now the main factor behind the country's political instability: as the rouble's purchasing power rapidly declines, more Russians become impoverished, and secessionist trends in Russia become more visible. The Baltic States, it should be noted, had to introduce their own currencies to protect themselves from Russia's inflation. Moreover, Russia is quite unable in the near future to introduce into circulation a gold-backed rouble.

---

1. Chairman of the board of ELBIM Bank; Full Member of the Academy of Economics, Finance and Law; Member of the International Union of Economists; Candidate of Medical Science.

There is a solution on offer, which would also see Russia making good use of the hard currency kept by ordinary Russians. ELBIM Bank proposes the introduction of a quasi-currency in Russia. Under this system foreign currency circulating in Russia would be replaced by international multi-currency debit (or 'pre-paid') cheques, known as IMD cheques, either with fixed denominations – bearer cheques – or cheques simply made payable to specified persons, or order cheques. Prices in Russian shops would be shown in US dollars, and would stabilise as no longer dependent on the rouble exchange rate. IMD cheques too are denominated in US dollars. They can be bought at ELBIM Bank's branches and exchange offices, or at other banks specially licensed by ELBIM. The cheques will be sold for or exchanged into any hard currency according to official rates; there will be no commission charge for this. Converting cheques into hard currency will be more attractive than converting them into roubles because the bank will charge a commission on transactions involving rouble amounts. Moreover the exchange rates used to convert IMD cheques into roubles will be less favourable than prevailing market rates. The cheques will be used very much like Visa and MasterCard plastic cards. They will be protected from forgery and will not require authorisation.

Today the absence of reliable telecommunications significantly impedes authorisation of plastic card transactions. As this problem is unlikely to be resolved in the next ten years, the widespread use of plastic cards in Russia will remain difficult.

At the moment 60 per cent of Russians are unable to acquire plastic cards because of low wages. IMD cheques will be more suitable for them because they may be denominated in any amount: students, pensioners or school children will be able to buy such cheques.

The system would help to solve many problems encountered during settlement of hard currency transactions both in Russia and abroad. The cheques are not currency, but represent the Bank's obligation to pay a specified amount, in any specified currency, to the bearer.

Like plastic cards, IMD cheques of unlimited value may be taken out of Russia freely, and brought back. They will help to facilitate the development of a project to build a large Russian shopping centre – HUB – at Shannon airport in Ireland. Russian businessmen and tourists will go to Ireland with IMD cheques, which will be accepted by the Bank of Ireland, with which ELBIM has established business relations. The same scheme can be applied in any country of the world, particularly the United States. IMD cheques could enable the US to accept more tourists from Russia, for example during the 1996 Atlanta Olympics.

Introduction of such cheques would give Russians a universal payment facility that can be easily converted into any hard currency. Foreigners too would have the opportunity to buy them before travelling to Russia.

During the information stage a specific type of the international market, the open economic environment, was created. It was subdivided into several regional markets. As various national currencies are used every day to settle transactions in these markets, it became necessary to introduce a new, universal payment facility, which, like gold, can reduce national currencies to a common denominator. Thus we argue that IMD cheques will be an important payment facility in the future. Hard currency circulating in Russia should be kept in banks in accordance with Russian legislation, with IMD cheques and IMD plastic cards used for transaction settlements.

Once people had to carry sacks of coins to settle large transactions; today many Russians have to carry sacks of paper money. The introduction of IMD cheques will enable a reduction in the amount of paper money in circulation. And the same model could be applied in any country of the world.

In addition to the cheques, IMD plastic cards are also issued by ELBIM Bank. Amounts placed in plastic card holders' accounts are converted into hard currency, at no commission. The direct transfer of wages to cardholders' accounts is very convenient, as they do not need to waste time in exchange offices and pay no commission for the conversion of their money into hard currency. Cardholders can withdraw their wages from their accounts without any restrictions on the withdrawal amount. Unfortunately, further introduction of IMD cards in Russia – as with other plastic cards – is impeded by the absence of reliable telecommunications.

The IMD system is now in use at over 500 outlets in Moscow, including the International Trade Centre, which began to accept IMD cheques and cards in its restaurants and shops – in addition to Visa and MasterCard – in September 1994. All their prices are now shown in US dollar equivalents.

The IMD cheque idea now has patents pending in Russia and in eight other countries. The cheques are protected from inflation even if purchased with Russia's inconvertible currency. They will play the role of an international financial Esperanto, and offer a new type of payment facility that reduces all hard currencies to a common denominator.

Unlike the introduction of the European Currency Unit (ECU), the introduction of the IMD cheque system would not change the existing relation between hard currencies. Rather it offers a model for a universal payment facility that can be used in the open economic environment of the future.

I believe that there is no need to replace the Russian government, the parliament or the president. What Russia does need is to replace its transaction settlement system. Unless the country introduces IMD cheques, it will face the greatest difficulty in resolving its economic problems. The cheques are, according to our model, the mirror image, the antithesis of gold. Transactions with cheques are similar to transactions with metal gold. The transactions are modelling each other.

AUDITING AND ACCOUNTING

Traditionally, Russian accounting tried to ensure the state's control over the use of resources by companies and banks. It was, in effect, mere bookkeeping and was the same everywhere, whether the books belonged to an enterprise, a bank or a government department. There was no inflation accounting, no proper auditing, only tax inspectors to contend with. This led to the inadequacy of most current bank accounting systems. There is little understanding of financial statements, primitive accounting principles, and few reporting or supervisory guidelines. Financial statements often do not present a proper picture of performance: they say little about solvency, liquidity, profitability or prudential criteria.

The first step to improving the situation came in 1991 when a set of new accounting principles and systems was adopted. The existing system is being adapted to bring it in line with international practices in terms of principles and presentation. A thorough reform of the accounting system will be carried out over the next few years to bring it up to international standards and a Russian Accounting Standards Board will design and implement the transformation. Auditing is in its early stages of development in Russia: there are some authorised Russian auditors and the top banks are now audited by the most important international accounting firms.

CAPITAL MARKETS

Russia's first stock exchanges opened in the summer of 1991 and, in fairly short order, there were well over 100 exchanges, mainly in Moscow, St Petersburg, Eastern Russia and the Urals. However, a lack of saleable securities, standard market practices and even investors inhibited early growth. The securities markets are very fragmented. The over-the-counter market now accounts for more than 90 per cent of total trading, while stock exchanges and the security departments of commodity exchanges and banks share the rest. There are still about 100 stock exchanges in Russia, but with little activity. Russia's expanse and poor telecommunications keep stock exchanges operating at the regional level and there is no system of national standards. Privatisation has boosted trading, mainly in the OTC market, but there is a marked lack of merchant banks, pension funds, mutual funds and other institutional investors. Some investment funds, usually small, have about 10 per cent of their assets in securities. Brokerage firms, with some exceptions, are poorly developed and largely unregulated.

The securities market has developed under a rapidly changing legal framework that came into being in little more than two years. These laws have been revised and will need yet more revision. The OTC market is virtually unregulated. There is little in the legislation that would land a securities violator in court, as the recent MMM scandal demonstrated. The authorities have to use the Criminal Code to start a legal action and it took the tax police to nail MMM. However, some effort is now underway at the legislative level to protect minority ownership rights, minimise conflicts of interest and enforce the fiduciary responsibilities of corporate managers.

The boom in Russia's capital markets that lasted throughout 1993 and 1994 settled down somewhat in early 1995 to what one observer described as 'a deep bull market'. But there are opportunities for recovery. Those who made vast profits trading in government bonds will look to the large new 1995 issue planned by the Ministry of Finance, while continuing privatisation by the cash route and the need of many privatised companies to raise capital will surely bring life back to the market. What was once a dearth of information on securities is fast turning to a plethora as several institutions increase their output of statistics and information. Recent legislation has painstakingly defined nine types of securities and updated aspects of securities law. The legislation also laid down the minimum requirements for share certificates, deals with the creation of shareholder registries and the development of standard documentation for the transfer of shares.

The number of exchanges is likely to shrink in the short term and no new ones will be licensed: the commodity exchange securities departments will probably go too. Meanwhile, future legislation will address the development of more regulatory capability. There are currently too many regulators and not enough regulations. The International Finance Corporation (IFC) has been working with the government to develop the appropriate legislation to build market institutions and regulate the system properly. But all new laws must be integrated with the company code, the commercial code and the banking laws and it must be appropriate for the country and, above all, enforceable. The World Bank has recommended that a comprehensive securities law should be centralised in a single body, and not be dispersed among several government agencies. This is likely to be the case, since the president has established a commission whose job description fits the bill very closely. The near future should also see regulations to provide equal conditions for banks and non-banks in the securities market.

Russia has already seen a futures market in privatisation vouchers and there is a rouble futures market running at the Moscow Commodities Exchange (see Exhibit 11.1). Observers forecast some pretty brisk development, especially if – as is expected – currency futures trading is concentrated in the Micex, Russia's best-developed exchange in terms of sophistication and technology. However, with all the improvements either achieved or promised, it will take about five years for Russia to have really modern securities and foreign exchange markets.

Exhibit 11.1

Rouble/US$ futures on Moscow Commodities Exchange

Maturity	*Average price 25/11/94*	*Average price 2/12/94*	*Change*	*Volume ($'000)*
Dec 1994	253,334	3,380	+46	4
Jan 1995	3,610	3,493	-117	55
Feb 1995	3,867	3,949	+82	33
Mar 1995	4,084	4,323	+239	82
Apr 1995	4,273	4,678	+406	77
May 1995	4,442	4,904	+462	50
Jun 1995	4,701	5,185	+484	76

Source: Moscow Times.

In 1996 Russia will face elections and, quite possibly, the exit of Boris Yeltsin from public life. The reforms he has, at times haltingly, presided over will have taken root and be difficult to reverse, whoever comes out the winner. In the unlikely event of Vladimir Zhirinovsky finding himself in the presidential chair all bets would be off; but his popularity has taken a dip and there are several viable alternatives. It is impossible to say whether the elections will bring in a liberal reformer, a reform-minded conservative or some other variant, but it is possible to forecast that the reforms are here to stay. It is enough to remember that they were in fact begun by the last Soviet regime to see that while few are happy with the results, fewer are ready to go back to the bad old days.

If the Russian economy recovers from its current depression, there can be little doubt that the reforms will continue and prosper. But if the economic situation worsens, there could be some tendency to pull back from the direct route to the free market. What might happen in that case must be pure speculation; but contingent scenarios exist. If the economy did get worse, as some confidently expect, and the banking sector was hit by a series of bankruptcies, as others have forecast, what are the most likely outcomes? According to Grigory Khanin, head of the economics faculty of the Siberian Independent University, who has made a study of the banking sector, there are four possible options for restructuring the system.

- Option one would be a partial return to an administrative command economy in those branches (of the banking system) that are still not ready for the market and privatisation. The banking system would have to be reconstructed to deal with this situation. The rest of the economy would function on market principles, while credit relations within it begin to play a minor role. Modern credit institutions would be slow to develop.
- Option two is internationalising the Russian credit system. Russia has not known a genuine credit system for about 80 years and might have been over-ambitious in attempting to do everything by itself. In pre-Revolutionary Russia, the biggest banks were joint ventures between Russian and foreign partners. Joint credit institutions could also become centres around which financial and industrial groups form.
- Option three presupposes that there is a sharp fall in inflation, stricter controls on the activities of commercial banks and other credit institutions, and greater opportunities for foreign competition. Then, once the more ailing credit institutions have met their inevitable end, would the current credit system have any chance of recovering and starting to grow.
- Option four is the doomsday one, that Russia would have to nationalise the entire credit system, partially as a protective measure and partially in answer to a wave of bankruptcies. The Central Bank would probably have to take on the task of issuing market credits itself, until the prerequisites for a two-tiered banking system were in place. Khanin adds that compensation for nationalised property would have to be paid and obligations to the clients upheld.

Khanin favours the first option, but others more hopeful would go for option three. In fact, most Russian bankers would see the future in just that way.

THE CO-PUBLISHERS

МОСТ-БАНК
MOST-BANK

Russia's new retail banking at Most-Bank

In the transition period of Russian society towards a market oriented economy, national banks' activities are crucial to the development of the country's economy and to the establishment of a modern and more sophisticated financial infrastructure. The overwhelming objective of the new banks is to integrate into a world banking community, thus re-establishing the economic links between the West and the newly emerging markets of Russia and the former Soviet Republics.

Analysing the modern financial market in Russia, one can see that there are several types of banking institutions. First of all, there are former state banks, which not only retained the staff and the organisational structure of their units, but also managed to keep their former clients. This first group of banks still obtain governmental loans at preferential rates. The second group of banks are represented by the institutions, established by former state enterprises, transformed into joint stock companies. The policy of these banks is oriented at satisfying the needs of a very close circle of corporate clients, founders of the banks. The third group is known by risky investment institutions, offering their clients unrealistically high interest rates and very often not meeting their obligations.

Against this background, Most-Bank occupies quite a unique position. The bank was established in 1991 by a group of private shareholders. In a very short period of time the bank managed to attract new clients due to the implementation of new technologies and expertise of its staff, the core of which came from the well-educated and well-trained younger generation of Vnesheconombank, the only former state bank with international banking experience.

In a relatively short period of time the bank has gained a high-profile reputation for its strong financial position, reliability and the top quality services it provides. For the years 1993 and 1994 the bank has been included in the Highest Reliabilty Group among Russian banks.

The bank is a financial core of Most Group, a large holding company comprising 42 legal entities and employing more than 12,000 staff.

The banking organisation has now developed into an institution with 12 branches in Moscow, three affiliated branches in St Petersburg, Yekateringburg and Krasnoyarsk and a representative office in London. At least three other regional branches are to be opened in the near future. The bank is audited by Price Waterhouse.

STRONG FIGURES

Growth and expansion has been continuing from the moment Most-Bank was founded. In 1994, growth continued to be impressive. Capital came to Rb136,576 million (75 per cent is hard currency denominated), an increase of 5.3 times and reserves standing at Rb129,419 million have risen 25.5 times as compared to the end of the 1993 financial year. Assets grew 4.5 times for the same period.

STRATEGY AND SERVICES

Most-Bank offers its clients universal banking services, combining traditional Russian banking operations with modern western banking techniques. Loan operations, which take a large share of

Below: Vladimir A. Goussinsky, President

the bank's assets, can be mentioned as one of the traditional services. The bank never chases doubtful revenues and prefers reliable borrowers. Short-term loans make up the most significant part of the portfolio and an overdraft is one of the forms of extending a loan.

Despite a very unfriendly investment environment in the country, the bank is among ten other Russian banks that also provide project finance with a stress on real estate development.

The policy of the bank rests on the principle of a combination of corporate finance and a retail banking institution. The latter sector of banking in Russia is currently underdeveloped but has massive potential in the medium to long term, and it is

an area of financial services where Most-Bank is active and has a great deal of relevant expertise. As Alexander Polyakov, first vice president points out, 'The goal of Most-Bank is clearly to become a fully-fledged retail bank. It is an ambitious goal, which will take years to achieve, but we are confident that we will succeed'.

Corporate clients of the bank include Siemens Nixdorf, New Arbat (supermarket), Kalinka/Stockman, Mercedes-Benz Avtomobili A.O.S.T., industrial companies, construction enterprises and a number of municipal organisations of social infrastructure and the medical sector.

The bank currently offers universal services such as rouble/foreign currency, cash settlement, securities transactions, currency exchange, money market operations, guaranty/warranty issuance, deposit accounts, gold transactions, project finance, correspondent banking and credit cards. From the above, Most-Bank is particularly active in three areas: securities, correspondent banking and credit card issuance and settlement.

THE STOCK MARKET AWAKENS

Most-Bank is activley involved in the development of the Russian securities market. In 1994 the activities of the bank on this market radically increased in terms of either types of operations and their volume.

Under the current circumstances of economic instability, one of the most reliable investments is an investment in government securities. From the moment the market of short-term government bond sprang up, the bank was among 16 banks and five brokers authorised by the Central Bank of Russia to carry out operations in this sector. The bank is widely recognised as one of the top prime dealers on the Russian T-bill market.

The bank is also authorised by the Central Bank to carry out transactions in gold and precious metals and in Internal Foreign Currency (Taiga) Bonds.

The bank actively participates in the privatisation of state and municipal enterprises, offering a full range of services from project development to issuance of shares and keeping shareholders' registry.

Most-Bank is among a few Russian banks rendering consulting services to its clients on the Russian stock market, among them the way of optimising and diversifying a client's investment portfolio.

PLASTIC CARDS

Most-Bank was the first bank is Russia to become a member of both the Visa and MasterCard payment systems, issuing all types of cards of the above systems. However, as the plastic cards sector is one of the most competitive in the Russian financial market, the bank has worked out a marketing strategy in two major directions: the introduction of well-known international plastic cards and the development of tailored products, meeting the requirements of target groups of consumers. One of these is MostCard, operated under the Cirrus/Maestro and Electron/Plus systems, which is a comparatively less expensive system than Visa/MasterCard, but can be used both in Russia and abroad. The bank's Multicarta Co. is the most advanced processing centre in Russia.

CORRESPONDENT NETWORK

Most-Bank has a large correspondent banking network, covering the world's major markets. From Europe to the United States and the Far East, the bank has established relations with leading banking institutions to satisfy the needs of its clients in international services.

The network comprises 33 major banks, including the bank of New York, Bank of America, Barclays Bank, Midland Bank, Crédit Lyonnais, Deutsche Bank, Dresdner Bank, Swiss Bank Corporation, Credit Suisse and the Bank of Tokyo.

Most-Bank has established correspondent relations with major commercial banks in Russia, such as Inkombank, Stolichny Bank of Savings, Menatep, National Credit Bank of Moscow and others.

In 1992 the bank became a member of the Moscow Interbank Currency Exchange. It enlarged the bank's forex capabilites and operations greatly, widening the scope of forex services at the same time.

The situation was developed further in 1993 when the bank joined the SWIFT system which has enabled the bank to carry out money market and forex transactions with greater speed and efficiency that was previously available. The bank also uses Reuters Dealing 2000 terminals and Telerate to speed up these types of operations still further.

The international division of the bank is active in a wide range of international operations, including settlements, the issuance of documentary L/Cs, payments for collection and guaranty/warranty issuance.

With the high speed development of a financial market in Russia, the policy of Most-Bank will be aimed at forecasting the requirements of its clients. Anyone will be heartily welcomed at the bank and get the necessary expert advice on any problems concerning Russian finance and the stock market.

Most-Bank

36 Novy Arbat Street
Moscow 121205
Russia
Tel: +7 (095) 203 2552
Tel: +7 (095) 290 8206
Fax: +7 (095) 290 9184

Commercial Bank 'Most-Bank' United Kingdom

Representative Office
Level 4, City Tower
40 Basinghall Street
London EC2V 5DE
Tel: +44 (171) 638 8652
Fax: +44 (171) 256 7816

The bank for the 21st century

DialogBank is one of the oldest private Russian commercial banks, founded in 1989. It has a full general banking licence that permits it to perform all traditional banking operations, both domestically and internationally. It is one of the most innovative and progressive banks in Russia, placing a heavy emphasis on automation and technology, with the goal of serving customers better in a difficult business and political environment. Clients include many well-known large multinational and Russian companies.

DialogBank is also a conservative bank that stresses service and safety. As of 30 June 1994, only 6.2 per cent of the bank's assets were in corporate loans as compared to the average Russian bank, which has between 30 and 50 per cent of its assets in commercial credits. The rest of the bank's liquid assets were deposited with its core international corespondent banks. DialogBank is a closed joint-stock bank with 10 shareholders, who – like the management team – are Russian and foreign. The offices are centrally located in Moscow and Nizhny Novgorod.

The bank's net assets at the end of 1994 came to over Rb482.3 billion, up from Rb146.3 billion a year previously. After-tax profits came to more than Rb23.5 billion, against Rb6.1 billion in 1993.

Peter Derby, President, Chief Executive Officer, DialogBank

CORPORATE SERVICES

The bank offers its services in any currency, with an emphasis on Russian roubles and US dollars. Services for corporate accounts include current (DDA) accounts, investment accounts, foreign exchange against the Russian rouble as well as other CIS currencies and the US dollar, deposits, trade finance services (including letters of credit, guarantees and collections), vault and cash operations, custodial services for stocks and bonds, funds transfer, Treasury bill (GKO) and MinFin (Taiga) bond trading, lending, and corporate finance advisory services. DialogBank has a full network of correspondent bank accounts in Russia, the CIS, and throughout the rest of the world. In 1995, the bank will introduce CrownNet, a state-of-the-art corporate cash management system that will allow customers to perform most banking transactions from their offices, instead of going to the bank every day, which is the current practice in Russia. CrownNet will be a highly secure and user-friendly product.

DialogBank net income, 1992–94

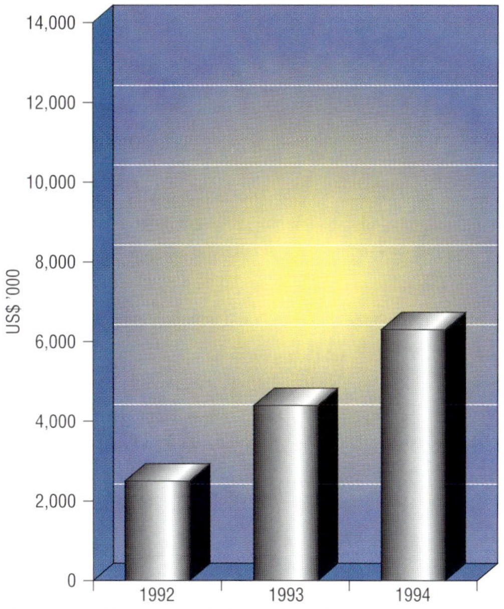

For a comparative inflation-adjusted analysis, these amounts have been converted into US dollar equivalents using the Moscow Interbank Currency Exchange Rate (MICEX) as of the close of trading for each respective year: 24 December 1992: Rb414.5/$1; 28 December 1993: Rb1,247/$1; 29 December 1994: Rb3,350/$1.

DialogBank stockholders' equity, 1992–94

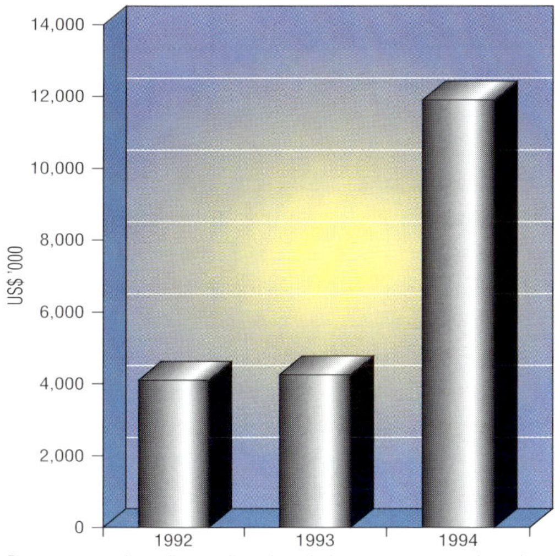

For a comparative inflation-adjusted analysis, these amounts have been converted into US dollar equivalents using the Moscow Interbank Currency Exchange Rate (MICEX) as of the close of trading for each respective year: 24 December 1992: Rb414.5/$1; 28 December 1993: Rb1,247/$1; 29 December 1994: Rb3,350/$1.

DialogBank assets, 1992–94

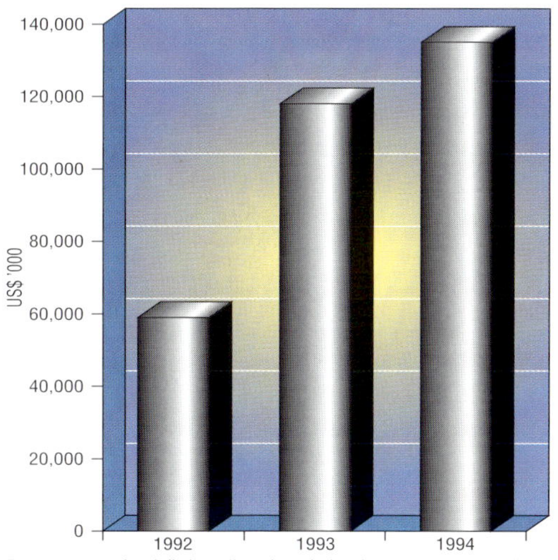

For a comparative inflation-adjusted analysis, these amounts have been converted into US dollar equivalents using the Moscow Interbank Currency Exchange Rate (MICEX) as of the close of trading for each respective year: 24 December 1992: Rb414.5/$1; 28 December 1993: Rb1,247/$1; 29 December 1994: Rb3,350/$1.

CONSUMER BANKING SERVICES

Consumer banking services include: Eurocard/Mastercard issuance and cash advances, DialogBank Debit Card issuance, incoming personal money transfers, safe deposit boxes, currency exchange point operations, including the encashment of all major travellers cheques and EuroCheques, and the sale of American Express travellers cheques. The bank also offers American Express emergency check cashing services. The DialogBank Debit Card is part of the Maestro/CIRRUS network. In 1995, DialogBank will start the installation of its ATMs in Moscow. These machines will have the ability to dispense both Russian roubles and US dollars.

OTHER SERVICES

DialogBank has a special department dedicated to servicing the particular needs of investors (i.e. investment banks and investment firms, emerging marker funds, etc.). The European Bank for Reconstruction and Development (EBRD), the International Finance Corporation (IFC) and the US Export-Import Bank have all selected DialogBank as a depository for major projects in Russia.

The bank is a founder-member and shareholder of the Moscow Interbank Currency Exchange (MICEX), Russia's largest currency exchange. It was one of the first Russian banks to go on-line with SWIFT and currently uses it for all international settlements and other banking activity. DialogBank was one of the first primary dealers in Russian Federation Treasury Bills, currently a Rb21 trillion market. It actively uses Reuters Dealing (code: DLGB) and News and Money 2000 and has a regularly updated contributor page (Page code: DLGB). The bank is also one of only a select few banks that have the right to trade Russian Ministry of Finance rouble-denominated gold-backed certificates.

TROIKA DIALOG

Troika Dialog is one of Russia's few, truly integrated investment banking institutions. The firm is an active trader and primary dealer in government securities as well as a leading participant in Russia's OTC share market. Troika Dialog provides clients with financial advisory services on mergers and acquisitions, the issuance of equity and debt, and structured direct investment. The firm's team-based approach brings together professionals from sales, trading, research and investment banking. Their efforts are supported by a dedicated legal and trade operations team that has demonstrated exceptional proficiency in an environment that has challenged all market participants.

PROFESSIONAL EXCELLENCE

The firm continues to evidence its commitment to raising the standards of business in Russia by emphasising in-house and outside training for its employees, selectively recruiting experienced professionals, and reinforcing the firm's infrastructure. Troika Dialog strongly supports the continuing development of Russia's capital markets through its involvement in the Professional Association of Securities Market Participants, the Moscow Times Index Board and the Depository Clearing Corporation (DCC). Troika Dialog's executive director is the vice chairman of the DCC. Troika Dialog's senior management is frequently consulted by the Russian government regarding privatisation and the continued development of the equity markets.

EQUITY TRADING AND SALES

Troika Dialog is recognised as an active and aggressive market leader in Russia's equity market and has had a pivotal role in developing secondary market trading for shares in Russia's largest corporations. Troika Dialog was one of the pioneers in the creation of Russia's OTC market.

Ruben Vardanyan
Executive
Director, Troika
Dialog

GOVERNMENT DEBT TRADING

In April 1994, Troika Dialog was awarded primary dealership status on the Moscow Interbank Currency Exchange (MICEX), one of only two investment banks to earn this distinction. Primary dealership was granted in recognition of the firm's professional integrity and continuing commitment to the development of the market's infrastructure. Troika Dialog's traders are among the most experienced in Russia, having been active in the market since its inception in May of 1993.

INVESTMENT BANKING

Troika Dialog is committed to long-term strategic investors interested in direct investment in Russia. We focus on our clients' strategic goals in a dynamic corporate and regulatory environment. We provide advice for our Russian and international clients on privatisation, acquisition, cross-border financing, tender offers and restructurings. Troika Dialog uses in-depth analysis to design investment programmes custom-tailored to each unique situation. Capitalising on the firm's trading expertise, we are able to provide clients with execution and implementation of their corporate strategies.

RESEARCH

Troika Dialog's research is focused on current, market sensitive analysis designed for firms active in the Russian capital markets. The firm's research is recognised for its objectivity and innovation, providing international institutional investors with information unavailable elsewhere. Clients of Troika Dialog receive a daily market summary that goes beyond share quotations, providing information and analysis of news and trends that impact the market.

ЭЛБИМ БАНК ELBIM BANK

ELBIM Bank was established in 1990 and received a general licence from the Central Bank of Russia in 1992, which authorises it to conduct business both inside and outside the country. In terms of shareholders' equity, ELBIM Bank is one of the top 20 Russian banks and the Rb32.5 billion registered as of 1 July 1994 had increased to Rb38.94 billion by 1 January 1995. The bank carries out all types of financial transactions, maintains rouble and foreign currency accounts, extends rouble and hard currency credit, and handles all kinds of international transactions, including securities, letters of credit, cheques and other payment facilities.

ELBIM Bank has over 150 shareholders, including the Russian Chamber of Commerce and Industry, the SOVINCENTR joint stock company, the MIG and Illyushin aircraft corporations, Central Telegraph, the St Petersburg nuclear power plant, Sheremetyevo-2 International Airport, TV-Centre in Ostankino, the Bolshoi Theatre and Sberbank, as well as many other banks, enterprises and individuals. In 1993, several foreign companies purchased equity. The bank's generally high profits have allowed it to pay high dividends to shareholders.

BALANCE SHEET AND RESERVE REQUIREMENTS

Total assets exceeded Rb538.4 billion on 1 January 1995, up from Rb271.8 billion in July. Over the same period, turnover soared from over Rb27.135 trillion to Rb82.625 trillion, and profits from Rb6.317 billion to Rb22.597 billion. In accordance with the Central Bank's obligatory reserve requirements, ELBIM Bank makes regular transfers to the Central Bank's credit resources fund, as well as maintaining its own reserves. In the period from 1 July 1994 to 1 January 1995 the funds and reserves category rose from Rb11.096 billion to Rb47.641 billion. For purposes of deposit and self-insurance, the bank makes regular transfers to the Commercial Bank Insurance Fund and the Commercial Bank Deposit Insurance Fund. In 1993, ELBIM Bank started to adjust its accounting procedures to international standards, as part of the drive to bring Russia's accounting procedures into line with international norms.

Sergei Morozov, General Director and Chairman of the Board

EXPANDING SERVICES

ELBIM Bank carries out settlements world-wide via a network of NOSTRO accounts and also operates more than 30 LORO accounts in foreign currency for other Russian banks. The bank is a member of the Eurocard/MasterCard system and issues ELBIM Bank Eurocard/MasterCard credit cards. Commercial cheques issued by foreign companies and banks are accepted by ELBIM Bank. The bank accepts all types of travellers cheques in any hard currency and sells travellers cheques issued by Thomas Cook, American Express and VISA. The bank operates 12 divisional offices throughout Moscow and branch offices in Novorossiysk and Gelendjik. It is currently developing currency exchange services and operates Bureau de Change outlets accepting major world currencies in the most active business locations in Moscow.

Olga Blinkova, President, Deputy Chairman of the Board

The volume of transactions handled by the branches is constantly growing, while their assets are rising due to attracting new clients and the introduction of new services. New customers were attracted mainly by a relatively high interest on deposits, the wide range of deposits accepted, and the possibility of collecting interest or withdrawing deposits at any time. ELBIM Bank also issues its own debit card for payment of goods and services. Travellers cheques now play an increasingly important role in the bank's payment transactions.

Together with establishing new branches in Moscow, ELBIM Bank has been developing its computer banking divisions to provide banking services to remote clients. This is now one of the most promising lines of the bank's development.

As of 1 January 1994, there were more than 6,500 hard currency accounts in the bank, of which about 300 were maintained by foreign companies operating in Russia, while 700 belonged to foreign citizens. Non-resident companies with accounts in ELBIM Bank include many world-renowned ones. The bank established a currency collection service to collect cash from its customers and organised some agencies for international and domestic cards and cheques. It also continued to develop its remote electronic banking service and also to cut charges on cash transactions and provide other customer incentives.

ELBIM BANK CHEQUES – A NEW MEANS OF PAYMENT

The developing market economy needs a very large amount of currency in circulation at all times. ELBIM Bank has proposed a system of international multi-currency debit cheques (IMD cheques) to be used in conjunction with banknotes. The cheques would be issued with a higher degree of protection than notes and a different paper would be used in printing.

Three types of cheques are currently being explored; name cheques (issued for a legal entity or an individual for the purpose of transfer to another firm or person); order cheques (cheques given directly to the payee); and bearer cheques (a cash substitute for multiple usage). The cheques would be guaranteed by ELBIM Bank and would be exchangeable in roubles or other currency. Step-by-step introduction of ELBIM Bank universal cheques, followed by increasing demand for them, would gradually expand the range of their application. The financial modulator in the form of universal quasi-currency IMD cheques is called financial "Esperanto" because it allows all the national hard currencies to be drawn to a single base according to the exchange rate on the date of the IMD cheque purchase.

Currently, CIS countries are facing financial difficulties while effecting settlements with foreign tourists and businesses. The introduction of a universal quasi-currency market within the territory of the former USSR could remove these difficulties. The only financial market viable in the Global Open Economic Space (GOES) is the quasi-currency one. On the one hand, the IMD cheques do not impede exchange speculations with national hard currencies, easily converting from one currency to another. In this function they are similar to any world currency while not actually being one. On the other hand, the IMD cheques allow ultimate payment for goods and services to be effected in any country in the world without exception, which makes the cheques similar in their function as a universal payment means to gold (as the world money) while actually not being gold.

The universal quasi-currency IMD cheques we are offering are an ultimate international non-monetary payment means which will allow the removal of all the contradictions when carrying out settlements within the GOES, and are in fact a novel compact means of payment in this present day "Age of Information".

According to MasterCard's estimates, plastic cards as a non-cash payment means service about 5 per cent of all retail purchases within Europe and 10 per cent thereof in the United States. The maintenance of plastic cards authorisation is complicated and requires expensive electronic computerised services, as well as a wide, well-established and reliable tele, radio and cable (hollow fibre) communication network. The Achilles' heel of the plastic cards is their compulsory authorisation and the impossibility to effect settlements between individuals. In order to do this, the card user has to use either a cash-dispensing machine or must go to a bank for cash (the "cash advance"). The cash-dispensing machine is an expensive piece of computerised equipment with high-tech hardware. Despite their advantages, plastic cards will never fully replace the need for cash. All the modern cash-dispensing machines are equipped with concealed cameras that record people's transactions. This is one of the low-efficient systems employed to protect against forgery and theft. Today, plastic cards, including the "smart" cards, are extremely appealing to forgers and fraudsters. Losses caused by well-made forged cards are on the increase, forcing banks to maintain special reserve funds to cover these losses. Electronic theft of money is a new problem for world finance and is much more sophisticated and harder to combat compared to cheque and bank note forgery.

The level of users of plastic cards is limited in principle by the prerequisite of long credit histories with the bank. This means that only those who are well-off are able to obtain cards. In any society this group is not a majority of the population, especially in Russia but also in other countries with developing markets (China, India, Mexico, Brazil and so on). The IMD cheques now offered lack the shortcomings associated with plastic cards and are available to all levels of society – from the richest multi-billionaire to the poorest pensioner as well as the schoolboy who pays for lunch with his IMD cheque.

The IMD cheques have one more important feature: they could mobilise cash that people are keeping at home. This is especially important in Russia where people prefer to keep their savings at home in a hard currency, mostly in US dollars. The amount of these home savings for the past 1.5 years has been estimated to be around US$25 billion. For the last 10 years this amount was around US$100 billion. If the Russian people are offered a new and highly liquid means of payment which is easily convertible into any currency and widely accepted with favourable conditions within the Russian and CIS market, the majority of this hard currency cash would move from people's home to bank accounts in Russia's commercial banks. If this were to happen retail prices would stabilise and become international as they would be equivalent to US dollars or any other hard currency. The amount of cash in roubles on the market will decrease sharply. The fall of the unconvertible Russian rouble will continue and the state will have to print more and more "Kerenkis" with a face value of millions of roubles. The IMD cheques could easily overcome this situation. Today one IMD cheque with the equivalent face value of US$100 is equal to almost Rb500,000. An IMD cheque with the equivalent face value of US$1,000 would be equal to Rb5 million. The need for the state to print more unconvertible Russian roubles would cease and only non-cash transactions would be left in the national economy. This would reduce the budget foreign currency funds' spending. The need to reform the financial system in Russia is now urgent.

INVESTMENT STRATEGY

Russian banks owning shares in manufacturing companies, as well as those with well-established ties with efficient businesses, are expected to gain an edge after the Russian economy begins to improve and domestic interest rates begin to fall. ELBIM Bank's investment strategy takes this into account. The bank has been investing in shares in other banks and trading and manufacturing companies, which currently produce the highest yields. ELBIM Bank holds shares in the Russian savings bank (Sberbank), Mosbusinessbank and Rosmedbank. It owns a stake in the large Moscow trading house GUM, and Permskie Motory, an aircraft manufacturer in Perm. ELBIM Bank is a major founder of the Russian Stock Exchange. In 1993, its total investment in various types of security grew seven-fold.

ELBIM Bank has supplied capital to more than 30 companies. Real estate and trading firms, as well as those implementing major commercial and industrial projects, account for 50 per cent of the bank's investment. The bank's specialists now analyse a large number of investment projects in order to form an investment portfolio that will ensure stable income to the bank and high dividends to its shareholders. In 1993, ELBIM Bank began trading in short-term government bonds and other securities on the secondary securities market. Securities trading is likely to play an important part in ELBIM Bank's activities as Russia's financial markets begin to stabilise.

CORRESPONDENT BANKS

As of 1 January 1995 ELBIM Bank had correspondent relations with 65 banks. Holders of LORO accounts include 27 Moscow-based commercial banks, as well as others in St Petersburg, Rostov-on-Don and other centres. Relations have been established with a number of East European and Japanese banks, while negotiations with banks in the Middle East are underway. ELBIM is connected to the SWIFT network.

MEZHCOMBANK

Sergey K. Ovsiannikov, Chairman of the board

MEZHCOMBANK opened in Moscow in 1990 and has quickly achieved a remarkable record of success. It has become one of the most efficient banks operating in Russia and enjoys a reputation for the first-class services it provides for large foreign trade companies. Maintaining a comprehensive range of services, combined with specialisation in international transactions, is the Bank's primary market strategy.

Despite a complex and increasingly competitive economic environment, the Bank has shown an accelerated pace of development and has the reputation for being one of the most reliable and profitable credit institutions in Russia. As Sergei Ovsiannikov, chairman of the Bank says: "A volatile economy and competition are teaching us to spend minutes where western banks have spent days, and to spend hours where western banks have spent years."

The result of this approach is the rapid growth of all main economic indicators of the Bank and the successful implementation of its strategy. During the last two years MEZHCOMBANK has opened two branches and a network of specialised offices in Moscow, and branches in St. Petersburg, Krasnoyarsk, Karelia, Kazan, Stavropol and Kirov.

The long-term programme of regional development adopted by the Bank envisages the establishment of the Bank's presence in major financial centres world-wide. In 1994 the first representative office was opened in Bahrain.

INTERNATIONAL SETTLEMENTS AND FOREIGN EXCHANGE

With a large network of correspondent banks abroad and in the former Soviet republics of the Ukraine, Belarus, Kazakhstan, Latvia and Estonia, MEZHCOMBANK offers importers and exporters a full range of financial documentary and payment services in the domestic and foreign markets.

International settlements are held in all major hard and soft currencies via the SWIFT network.

MEZHCOMBANK acts as a clearing centre for rouble settlements of banks in the Ukraine, Estonia, Latvia and Kazakhstan.

Connection to the Reuters Dealing 2000 trading system allows the dealing department of the Bank to effectively conduct foreign exchange, deposit, bank note and other operations with numerous partners in global financial centres. Bilateral foreign exchange trading limits and credit lines with large domestic and foreign banks allow MEZHCOMBANK to further expand the scale of its operations.

The Bank is one of the first founders of the Moscow Interbank Currency Exchange (MICEX) and an active trader in all currencies quoted on the MICEX.

New office of Mezhcombank in St Petersburg

LENDING OPERATIONS

In 1994 MEZHCOMBANK successfully expanded its lending operations both in roubles and in foreign currencies. The total value of the Bank's loan portfolio nearly increased four-fold during 1994.

MEZHCOMBANK is extensively involved in attracting new clients oriented towards exporting their products and is strengthening its business links with large foreign trade companies in need of foreign currency loans.

The Bank is also active in long-term financing (up to four years) of investment projects associated with development of export production and participates in issuing syndicated loans together with other banks.

To ensure that the overall credit portfolio produces the highest return possible within acceptable levels of risk, the Bank's experts use modern methods of risk assessment and evaluation of the creditworthiness of all borrowers and business partners. They also work to develop feasibility studies of projects and other documents based on existing banking practices. The quality of expertise is reflected in a very low ratio of non-performing loans that stood at just 0.7 per cent of the total credit portfolio in 1994.

SECURITIES

In 1994 MEZHCOMBANK substantially increased its activity in the securities market and in the investment banking sector. MEZHCOMBANK was among the first 24 commercial banks and brokerage companies authorised by the Central Bank of Russia to act as primary dealers in the government short-term bond market (GSTB).

MEZHCOMBANK also operates in the government 3 per cent hard currency loan bond market (MinFin bonds), acts as a custodian of the bonds for its clients and conducts trust management of its clients' rouble- and foreign currency-denominated deposits.

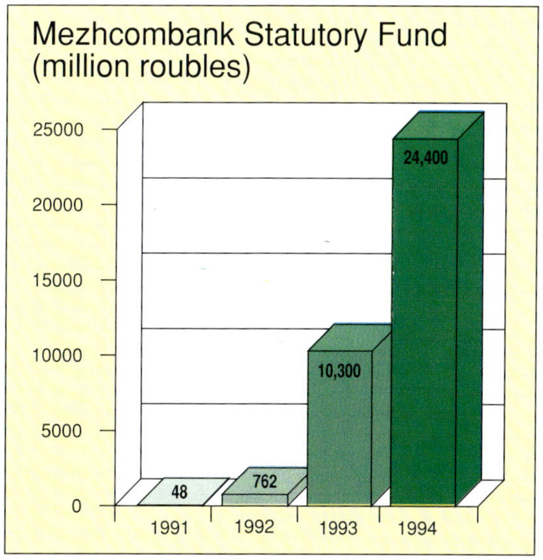

The bank closely follows the situation in the share market of privatised companies which emerged at the beginning of 1994. Plans to establish a brokerage unit in shares and to develop equity research facilities are currently on the bank's agenda.

The ability to manoeuvre in the different sectors of the market and to make use of its temporary inefficiencies revealed by the analysis of real-time market data allowed the bank to derive additional income and introduce highly profitable asset management services for its clients in the domestic market at times when investment in western money markets proved unfavourable.

MEZHCOMBANK currently manages, on a discretionary basis, a considerable amount of funds for both domestic and foreign businesses operating in the Russian market. By combining detailed knowledge of the Russian money markets with advanced portfolio management techniques, MEZHCOMBANK does its best to decrease risks and maximise returns on its clients investments.

MEZHCOMBANK provides consulting services to corporations and individuals wishing to make investments in Russia. Our knowledge of clientele in many regions of Russia, combined with close monitoring of the country's economic situation, allows us to find promising investment opportunities.

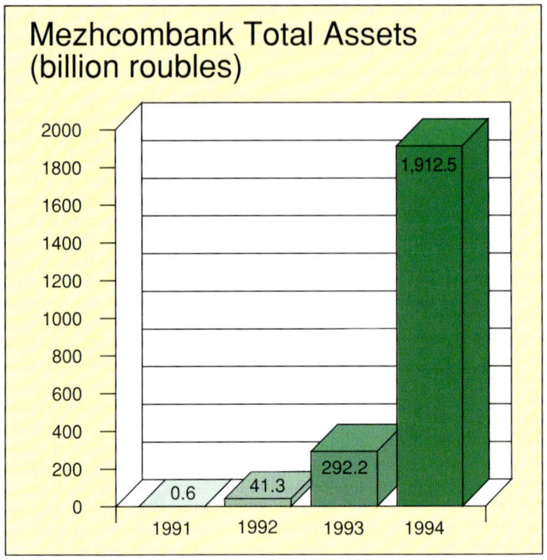

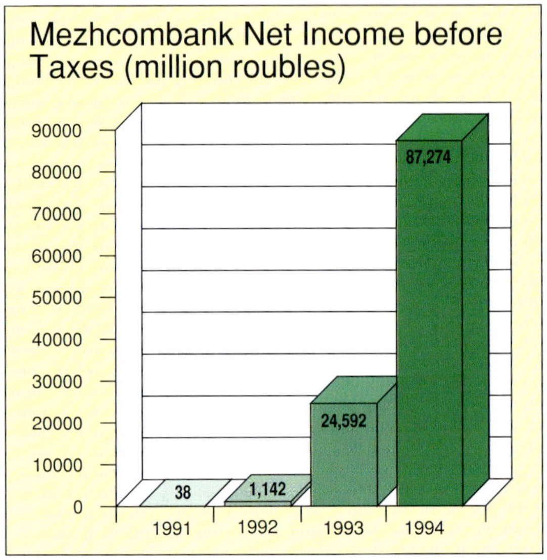

RETAIL BANKING

Although the preference in the domestic market is given to major foreign trade and industrial enterprises, the development of retail banking is considered to be very important within the strategy of universalisation. Among the most significant achievements in this area, the following should be mentioned:

- MEZHCOMBANK occupies a leading position in the emerging cheque market in Russia and plays a pioneering role in its development.
- The Bank implemented its own debit card scheme, tailored as a cash card for payroll payment services.
- The Bank is also a principle licensee for Eurocard/MasterCard and issues three types of credit cards for the employees of its corporate clients.
- MEZHCOMBANK was the first in Russia to become an agent for American Express.

STAFF POLICY

Special attention to the individual needs of employees, career planning, profit-sharing programmes and other team-building efforts made MEZHCOMBANK's staff widely renowned for highly professional standards, corporate loyalty and team spirit. The existing practice of on-the-job training allowed the bank to increase its staff dramatically without any adverse effect on the quality of service, which MEZHCOMBANK traditionally maintains at a superior level.

CONTACTS:

19 Chernyakhovskogo Str.,
Moscow 125319
Russia
Tel: (095) 152 04 19   Fax: (095) 155 72 33
SWIFT Code: MEZHRUMM
Telex: 612642 MECOM RU
REUTERS Code: MEZH

Price Waterhouse

Price Waterhouse is one of the world's leading providers of independent audit business advisory services. The firm was founded in 1849 by Samuel Lowell Price, who practised as an accountant in the City of London. In 1865 Samuel Price was joined by Edwin Waterhouse. Today the world organisation has 2,600 partners and employs some 48,000 people in over 450 offices providing professional services to clients in more than 110 different countries, including all the major and financial centres.

Price Waterhouse's worldwide expansion has closely followed that of the international banking market and our services have developed through our close association with the financial communities in the major financial centres of the world. Specialist banking and finance groups have been established to serve each of these financial communities. Their specialist knowledge and their direct experience within the banking sector enables them to deliver the highest quality service. The banking sector is currently the fastest growing area of our practice and accounts for over 20 per cent of our worldwide fees.

All of the partners in Price Waterhouse around the world are partners in the Price Waterhouse World Firm as well as their local firm. This enables us to give high quality service delivery from our multi-disciplinary teams on a worldwide basis – a real advantage for our clients.

The distinctive structure of Price Waterhouse in Europe and around the world enables us to draw immediately upon worldwide knowledge and experience for the benefit of our clients, wherever they are located. We use this ability to ensure that the best people are available to service our clients, regardless of where they are located. This global commitment to client service has led to Price Waterhouse becoming a major force in the banking market.

Our audit clients include:

- 16 of the world's top 100 banks
- 2 of the UK clearing banks
- 4 of the major New York based money centre banks
- The World Bank

In addition we also audit a large number of regional and/or smaller banks and savings institutions throughout Europe. We have been appointed auditors to banks in Russia, Belarus, Kazakhstan, the Czech and Slovak republics, Hungary, Poland and Romania.

PRICE WATERHOUSE IN RUSSIA

Price Waterhouse's first overseas office was in New York. The second, opened in 1916, was in St Petersburg. Unfortunately, that office was forced to close in 1917. We returned to Russia in 1989 when we opened our Moscow office. We now employ over 500 staff in Moscow and foresee considerable future growth. Our work in Russia includes a substantial and growing base of audit work, as well as tax and legal work and privatisation projects.

In addition to our Moscow office we have offices in Togliatti (where a staff of 40 people

Our Geographical Spread in the Former Soviet Union

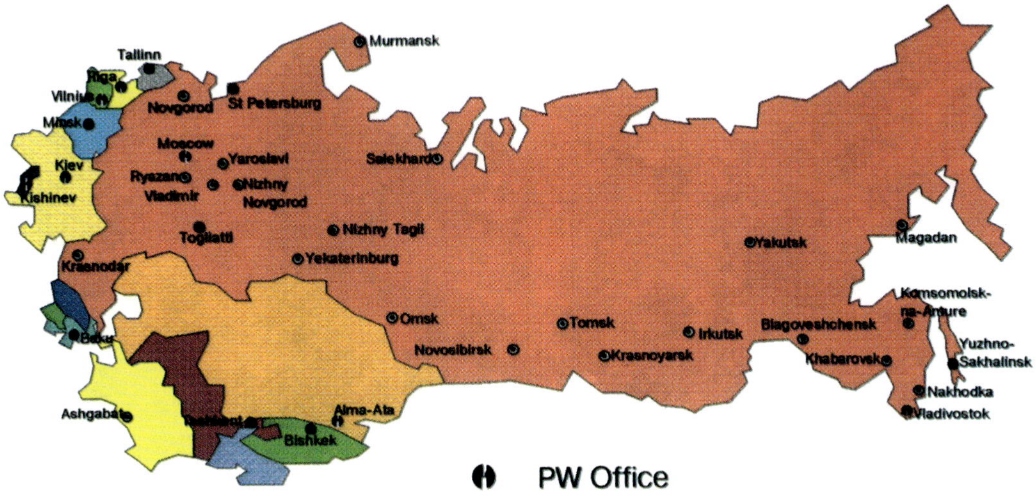

service one of our major clients, Avtovaz), Sakhalin Island, Vladivostok and St Petersburg, and we already have a presence in Ekaterinburg.

We also have offices in other republics of the former Soviet Union. In January 1993 we opened an office in Almaty, in June 1993 we opened an office in Minsk, and in February 1995 in Baku. We are currently in the process of opening an office in Kiev.

THE PRICE WATERHOUSE FINANCIAL SERVICES PRACTICE IN RUSSIA

Since 1989 the Price Waterhouse Russian Financial Services Group has grown quickly and now has almost 60 professional staff dedicated full time to the provision of advice to banks. Of these, approximately 15 staff are expatriates with extensive experience of western banking which complements in a highly effective way their rapidly developing experience of working with Russian banks. The group includes specialists in audit, tax and business advisory services.

Our Financial Services Practice in Russia is headed by Jonathan Hayward. A British citizen, Jonathan joined Price Waterhouse London in 1982 after qualifying as a Chartered Accountant. He moved to Moscow in 1992 and is responsible for all bank and other financial institution audits in Russia. He also has wide experience in other countries in Europe and completed the first audit of a private bank in Czechoslovakia. Mr Hayward has experience of statutory audit work, regulatory work, internal audits, special investigations and consultancy work. Clients have included Lloyds Bank, JP Morgan and Chase Manhattan. He has worked with the Bank of England to assess the practicality of certain of its banking supervision requirements and has lectured widely on banking and audit topics.

Our Russian staff include a number of individuals who provide a valuable insight from a position of extensive experience of Russian banking. They include the former Chief Internal Auditor of a major Russian bank and the former Head of Strategic Planning at another leading bank. Our audit staff are recruited from the top institutes and meet exacting recruitment standards before joining the firm. After joining, they follow a detailed training programme.

Michael Eggleton, an expatriate manager with extensive international experience of banking and investment fund taxation issues was assigned to the Financial Services Group in 1993. He works closely with other parts of the Price Waterhouse Tax Department which includes a number of highly experienced tax advisers. Natalia Milchikova is our senior adviser on Russian tax matters. Prior to joining PW, she was Chief Expert at the USSR Ministry of Finance Tax Directorate, where she was responsible for much of the USSR tax legislation. We have also developed a western-style VAT practice in Moscow. Ruth Cook, our Russian-speaking VAT and indirect tax director, is one of the lead advisers to the Russian authorities in rewriting the VAT law.

Our Financial Services group is based in Moscow. However, we have full-time banking audit managers resident in Vladivostok, Togliatti and St Petersburg for the purpose of servicing banks in those regions.

Our experience of working with Russian banks is now extensive. Through a combination of our western and Russian experience we are in a position to provide a wide range of valuable services to Russian financial institutions.

PRICE WATERHOUSE FINANCIAL SERVICES IN RUSSIA

We have provided audit and/or consultancy services to approximately 25 Russian banks, including the two largest in Russia.

Consultancy projects for both audit and non-audit clients have included:

- diagnostic reviews
- accounts conforming with International Accounting Standards

- review of Instruction No. 17 accounts
- due diligence reports for potential investors
- development of Internal Audit Department
- accountancy training
- taxation advice credit risk management training
- strategic reviews and business plans
- strategic planning training
- organisation restructuring and development of job descriptions
- skills and training needs analysis
- advice on remuneration policies
- assessment of Management Information Systems and identification of requirements
- development of risk management policies and procedures
- development of a Financial Control Department
- customer service review
- Information Systems consulting
- special investigation work of a loss-making branch
- investigation of troubled borrowers

TO FIND OUT MORE ABOUT PRICE WATERHOUSE IN RUSSIA PLEASE CONTACT:

- Price Waterhouse Russia (Partner: Jim Kilzer)
  Nikolo-Yamskaya, 15
  (formerly Ulyanovskaya)
  Moscow 109240
  Russia

  Telephone: (7095) 230 61 85
  Telefax: (7095) 230 61 86

- Price Waterhouse London (Partner: Paul McMahon)
  East European Services
  Southwark Towers
  32 London Bridge Street
  London SE1 9SY
  United Kingdom

  Telephone: (44171) 939 3000
  Telefax: (44171) 403 3873

- Price Waterhouse Washington (Partner: Michelle Siren)
  East European Services
  1801 K Street NW
  Washington DC 20006
  USA

  Telephone: (1202) 296 0800
  Telefax: (1202) 466 3918

Promstroybank of Russia, established in 1922, is the legal successor of Promstroybank of USSR. Since 1991 is has been a joint stock commercial and investment bank for industry and construction. Its shareholders comprise approximately 1,000 legal entities and more than 5,000 individuals. The share of the state in the bank's authorised capital is at present less than 2 per cent. The bank is acting as an agent of the Government of the Russian Federation for the implementation of the state investment and conversion programmes. The Promstroybank of Russia Holding Group incorporates, besides the head bank and its branches, 11 subsidiaries, thus enabling the bank to be represented in the major part of the country's territory.

Promstroybank of Russia is a recognised leader among the Russian bank community in terms of reliability and scale of activities: following the year-end results of 1994, the bank ranked first among the 150 largest Russian banks by the five basic parameters in aggregate (assets, equity, rouble deposits attracted, the outstanding balance of loans issued, balance profit); for the last few years, its reliability has been consistently rated as A3.

BALANCE SHEET

The results of Promstroybank of Russia's activities in 1994 are as follows:

- authorised capital – Rb40 billion;
- compared to 1993, the bank equity increased in 1994 from Rb77.6 billion up to Rb310.4 billion;
- total assets reached Rb4.2 trillion, which is 2.1 times more than in 1993;
- balance profit — Rb303 billion, which is 3.4 as much as in 1993.

The annual meeting of the bank's shareholders, held in March 1995, took the decision to increase the authorised capital to Rb100 billion.

STRATEGY

Throughout almost 70 years, Promostroybank of Russia used to be the main investment bank of the USSR. Under the new political and economic conditions established after the breakup of the Soviet Union in 1991, the bank was transformed into an universal commercial bank. The strategic business plan developed with the active participation of KPMG experts and approved in May 1993, targets the transformation of Promstroybank of Russia into an universal client-oriented bank which complies fully with international standards.

CUSTOMERS AND SERVICES

Within a short period of time, Promstroybank of Russia has been able to transform its activities and is currently able to provide its customers with a wide range of traditional services according to international banking pratices. Clients include large industrial companies, medium-sized and small private firms, joint ventures, and hundreds of thousands of private individuals. The bank offers

Sitting (left to right): **Mikhail N. Novikov,** First Deputy Chairman of the Board; **Nina M. Babkina,** Director, International Settlements Department; **Yakov N. Dubenetsky,** Chairman of the Board; **Stanislav I. Degtiarev,** First Deputy Chairman of the Board; **Yuri A. Balagurov,** Deputy Chairman of the Board.
Standing (left to right): **Nikolay M. Zavarikhin,** Head of Auditing Division; **Viktor N. Ogorev,** Director, Investment Department; **Alexander P. Zubkov,** Deputy Chairman of the Board; **Yuri V. Uvarov,** Deputy Chairman of the Board; **Artur V. Zhuravlev,** Deputy Chairman of the Board; **Andrey N. Kudinov,** Director, Economic Planning Department; **Sergey A. Moiseev,** Director, Bookkeeping and Settlements Department; **Alexander M. Masterkov,** Director, Administrative Department.

services in the areas of invesment and project financing, as well as medium-term and short-term credit both in roubles and in foreign currencies. The bank opens and holds foreign currency accounts of legal entities and individuals, as well as the correspondent accounts of banks. Subject to instructions from its customers, it performs the transfer of funds within the country and abroad, collection and LC operations, acceptance of bills of exchange, executes reimbursement orders, executes the purchase, sale and encashment of travellers cheques, as well as the conversion of funds into payment currencies.

The bank offers its clients the services provided by its wide correspondent network which incorporates over 150 banks in Russia, CIS and the Baltic region, as well as almost 200 foreign banks. The membership to the SWIFT and REUTER-2000 systems enables the bank to perform operations in compliance with international standards, while the modern means of telecommunications combined with the data-processing involving the electronic signature make it possible for the bank to operate in real time.

The bank has already obtained permission to open its representative office in the United

Kingdom, and similar matters are being settled with the Federal Reserve Board of the United States.

SERVICES FOR INDIVIDUALS

Until 1991 the bank practically carried out no work with private individuals, concentrating instead on services to large industrial enterprises. However, in accordance with the newly adopted strategy, the bank leads the policy aimed at becoming the market leader of services to the general public. By the middle of 1994, Promstroybank of Russia was one of the market leaders in the area of bank operations with individuals. Currently, along with the expansion of the range of services and the increase of their appeal to the general public, the bank is taking steps to spread its services over more territory. The continuous growth of the number of private customers testifies to the high confidence they have in the bank and proves the image it has as a reliable and trustworthy financial institution. By the beginning of 1995, the number of private customers' accounts held with the bank had grown more than twofold compared to the beginning of 1994. By April 1995, the bank had completed the first stage of the development of the clearing system based on the "smart card" technology, and was preparing its implementation.

THE HOLDING GROUP

The Holding Group, the first holding in Russian banking practices, incorporates along with Promstroybank of Russia (Moscow), Amurpromstroybank (Blagoveshchensk), Arcticpromstroybank (Murmansk), Arkhangelskpromstroybank (Arkhangelsk), Belgorodpromstroybank (Belgorod), Dalpromstroybank (Khabarovsk), Kavkazpromstroybank (Cherkessk), Makhachkala-

Promstroybank of Russia, Moscow

promstroybank (Makhachkala), Omskpromstroybank (Omsk), Rostpromstroybank (Rostov-on-Don), Stavropolpromstroybank (Stavropol), Yugpromstroybank (Tskhinval). It is able, therefore, to accumulate large financial resources, making it possible to execute large-scale investments and solve problems common to the participating banks.

BANK SYSTEM DEVELOPMENT

The bank is intensively widening the geographical coverage of its activities. For example, 14 new branches were established in 1994 alone, which made it possible to spread the bank's activities to such industrial centres as Orel, Cheliabinsk and Irkutsk. As of the beginning of 1995, the bank network comprised 73 branches, and the inclusion of 117 branches of 11 subsidiaries of the Promstroybank of Russia Holding Group incorporates over 200 institutions.

Promstroybank of Russia pays serious attention to the consolidation of the activities of the banking community in Russia. The bank is a member of the Russian Banks Association and the Moscow Bank Union. The Chairman of the Board of the bank has been elected the chairman of the Council of the "Russia" Association of Banks for industry and construction. The bank plays an active part in the development and improvement of banking legislation. The bank's experts are invited on a regular basis to be consultants to the state Duma, the Federal Assembly as well as other state and public organisations.

TRAINING AND INFORMATION

Large-scale and complex tasks facing the bank explain the special attention given to improving the professional skills of the staff. During the last two years, more than half of the bank's staff have participated in the training courses at the bank's own training centre, as well as at the leading educational establishments of Russia, Europe and North America, and in the foreign correspondent banks.

Promstroybank of Russia acts as an active sponsor for domestic science and culture and allocates part of its profits for various charity and social programmes.

Being a reliable partner to its customers, Promstroybank of Russia is looking into the future with certitude and optimism.

PROMSTROYBANK OF RUSSIA

13, Tverskoy Blvd.,
Moscow 103867
Russia

Telephone: (7 095) 229-2292/200-7287
Fax: (7 095) 200-6507/200-3133
Telex: 411943 PSB RU
SWIFT Code: PRSTRUMM
REUTERS: PSBR